Vibrant Matter

A John Hope Franklin Center Book

JANE BENNETT

Vibrant Matter

A Political Ecology of Things

Duke University Press Durham and London 2010

© 2010 Duke University Press
All rights reserved
Printed in the United States of America
on acid-free paper ∞
Designed by C. H. Westmoreland
Typeset in Whitman
by Tseng Information Systems, Inc.

Library of Congress Cataloging-in-Publication Data
Bennett, Jane, 1957–
Vibrant matter : a political ecology of things /
Jane Bennett.
p. cm.
Includes bibliographical references and index.
ISBN 978-0-8223-4619-7 (cloth : alk. paper)
ISBN 978-0-8223-4633-3 (pbk. : alk. paper)
1. Human ecology—Political aspects.
2. Human ecology—Philosophy.
3. Environmentalism—Philosophy. I. Title.
GF21.B465 2010
304.2—dc22   2009037177

Contents

Preface

This book has a philosophical project and, related to it, a political one. The philosophical project is to think slowly an idea that runs fast through modern heads: the idea of matter as passive stuff, as raw, brute, or inert. This habit of parsing the world into dull matter (it, things) and vibrant life (us, beings) is a "partition of the sensible," to use Jacques Rancière's phrase.[1] The quarantines of matter and life encourage us to ignore the vitality *of* matter and the lively powers *of* material formations, such as the way omega-3 fatty acids can alter human moods or the way our trash is not "away" in landfills but generating lively streams of chemicals and volatile winds of methane as we speak.[2] I will turn the figures of "life" and "matter" around and around, worrying them until they start to seem strange, in something like the way a common word when repeated can become a foreign, nonsense sound. In the space created by this estrangement, a *vital materiality* can start to take shape.

Or, rather, it can take shape again, for a version of this idea already found expression in childhood experiences of a world populated by animate things rather than passive objects. I will try to reinvoke this sense, to awaken what Henri Bergson described as "a latent belief in the spontaneity of nature."[3] The idea of vibrant matter also has a long (and if not latent, at least not dominant) philosophical history in the West. I will reinvoke this history too, drawing in particular on the concepts and claims of Baruch Spinoza, Friedrich Nietzsche, Henry David Thoreau, Charles Darwin, Theodor Adorno, Gilles Deleuze, and the early twentieth-century vitalisms of Bergson and Hans Driesch.

The political project of the book is, to put it most ambitiously, to encourage more intelligent and sustainable engagements with vibrant matter and lively things. A guiding question: How would political responses to public problems change were we to take seriously the vitality of (nonhuman) bodies? By "vitality" I mean the capacity of things — edibles, commodities, storms, metals — not only to impede or block the will and designs of humans but also to act as quasi agents or forces with trajectories, propensities, or tendencies of their own. My aspiration is to articulate a vibrant materiality that runs alongside and inside humans to see how analyses of political events might change if we gave the force of things more due. How, for example, would patterns of consumption change if we faced not litter, rubbish, trash, or "the recycling," but an accumulating pile of lively and potentially dangerous matter? What difference would it make to public health if eating was understood as an encounter between various and variegated bodies, some of them mine, most of them not, and none of which always gets the upper hand? What issues would surround stem cell research in the absence of the assumption that the only source of vitality in matter is a soul or spirit? What difference would it make to the course of energy policy were electricity to be figured not simply as a resource, commodity, or instrumentality but also and more radically as an "actant"?

The term is Bruno Latour's: an actant is a source of action that can be either human or nonhuman; it is that which has efficacy, can *do* things, has sufficient coherence to make a difference, produce effects, alter the course of events. It is "any entity that modifies another entity in a trial," something whose "competence is deduced from [its] performance" rather than posited in advance of the action.[4] Some actants are better described as protoactants, for these performances or energies are too small or too fast to be "things."[5] I admire Latour's attempt to develop a vocabulary that addresses multiple modes and degrees of effectivity, to begin to describe a more *distributive* agency. Latour strategically elides what is commonly taken as distinctive or even unique about humans, and so will I. At least for a while and up to a point. I lavish attention on specific "things," noting the distinctive capacities or efficacious powers of particular material configurations. To attempt, as I do, to present human and nonhuman actants on a less vertical plane than is common is to bracket the question of the human and to elide the rich and diverse literature on subjectivity and its genesis, its conditions of possibility, and its boundaries. The philosophical project of naming where subjectivity begins and ends is too often bound up with fantasies of a human uniqueness in the eyes of God, of escape from materiality, or of mastery of nature; and even where it is not, it remains an aporetic or quixotic endeavor.

In what follows the otherwise important topic of subjectivity thus gets short shrift so that I may focus on the task of developing a vocabulary and syntax for, and thus a better discernment of, the active powers issuing from nonsubjects. I want to highlight what is typically cast in the shadow: the material agency or effectivity of nonhuman or not-quite-human things. I will try to make a meal out of the stuff left out of the feast of political theory done in the anthropocentric style. In so doing, I court the charge of performative self-contradiction: is it not a human subject who, after all, is articulating this theory of vibrant matter? Yes and no, for I will argue that what looks like a performative contradiction may well dissipate if one considers revisions in operative notions of matter, life, self, self-interest, will, and agency.

Why advocate the vitality of matter? Because my hunch is that the image of dead or thoroughly instrumentalized matter feeds human hubris and our earth-destroying fantasies of conquest and consumption. It does so by preventing us from detecting (seeing, hearing, smelling, tasting, feeling) a fuller range of the nonhuman powers circulating around and within human bodies. These material powers, which can aid or destroy, enrich or disable, ennoble or degrade us, in any case call for our attentiveness, or even "respect" (provided that the term be stretched beyond its Kantian sense). The figure of an intrinsically inanimate matter may be one of the impediments to the emergence of more ecological and more materially sustainable modes of production and consumption. My claims here are motivated by a self-interested or conative concern for *human* survival and happiness: I want to pro-mote greener forms of human culture and more attentive encounters between people-materialities and thing-materialities. (The "ecological" character of a vital materialism is the focus of the last two chapters.)

In the "Treatise on Nomadology," Deleuze and Félix Guattari experi-ment with the idea of a "material vitalism," according to which vitality is immanent in matter-energy.[6] That project has helped inspire mine. Like Deleuze and Guattari, I draw selectively from Epicurean, Spino-zist, Nietzschean, and vitalist traditions, as well as from an assortment of contemporary writers in science and literature. I need all the help I can get, for this project calls for the pursuit of several tasks simul-taneously: (1) to paint a positive ontology of vibrant matter, which stretches received concepts of agency, action, and freedom sometimes to the breaking point; (2) to dissipate the onto-theological binaries of life/matter, human/animal, will/determination, and organic/inorganic using arguments and other rhetorical means to induce in human bodies an aesthetic-affective openness to material vitality; and (3) to sketch a style of political analysis that can better account for the contributions of nonhuman actants.

In what follows, then, I try to bear witness to the vital materialities that flow through and around us. Though the movements and effectivity of stem cells, electricity, food, trash, and metals are crucial to political life (and human life per se), almost as soon as they appear in public (often at first by disrupting human projects or expectations), these ac-tivities and powers are represented as human mood, action, meaning, agenda, or ideology. This quick substitution sustains the fantasy that "we" really are in charge of all those "its" — its that, according to the tradition of (nonmechanistic, nonteleological) materialism I draw on, reveal themselves to be potentially forceful agents.

Spinoza stands as a touchstone for me in this book, even though he himself was not quite a materialist. I invoke his idea of conative bodies that strive to enhance their power of activity by forming alliances with other bodies, and I share his faith that everything is made of the same substance. Spinoza rejected the idea that man "disturbs rather than fol-lows Nature's order," and promises instead to "consider human actions and appetites just as if it were an investigation into lines, planes, or bodies."[7] Lucretius, too, expressed a kind of monism in his *De Rerum*

Natura: everything, he says, is made of the same quirky stuff, the same building blocks, if you will. Lucretius calls them primordia; today we might call them atoms, quarks, particle streams, or matter-energy. This same-stuff claim, this insinuation that deep down everything is connected and irreducible to a simple substrate, resonates with an *ecological sensibility*, and that too is important to me. But in contrast to some versions of deep ecology, my monism posits neither a smooth harmony of parts nor a diversity unified by a common spirit. The formula here, writes Deleuze, is "ontologically one, formally diverse."[8] This is, as Michel Serres says in *The Birth of Physics*, a turbulent, immanent field in which various and variable materialities collide, congeal, morph, evolve, and disintegrate.[9] Though I find Epicureanism to be too simple in its imagery of individual atoms falling and swerving in the void, I share its conviction that there remains a natural *tendency* to the way things are — and that human decency and a decent politics are fostered if we tune in to the strange logic of turbulence.

Impersonal Affect

When I wrote *The Enchantment of Modern Life*, my focus was on the ethical relevance of human affect, more specifically, of the mood of enchantment or that strange combination of delight and disturbance. The idea was that moments of sensuous enchantment with the everyday world — with nature but also with commodities and other cultural products — might augment the motivational energy needed to move selves from the endorsement of ethical principles to the actual practice of ethical behaviors.

The theme of that book participated in a larger trend within political theory, a kind of ethical and aesthetic turn inspired in large part by feminist studies of the body and by Michel Foucault's work on "care of the self." These inquires helped put "desire" and bodily practices such as physical exercise, meditation, sexuality, and eating back on the ethical radar screen. Some in political theory, perhaps most notably Nancy Fraser in *Justice Interruptus*, criticized this turn as a retreat to soft, psycho-cultural issues of identity at the expense of the hard, political issues of economic justice, environmental sustainability, human rights, or democratic governance. Others (I am in this camp) replied that the bodily disciplines through which ethical sensibilities and social relations are formed and reformed are *themselves* political and constitute a whole (underexplored) field of "micropolitics" without which any principle or policy risks being just a bunch of words. There will be no greening of the economy, no redistribution of wealth, no enforcement or extension of rights without human dispositions, moods, and cultural ensembles hospitable to these effects.

The ethical turn encouraged political theorists to pay more attention to films, religious practices, news media rituals, neuroscientific experiments, and other noncanonical means of ethical will formation. In the process, "ethics" could no longer refer primarily to a set of doctrines; it had to be considered as a complex set of relays between moral contents, aesthetic-affective styles, and public moods. Here political theorists affirmed what Romantic thinkers (I am thinking of Jean-Jacques Rousseau, Friedrich Schiller, Nietzsche, Ralph Waldo Emerson, Thoreau, and Walt Whitman) had long noted: if a set of moral principles is actually to be lived out, the right mood or landscape of affect has to be in place.

I continue to think of affect as central to politics and ethics, but in this book I branch out to an "affect" not specific to human bodies. I want now to focus less on the enhancement to human relational capacities resulting from affective catalysts and more on the catalyst itself as it exists in nonhuman bodies. This power is not transpersonal or intersubjective but impersonal, an affect intrinsic to forms that cannot be imagined (even ideally) as persons. I now emphasize even more how the figure of enchantment points in two directions: the first toward the humans who *feel* enchanted and whose agentic capacities may be thereby strengthened, and the second toward the agency of the things that *produce* (helpful, harmful) effects in human and other bodies.[10] Organic and inorganic bodies, natural and cultural objects (these distinctions are not particularly salient here) *all* are affective. I am here drawing on a Spinozist notion of affect, which refers broadly to the capacity of any body for activity and responsiveness. Deleuze and Guattari put the point this way: "We know nothing about a body until we know what it can do, in other words, what its affects are, how they can or cannot enter into composition with other affects, with the affects of another body, . . . to destroy that body or to be destroyed by it, . . . to exchange actions and passions with it or to join with in composing a more powerful body."[11] Or, according to David Cole, "affects entail the colliding of particle-forces delineating the impact of one body on another; this could also be explained as the capacity to feel force before [or without] subjective emotion. . . . Affects create a field of forces that do not tend to congeal into subjectivity."[12] What I am calling impersonal affect or material vibrancy is not a spiritual supplement or "life force" added to the matter said to house it. Mine is not a vitalism in the traditional sense; I equate affect with materiality, rather than posit a separate force that can enter and animate a physical body.

My aim, again, is to theorize a vitality intrinsic to materiality as such, and to detach materiality from the figures of passive, mechanistic, or divinely infused substance. This vibrant matter is *not* the raw material for the creative activity of humans or God. It is my body, but also the bodies of Baltimore litter (chapter 1), Prometheus's chains (chapter 4), and Darwin's worms (chapter 7), as well as the not-quite-bodies of electricity (chapter 2), ingested food (chapter 3), and stem cells (chapters 5 and 6).

A Note on Methodology

I pursue a materialism in the tradition of Democritus-Epicurus-Spinoza-Diderot-Deleuze more than Hegel-Marx-Adorno. It is important to follow the trail of human power to expose social hegemonies (as historical materialists do). But my contention is that there is also public value in following the scent of a nonhuman, thingly power, the material agency of natural bodies and technological artifacts. Here I mean "to follow" in the sense in which Jacques Derrida develops it in the context of his meditation on animals. Derrida points to the intimacy between being and following: to be (anything, anyone) is always to be following (something, someone), always to be in response to call from something, however nonhuman it may be.[13]

What method could possibly be appropriate for the task of speaking a word for vibrant matter? How to describe without thereby erasing the independence of things? How to acknowledge the obscure but ubiquitous intensity of impersonal affect? What seems to be needed is a certain willingness to appear naive or foolish, to affirm what Adorno called his "clownish traits."[14] This entails, in my case, a willingness to theorize events (a blackout, a meal, an imprisonment in chains, an experience of litter) as encounters between ontologically diverse actants, some human, some not, though all thoroughly material.[15]

What is also needed is a cultivated, patient, sensory attentiveness to nonhuman forces operating outside and inside the human body. I have tried to learn how to induce an attentiveness to things and their affects from Thoreau, Franz Kafka, and Whitman, as well as from the eco- and ecofeminist philosophers Romand Coles, Val Plumwood, Wade Sikorski, Freya Mathews, Wendell Berry, Angus Fletcher, Barry Lopez, and Barbara Kingsolver. Without proficiency in this countercultural kind of perceiving, the world appears as if it consists only of active human subjects who confront passive objects and their law-governed mechanisms. This appearance may be indispensable to the action-oriented perception on which our survival depends (as Nietzsche and Bergson each in his own way contends), but it is also dangerous and counterproductive to live this fiction all the time (as Nietzsche and Bergson also note), and neither does it conduce to the formation of a "greener" sensibility.

For *this* task, demystification, that most popular of practices in critical theory, should be used with caution and sparingly, because demystification presumes that at the heart of any event or process lies a *human* agency that has illicitly been projected into things. This hermeneutics of suspicion calls for theorists to be on high alert for signs of the secret truth (a human will to power) below the false appearance of nonhuman agency. Karl Marx sought to demystify commodities and prevent their fetishization by showing them to be invested with an agency that belongs to humans; patriotic Americans under the Bush regime exposed the self-interest, greed, or cruelty inside the "global war on terror" or inside the former attorney general Alberto Gonzales's version of the rule of law; the feminist theorist Wendy Brown demystifies when she promises to "remove the scales from our eyes" and reveal that "the discourse of tolerance . . . [valorizes] the West, othering the rest . . . while feigning to do no more than . . . extend the benefits of liberal thought and practices."[16]

Demystification is an indispensable tool in a democratic, pluralist politics that seeks to hold officials accountable to (less unjust versions of) the rule of law and to check attempts to impose a system of (racial, civilizational, religious, sexual, class) domination. But there are limits to its political efficacy, among them that exposés of illegality, greed,

mendacity, oligarchy, or hypocrisy do not reliably produce moral outrage and that, if they do, this outrage may or may not spark ameliorative
action. Brown, too, acknowledges that even if the exposé of the "false
conceits" of liberal tolerance were to weaken the "justification" for the
liberal quest for empire, it would not necessarily weaken the "motivation" for empire.[17] What is more, ethical political action on the part of
humans seems to require not only a vigilant critique of existing institutions but also positive, even utopian alternatives.[18] Jodi Dean, another
advocate for demystification, recognizes this liability: "If all we can do
is evaluate, critique, or demystify the present, then what is it that we are
hoping to accomplish?"[19] A relentless approach toward demystification
works against the possibility of positive formulations. In a discussion
of the François Mitterand government, Foucault broke with his former
tendency to rely on demystification and proposed specific reforms in
the domain of sexuality: "I've become rather irritated by an attitude,
which for a long time was mine, too, and which I no longer subscribe
to, which consists in saying: our problem is to denounce and criticize:
let them get on with their legislation and reforms. That doesn't seem
to me like the right attitude."[20] The point, again, is that we need both
critique and positive formulations of alternatives, alternatives that will
themselves become the objects of later critique and reform.

What demystification uncovers is always something human, for example, the hidden quest for domination on the part of some humans
over others, a human desire to deflect responsibility for harms done,
or an unjust distribution of (human) power. Demystification tends to
screen from view the vitality of matter and to reduce *political* agency to
human agency. Those are the tendencies I resist.

The capacity to detect the presence of impersonal affect requires that
one is caught up in it. One needs, at least for a while, to suspend suspicion and adopt a more open-ended comportment. If we think we already know what is out there, we will almost surely miss much of it.

Materialisms

Several years ago I mentioned to a friend that Thoreau's notion of the
Wild had interesting affinities with Deleuze's idea of the virtual and
with Foucault's notion of the unthought. All three thinkers are trying

to acknowledge a force that, though quite real and powerful, is intrinsically resistant to representation.[21] My friend replied that she did not much care for French poststructuralism, for it "lacked a materialist perspective." At the time I took this reply as a way of letting me know that she was committed to a Marx-inspired, egalitarian politics. But the comment stuck, and it eventually provoked these thoughts: Why did Foucault's concern with "bodies and pleasures" or Deleuze's and Guattari's interest in "machinic assemblages" not count as *materialist*? How did Marx's notion of materiality—as economic structures and exchanges that provoke many other events—come to stand for the materialist perspective per se? Why is there not a more robust debate between contending philosophies of materiality or between contending accounts of how materiality matters to politics?

For some time political theory has acknowledged that materiality matters. But this materiality most often refers to human social structures or to the human meanings "embodied" in them and other objects. Because politics is itself often construed as an exclusively human domain, what registers on it is a set of material constraints on or a context for human action. Dogged resistance to anthropocentrism is perhaps the main difference between the vital materialism I pursue and this kind of historical materialism.[22] I will emphasize, even overemphasize, the agentic contributions of nonhuman forces (operating in nature, in the human body, and in human artifacts) in an attempt to counter the narcissistic reflex of human language and thought. We need to cultivate a bit of anthropomorphism—the idea that human agency has some echoes in nonhuman nature—to counter the narcissism of humans in charge of the world.

In chapter 1, "The Force of Things," I explore two terms in a vital materialist vocabulary: *thing-power* and the *out-side*. Thing-power gestures toward the strange ability of ordinary, man-made items to exceed their status as objects and to manifest traces of independence or aliveness, constituting the outside of our own experience. I look at how found objects (my examples come from litter on the street, a toy creature in a Kafka story, a technical gadget used in criminal investigations) can become vibrant things with a certain effectivity of their own, a perhaps small but irreducible degree of independence from the words, images, and feelings they provoke in us. I present this as a liveliness intrinsic to the materiality of the thing formerly known as an object. This raises a metaquestion: is it really possible to theorize this vibrancy, or is it (as Adorno says it is) a quest that is not only futile but also tied to the hubristic human will to comprehensive knowledge and the violent human will to dominate and control? In the light of his critique, and given Adorno's own efforts in *Negative Dialectics* to "grope toward the preponderance of the object," I defend the "naive" ambition of a vital materialism.[23]

The concept of thing-power offers an alternative to the object as a way of encountering the nonhuman world. It also has (at least) two liabilities: first, it attends only to the vitality of stable or fixed entities (things), and second, it presents this vitality in terms that are too individualistic (even though the individuals are not human beings). In chapter 2, "The Agency of Assemblages," I enrich the picture of material agency through the notion of "assemblages," borrowed from Deleuze and Guattari. The locus of agency is always a human-nonhuman working group. I move from the vitality of a discrete thing to vitality as a (Spinozist) function of the tendency of matter to conglomerate or form heterogeneous groupings. I then explore the agency of human-nonhuman assemblages through the example of the electrical power grid, focusing on a 2003 blackout that affected large sections of North America.

In chapter 3, "Edible Matter," I repeat the experiment by focusing on food. Drawing on studies of obesity, recent food writing, and on ideas formulated by Thoreau and Nietzsche on the question of diet, I present the case for edible matter as an actant operating inside and alongside humankind, exerting influence on moods, dispositions, and decisions. I here begin to defend a conception of self, developed in later chapters, as itself an impure, human-nonhuman assemblage. I also consider, but ultimately eschew, the alternative view that the vibrancy I posit in matter is best attributed to a nonmaterial source, to an animating spirit or "soul."

Chapter 4, "A Life of Metal," continues to gnaw away at the life/matter binary, this time through the concept of "*a* life." I take up the hard case for a (nonmechanistic) materialism that conceives of matter as intrinsically lively (but not ensouled): the case of inorganic matter. My example is metal. What can it mean to say that metal—usually the avatar of a rigid and inert substance—is vibrant matter? I compare the "adamantine chains" that bind Aeschylus's Prometheus to a rock to the polycrystalline metal described by the historian of science Cyril Smith.

Vital materialism as a doctrine has affinities with several nonmodern (and often discredited) modes of thought, including animism, the Romantic quest for Nature, and vitalism. Some of these affinities I embrace, some I do not. I reject the life/matter binary informing classical vitalism. In chapters 5 and 6 I ask why this divide has been so persistent and defended so militantly, especially as developments in the natural sciences and in bioengineering have rendered the line between organic and inorganic, life and matter, increasingly problematic. In Chapter 5, "Neither Mechanism nor Vitalism," I focus on three fascinating attempts to name the "vital force" in matter: Immanuel Kant's *Bildungstrieb*, the embryologist Driesch's entelechy, and Bergson's *élan vital*. Driesch and Bergson both sought to infuse philosophy with the science of their day, and both were skeptical about mechanistic models of nature. To me, their vitalisms constituted an invaluable holding action, maintaining an open space that a philosophy of vibrant materiality could fill.

In Chapter 6, "Stems Cells and the Culture of Life," I explore the latter-day vitalism of George W. Bush and other evangelical defenders of a "culture of life" as expressed in political debates about embryonic stem cell research during the final years of the Bush adminstration. I appreciate the pluripotentiality of stem cells but resist the effort of culture-of-life advocates to place these cells on one side of a radical divide between life and nonlife.

Chapter 7, "Political Ecologies," was the most difficult to conceive and write, because there I stage a meeting between the (meta)physics of vital materialism and a political theory. I explore how a conception of vibrant matter could resound in several key concepts of political theory, including the "public," "political participation," and "the political." I begin with a discussion of one more example of vibrant matter, the inventive worms studied by Darwin. Darwin treats worms as actants operating not only in nature but in *history*: "Worms have played a more important part in the history of the world than most persons would at first assume."[24] Darwin's anthropomorphizing prompts me to consider the reverse case: whether a polity might itself be a kind of ecosystem. I use (and stretch) John Dewey's model of a public as the emergent effect of a problem to defend such an idea. But I also consider the objection to it posed by Rancière, who both talks about dissonances coming from outside the regime of political intelligibility and models politics as a unique realm of exclusively human endeavor. I end the chapter by endorsing a definition of politics as a political *ecology* and a notion of publics as human-nonhuman collectives that are provoked into existence by a shared experience of harm. I imagine this public to be one of the "disruptions" that Rancière names as the quintessentially political act.

In the last chapter, "Vitality and Self-interest," I gather together the various links between ecophilosophy and a vital materialism. What are some tactics for cultivating the experience of our *selves* as vibrant matter? The task is to explore ways to engage effectively and sustainably this enchanting and dangerous matter-energy.

Acknowledgments

This book is the effect of a fortuitous assemblage of friends, colleagues, interlocutors, and other things. No author could hope for a better editor than Courtney Berger of Duke University Press. I am grateful for the lively intelligence of the students in my seminar "Materialisms and Politics" in 2007: Kellan Anfinson, Cara Daggett, Derek Denman, Suzanne Gallant, Scott Gottbreht, Anatoli Ignatov (who also provided high-quality assistance in preparing the manuscript and the index), Suvi Irvine, Meica Magnani, Stephen Peyser, Chas Phillips, Hannah Son, and Filip Wojciechowski. Rebecca Brown, Jennifer Culbert, Veena Das, Hent de Vries, Paola Marrati, Bill Connolly, Katrin Pahl, Sam Chambers, and John Marshall infected my ideas. I thank them for that and for helping to form such an intellectually (and socially) vibrant milieu at Johns Hopkins University. I also give my profound thanks to John Buell, Jairus Grove, and Jennifer Lin for their analyses, turns of phrase, references, and for urging me to stand my ground and, when I didn't, defending it for me; and to Bhrigu Singh for gently, repeatedly reminding me about violence. I am grateful to other theorist friends who criticized and strengthened my talks, essays, and chapters over the last several years: Anders Berg-Sørensen, Malcolm Bull, Diana Coole, Eu Jin Chua, Jodi Dean, Bill Dixon, Thomas Dumm, Kathy Ferguson, Kennan Ferguson, Stefanie Fishel, Jason Frank, Jonathan Goldberg, Aaron Goodfellow, Bonnie Honig, Steven Johnston, Gulshan Khan, Dot Kwek, Daniel Levine, Patchen Markell, Lida Maxwell, Melissa Orlie, Davide Panagia, Bican Polat, Matt Scherer, Mort Schoolman, Nicholas Tampio, Lars Tønder, Stephen White, Mabel Wong, and Linda Zerilli. Thanks to David Howarth and Aletta Norval for the inspirational Conference on Political Theory at the University of Essex, to Noortje Marres for the great Physique of the Public conference at Goldsmiths College, and to Chris Pierson for the truly interdisciplinary discussions he organized at the University of Nottingham's Stem Cell Identities, Governance, and Ethics conference. The book has also profited from my lucky encounter with an extraordinary group of geographers, including David Campbell, Derek McCormack, Sarah Whatmore, Emma Roe, Nick Bingham, Nigel Thrift, Ben Anderson, Jamie Lorimer, and J. D. Dewsbury, as well as the members of the Theoretical Archaeology Group at Columbia University. I am especially indebted to Rom Coles for his careful, critical, and wise reading of the entire manuscript. Finally, I am grateful, once again, to my best friend, Bill Connolly, whose comments always enriched the next draft and who gave me courage to pursue the project on those occasions when I lost faith in it.

Vibrant Matter

I must let my senses wander as my thought,
my eyes see without looking. . . .
Go not to the object; let it come to you.

HENRY THOREAU,
The Journal of Henry David Thoreau

It is never we who affirm or deny something of a thing;
it is the thing itself that affirms or denies something of itself in us.

BARUCH SPINOZA, *Short Treatise II*

The Force of Things

In the wake of Michel Foucault's death in 1984, there was an explosion of scholarship on the body and its social construction, on the operations of biopower. These genealogical (in the Nietzschean sense) studies exposed the various micropolitical and macropolitical techniques through which the human body was disciplined, normalized, sped up and slowed down, gendered, sexed, nationalized, globalized, rendered disposable, or otherwise composed. The initial insight was to reveal how cultural practices produce what is experienced as the "natural," but many theorists also insisted on the *material recalcitrance* of such cultural productions.[1] Though gender, for example, was a congealed bodily effect of historical norms and repetitions, its status as artifact does *not* imply an easy susceptibility to human understanding, reform, or control. The point was that cultural forms are themselves powerful, material assemblages with *resistant force*.

In what follows, I, too, will feature the negative power or recalcitrance of things. But I will also seek to highlight a positive, productive power of their own. And, instead of focusing on collectives conceived primarily as conglomerates of *human* designs and practices ("discourse"), I will highlight the active role of *nonhuman* materials in public life. In short, I will try to give voice to a thing-power. As W. J. T. Mitchell notes, "objects are the way things appear to a subject—that is, with a name, an identity, a gestalt or stereotypical template. . . . Things, on the other hand, . . . [signal] the moment when the object becomes the Other, when the sardine can looks back, when the mute idol speaks, when the subject experiences the object as uncanny and feels the need for what Foucault calls 'a metaphysics of the object, or, more exactly, a metaphysics of that never objectifiable depth from which objects rise up toward our superficial knowledge.'"[2]

Thing-Power, or the Out-Side

Spinoza ascribes to bodies a peculiar vitality: "Each thing [*res*], as far as it can by its own power, strives [*conatur*] to persevere in its own being."[3] *Conatus* names an "active impulsion" or trending tendency to persist.[4] Although Spinoza distinguishes the human body from other bodies by noting that its "virtue" consists in "nothing other than to live by the guidance of reason,"[5] every nonhuman body shares with every human body a conative nature (and thus a "virtue" appropriate to its material configuration). Conatus names a power present in *every* body: "Any thing whatsoever, whether it be more perfect or less perfect, will always be able to persist in existing with that same force whereby it begins to exist, so that in this respect all things are equal."[6] Even a falling stone, writes Spinoza, "is endeavoring, as far as in it lies, to continue in its motion."[7] As Nancy Levene notes, "Spinoza continually stresses this continuity between human and other beings," for "not only do human beings not form a separate imperium unto themselves; they do not even command the imperium, nature, of which they are a part."[8]

The idea of thing-power bears a family resemblance to Spinoza's conatus, as well as to what Henry David Thoreau called the Wild or that uncanny presence that met him in the Concord woods and atop Mount Ktaadn and also resided in/as that monster called the railroad and that alien called his Genius. Wildness was a not-quite-human force that addled and altered human and other bodies. It named an irreducibly strange dimension of matter, an *out-side*. Thing-power is also kin to what Hent de Vries, in the context of political theology, called "the absolute" or that "intangible and imponderable" recalcitrance.[9] Though the absolute is often equated with God, especially in theologies emphasizing divine omnipotence or radical alterity, de Vries defines it more open-endedly as "that which tends to loosen its ties to existing contexts."[10] This definition makes sense when we look at the etymology of *absolute*: *ab* (off) + *solver* (to loosen). The absolute is that which is *loosened off* and on the loose. When, for example, a Catholic priest performs the act of ab-solution, he is the vehicle of a divine agency that loosens sins from their attachment to a particular soul: sins now stand apart, displaced foreigners living a strange, impersonal life of their own. When de Vries speaks of the absolute, he thus tries to point to what no speaker could possibly see, that is, a some-thing that is not an object of knowledge, that is detached or radically free from representation, and thus no-thing at all. Nothing but the force or effectivity of the detachment, that is.

De Vries's notion of the absolute, like the thing-power I will seek to express, seeks to acknowledge that which refuses to dissolve completely into the milieu of human knowledge. But there is also a difference in emphasis. De Vries conceives this exteriority, this out-side, primarily as an epistemological limit: in the presence of the absolute, we cannot *know*. It is from human thinking that the absolute has detached; the absolute names the limits of *intelligibility*. De Vries's formulations thus give priority to humans as knowing bodies, while tending to overlook things and what *they* can do. The notion of thing-power aims instead to attend to the it as actant; I will try, impossibly, to name the moment of independence (from subjectivity) possessed by things, a moment that must be there, since things do in fact affect other bodies, enhancing or weakening their power. I will shift from the language of epistemology to that of ontology, from a focus on an elusive recalcitrance hovering between immanence and transcendence (the absolute) to an active, earthy, not-quite-human capaciousness (vibrant matter). I will try to give voice to a vitality intrinsic to materiality, in the process absolving matter from its long history of attachment to automatism or mechanism.[11]

The strangely vital things that will rise up to meet us in this chapter— a dead rat, a plastic cap, a spool of thread—are characters in a speculative onto-story. The tale hazards an account of materiality, even though it is both too alien and too close to see clearly and even though linguistic means prove inadequate to the task. The story will highlight the extent to which human being and thinghood overlap, the extent to which the us and the it slip-slide into each other. One moral of the story is that we are also nonhuman and that things, too, are vital players in the world. The hope is that the story will enhance receptivity to the impersonal life that surrounds and infuses us, will generate a more subtle awareness of the complicated web of dissonant connections between bodies, and will enable wiser interventions into that ecology.

Thing-Power I: Debris

On a sunny Tuesday morning on 4 June in the grate over the storm drain to the Chesapeake Bay in front of Sam's Bagels on Cold Spring Lane in Baltimore, there was:

one large men's black plastic work glove
one dense mat of oak pollen
one unblemished dead rat
one white plastic bottle cap
one smooth stick of wood

Glove, pollen, rat, cap, stick. As I encountered these items, they shimmied back and forth between debris and thing—between, on the one hand, stuff to ignore, except insofar as it betokened human activity (the workman's efforts, the litterer's toss, the rat-poisoner's success), and, on the other hand, stuff that commanded attention in its own right, as existents in excess of their association with human meanings, habits, or projects. In the second moment, stuff exhibited its thing-power: it issued a call, even if I did not quite understand what it was saying. At the very least, it provoked affects in me: I was repelled by the dead (or was it merely sleeping?) rat and dismayed by the litter, but I also felt something else: a nameless awareness of the impossible singularity of *that* rat, *that* configuration of pollen, *that* otherwise utterly banal, mass-produced plastic water-bottle cap.

I was struck by what Stephen Jay Gould called the "excruciating complexity and intractability" of nonhuman bodies,[12] but, in being *struck*, I realized that the capacity of these bodies was not restricted to a passive "intractability" but also included the ability to make things happen, to produce effects. When the materiality of the glove, the rat, the pollen, the bottle cap, and the stick started to shimmer and spark, it was in part because of the contingent tableau that they formed with each other, with the street, with the weather that morning, with me. For had the sun not glinted on the black glove, I might not have seen the rat; had the rat not been there, I might not have noted the bottle cap, and so on. But they *were* all there just as they were, and so I caught a glimpse of an energetic vitality inside each of these things, things that I generally conceived as inert. In this assemblage, *objects* appeared as *things*, that is, as vivid entities not entirely reducible to the contexts in which (human) subjects set them, never entirely exhausted by their semiotics. In my encounter with the gutter on Cold Spring Lane, I glimpsed a culture of things irreducible to the culture of objects.[13] I achieved, for a moment, what Thoreau had made his life's goal: to be able, as Thomas Dumm puts it, "to be surprised by what we see."[14]

This window onto an eccentric out-side was made possible by the fortuity of that particular assemblage, but also by a certain anticipatory readiness on my in-side, by a perceptual style open to the appearance of thing-power. For I came on the glove-pollen-rat-cap-stick with Thoreau in my head, who had encouraged me to practice "the discipline of looking always at what is to be seen"; with Spinoza's claim that all things are "animate, albeit in different degrees"; and with Maurice Merleau-Ponty, whose *Phenomenology of Perception* had disclosed for me "an immanent or incipient significance in the living body [which] extends, . . . to the whole sensible world" and which had shown me how "our gaze, prompted by the experience of our own body, will discover in all other 'objects' the miracle of expression."[15]

As I have already noted, the items on the ground that day were vibratory—at one moment disclosing themselves as dead stuff and at the next as live presence: junk, then claimant; inert matter, then live wire. It hit me then in a visceral way how American materialism, which requires buying ever-increasing numbers of products purchased in ever-shorter cycles, is *anti*materiality.[16] The sheer volume of commodities, and the hyperconsumptive necessity of junking them to make room for new ones, conceals the vitality of matter. In *The Meadowlands*, a late twentieth-century, Thoreauian travelogue of the New Jersey garbage hills outside Manhattan, Robert Sullivan describes the vitality that persists even in trash: •

> The . . . garbage hills are alive. . . . there are billions of microscopic organisms thriving underground in dark, oxygen-free communities. . . . After having ingested the tiniest portion of leftover New Jersey or New York, these cells then exhale huge underground plumes of carbon dioxide and of warm moist methane, giant stillborn tropical winds that seep through the ground to feed the Meadowlands' fires, or creep up into the atmosphere, where they eat away at the . . . ozone. . . . One afternoon I . . . walked along the edge of a garbage hill, a forty-foot drumlin of compacted trash that owed its topography to the waste of the city of Newark. . . . There had been rain the night before, so it wasn't long before I found a little leachate seep, a black ooze trickling down the slope of the hill, an espresso of refuse. In a few hours, this stream would find its way down into the . . . groundwater of the Meadowlands; it would mingle with toxic streams. . . . But in this moment, here at its birth, . . . this little seep was pure pollution, a pristine stew of oil and grease, of cyanide and arsenic, of cadmium, chromium, copper, lead, nickel, silver, mercury, and zinc. I touched this fluid—my fingertip was a bluish caramel color—and it was warm and fresh. A few yards away, where the stream collected into a benzene-scented pool, a mallard swam alone.[17]

Sullivan reminds us that a vital materiality can never really be thrown "away," for it continues its activities even as a discarded or unwanted commodity. For Sullivan that day, as for me on that June morning, thing-power rose from a pile of trash. Not Flower Power, or Black Power, or Girl Power, but *Thing-Power*: the curious ability of inanimate things to animate, to act, to produce effects dramatic and subtle.

Thing-Power II: Odradek's Nonorganic Life

A dead rat, some oak pollen, and a stick of wood stopped me in my tracks. But so did the plastic glove and the bottle cap: thing-power arises from bodies inorganic as well as organic. In support of this contention, Manuel De Landa notes how even inorganic matter can "self-organize":

Inorganic matter-energy has a wider range of alternatives for the generation of structure than just simple phase transitions. . . . In other words, even the humblest forms of matter and energy have the potential for *self-organization* beyond the relatively simple type involved in the creation of crystals. There are, for instance, those coherent waves called solitons which form in many different types of materials, ranging from ocean waters (where they are called tsunamis) to lasers. Then there are . . . stable states (or attractors), which can sustain coherent cyclic activity. . . . Finally, and unlike the previous examples of nonlinear self-organization where true innovation cannot occur, there [are] . . . the different combinations into which entities derived from the previous processes (crystals, coherent pulses, cyclic patterns) may enter. When put together, these forms of spontaneous structural generation suggest that inorganic matter is much more variable and creative than we ever imagined. And this insight into matter's inherent creativity needs to be fully incorporated into our new materialist philosophies.[18]

I will in chapter 4 try to wrestle philosophically with the idea of impersonal or nonorganic life, but here I would like to draw attention to a literary dramatization of this idea: to Odradek, the protagonist of Franz Kafka's short story "Cares of a Family Man." Odradek is a spool of thread who/that can run and laugh; this animate wood exercises an impersonal form of vitality. De Landa speaks of a "spontaneous structural generation" that happens, for example, when chemical systems at far-from-equilibrium states inexplicably choose one path of development rather than another. Like these systems, the material configuration that is Odradek straddles the line between inert matter and vital life.

For this reason Kafka's narrator has trouble assigning Odradek to an ontological category. Is Odradek a cultural artifact, a tool of some sort? Perhaps, but if so, its purpose is obscure: "It looks like a flat star-shaped spool of thread, and indeed it does seem to have thread wound upon it; to be sure, these are only old, broken-off bits of thread, knotted and tangled together, of the most varied sorts and colors. . . . One is tempted to believe that the creature once had some sort of intelligible shape and is now only a broken-down remnant. Yet this does not seem to be the case; . . . nowhere is there an unfinished or unbroken surface to suggest anything of the kind: the whole thing looks senseless enough, but in its own way perfectly finished."[19]

Or perhaps Odradek is more a subject than an object—an organic creature, a little person? But if so, his/her/its embodiment seems rather unnatural: from the center of Odradek's star protrudes a small wooden crossbar, and "by means of this latter rod . . . and one of the points of the star . . . , the whole thing can stand upright as if on two legs."[20]

On the one hand, like an active organism, Odradek appears to move deliberately (he is "extraordinarily nimble") and to speak intelligibly: "He lurks by turns in the garret, the stairway, the lobbies, the entrance hall. Often for months on end he is not to be seen; then he has presumably moved into other houses; but he always comes faithfully back to our house again. Many a time when you go out of the door and he happens just to be leaning directly beneath you against the banisters you feel inclined to speak to him. Of course, you put no difficult questions to him, you treat him — he is so diminutive that you cannot help it — rather like a child. 'Well, what's your name?' you ask him. 'Odradek,' he says. 'And where do you live?' 'No fixed abode,' he says and laughs." And yet, on the other hand, like an inanimate object, Odradek produced a so-called laughter that "has no lungs behind it" and "sounds rather like the rustling of fallen leaves. And that is usually the end of the conversation. Even these answers are not always forthcoming; often he stays mute for a long time, as wooden as his appearance."[21]

Wooden yet lively, verbal yet vegetal, alive yet inert, Odradek is ontologically multiple. He/it is a vital materiality and exhibits what Gilles Deleuze has described as the persistent "hint of the animate in plants, and of the vegetable in animals."[22] The late-nineteenth-century Russian scientist Vladimir Ivanovich Vernadsky, who also refused any sharp distinction between life and matter, defined organisms as "special, distributed forms of the common mineral, water. . . . Emphasizing the continuity of watery life and rocks, such as that evident in coal or fossil limestone reefs, Vernadsky noted how these apparently inert strata are 'traces of bygone biospheres.'"[23] Odradek exposes this continuity of watery life and rocks; he/it brings to the fore the becoming of things.

Thing-Power III: Legal Actants

I may have met a relative of Odradek while serving on a jury, again in Baltimore, for a man on trial for attempted homicide. It was a small glass vial with an adhesive-covered metal lid: the Gunpowder Residue

Sampler. This object/witness had been dabbed on the accused's hand hours after the shooting and now offered to the jury its microscopic evidence that the hand had either fired a gun or been within three feet of a gun firing. Expert witnesses showed the sampler to the jury several times, and with each appearance it exercised more force, until it became vital to the verdict. This composite of glass, skin cells, glue, words, laws, metals, and human emotions had become an actant. *Actant*, recall, is Bruno Latour's term for a source of action; an actant can be human or not, or, most likely, a combination of both. Latour defines it as "something that acts or to which activity is granted by others. It implies no special motivation of human individual actors, nor of humans in general."[24] An actant is neither an object nor a subject but an "intervener,"[25] akin to the Deleuzean "quasi-causal operator."[26] An operator is that which, by virtue of its particular location in an assemblage and the fortuity of being in the right place at the right time, makes the difference, makes things happen, becomes the decisive force catalyzing an event.

Actant and *operator* are substitute words for what in a more subject-centered vocabulary are called agents. Agentic capacity is now seen as differentially distributed across a wider range of ontological types. This idea is also expressed in the notion of "deodand," a figure of English law from about 1200 until it was abolished in 1846. In cases of accidental death or injury to a human, the nonhuman actant, for example, the carving knife that fell into human flesh or the carriage that trampled the leg of a pedestrian—became deodand (literally, "that which must be given to God"). In recognition of *its* peculiar efficacy (a power that is less masterful than agency but more active than recalcitrance), the deodand, a materiality "suspended between human and thing,"[27] was surrendered to the crown to be used (or sold) to compensate for the harm done. According to William Pietz, "any culture must establish some procedure of compensation, expiation, or punishment to settle the debt created by unintended human deaths whose direct cause is not a morally accountable person, but a nonhuman material object. This was the issue thematized in public discourse by . . . the law of deodand."[28]

There are of course differences between the knife that impales and the man impaled, between the technician who dabs the sampler and the sampler, between the array of items in the gutter of Cold Spring Lane and me, the narrator of their vitality. But I agree with John Frow that these differences need "to be flattened, read horizontally as a juxtaposition rather than vertically as a hierarchy of being. It's a feature of our world that we can and do distinguish . . . things from persons. But the sort of world we live in makes it constantly possible for these two sets of kinds to exchange properties."[29] And to note this fact explicitly, which is also to begin to *experience* the relationship between persons and other materialities more horizontally, is to take a step toward a more ecological sensibility.

Thing-Power IV: Walking, Talking Minerals

Odradek, a gunpowder residue sampler, and some junk on the street can be fascinating to people and can thus seem to come alive. But is this evanescence a property of the stuff or of people? Was the thing-power of the debris I encountered but a function of the subjective and intersubjective connotations, memories, and affects that had accumulated around my ideas of these items? Was the real agent of my temporary immobilization on the street that day *humanity*, that is, the cultural meanings of "rat," "plastic," and "wood" in conjunction with my own idiosyncratic biography? It could be. But what if the swarming activity inside my head was *itself* an instance of the vital materiality that also constituted the trash?

I have been trying to raise the volume on the vitality of materiality per se, pursuing this task so far by focusing on nonhuman bodies, by, that is, depicting them as actants rather than as objects. But the case for matter as active needs also to readjust the status of human actants: not by denying humanity's awesome, awful powers, but by presenting these powers as evidence of our own constitution as vital materiality. In other words, human power is itself a kind of thing-power. At one level this claim is uncontroversial: it is easy to acknowledge that humans are composed of various material parts (the minerality of our bones, or the metal of our blood, or the electricity of our neurons). But it is more challenging to conceive of these materials as lively and self-organizing, rather than as passive or mechanical means under the direction of something nonmaterial, that is, an active soul or mind.

Perhaps the claim to a vitality intrinsic to matter itself becomes more plausible if one takes a long view of time. If one adopts the perspective of evolutionary rather than biographical time, for example, a mineral efficacy becomes visible. Here is De Landa's account of the emergence of our bones: "Soft tissue (gels and aerosols, muscle and nerve) reigned supreme until 5000 million years ago. At that point, some of the conglomerations of fleshy matter-energy that made up life underwent a sudden *mineralization*, and a new material for constructing living creatures emerged: bone. It is almost as if the mineral world that had served as a substratum for the emergence of biological creatures was reasserting itself."[30] Mineralization names the creative agency by which bone was produced, and bones then "made new forms of movement control possible among animals, freeing them from many constraints and literally setting them into motion to conquer every available niche in the air, in water, and on land."[31] In the long and slow time of evolution, then, mineral material appears as the mover and shaker, the active power, and the human beings, with their much-lauded capacity for self-directed action, appear as *its* product.[32] Vernadsky seconds this view in his description of humankind as a particularly potent mix of minerals: "What struck [Vernadsky] most was that the material of Earth's crust has been packaged into myriad moving beings whose reproduction and growth build and break down matter on a global scale. People, for example, redistribute and concentrate oxygen . . . and other elements of Earth's crust into two-legged, upright forms that have an amazing propensity to wander across, dig into and in countless other ways alter Earth's surface. *We are walking, talking minerals*."[33]

Kafka, De Landa, and Vernadsky suggest that human individuals are themselves composed of vital materials, that our powers are thing-power. These vital materialists do not claim that there are no differences between humans and bones, only that there is no necessity to describe these differences in a way that places humans at the ontological center or hierarchical apex. Humanity can be distinguished, instead, as Jean-François Lyotard suggests, as a *particularly rich and complex* collection of materials: "Humankind is taken for a complex material system; consciousness, for an effect of language; and language for a highly complex material system."[34] Richard Rorty similarly defines humans as very complex animals, rather than as animals "with an extra added ingredient called 'intellect' or 'the rational soul.'"[35]

The fear is that in failing to affirm human uniqueness, such views authorize the treatment of people as mere things; in other words, that a strong distinction between subjects and objects is needed to prevent the instrumentalization of humans. Yes, such critics continue, objects possess a certain power of action (as when bacteria or pharmaceuticals enact hostile or symbiotic projects inside the human body), and yes, some subject-on-subject objectifications are permissible (as when persons consent to use and be used as a means to sexual pleasure), but the *ontological* divide between persons and things must remain lest one have no *moral* grounds for privileging man over germ or for condemning pernicious forms of human-on-human instrumentalization (as when powerful humans exploit illegal, poor, young, or otherwise weaker humans).

How can the vital materialist respond to this important concern? First, by acknowledging that the framework of subject versus object has indeed at times worked to prevent or ameliorate human suffering and to promote human happiness or well-being. Second, by noting that its successes come at the price of an instrumentalization of nonhuman nature that can itself be unethical and can itself undermine long-term human interests. Third, by pointing out that the Kantian imperative to treat humanity always as an end-in-itself and never merely as a means does not have a stellar record of success in preventing human suffering or promoting human well-being: it is important to raise the question of its actual, historical efficacy in order to open up space for forms of ethical practice that do not rely upon the image of an intrinsically *hierarchical* order of things. Here the materialist speaks of promoting healthy and enabling instrumentalizations, rather than of treating people as ends-in-themselves, because to face up to the compound nature of the human self is to find it difficult even to make sense of the notion of a single end-in-itself. What instead appears is a swarm of competing ends being pursued simultaneously in each individual, some of which are healthy to the whole, some of which are not. Here the vital materialist, taking a cue from Nietzsche's and Spinoza's ethics, favors physiological over moral descriptors because she fears that moralism can itself become a source of unnecessary human suffering.[36]

We are now in a better position to name that other way to promote human health and happiness: *to raise the status of the materiality of which we are composed.* Each human is a heterogeneous compound of wonderfully vibrant, dangerously vibrant, matter. If matter itself is lively, then not only is the difference between subjects and objects minimized, but the status of the shared materiality of all things is elevated. All bodies become more than mere objects, as the thing-powers of resistance and protean agency are brought into sharper relief. Vital materialism would thus set up a kind of safety net for those humans who are now, in a world where Kantian morality is the standard, routinely made to suffer because they do not conform to a particular (Euro-American, bourgeois, theocentric, or other) model of personhood. The ethical aim becomes to distribute value more generously, to bodies as such. Such a newfound attentiveness to matter and its powers will not solve the problem of human exploitation or oppression, but it can inspire a greater sense of the extent to which all bodies are kin in the sense of inextricably enmeshed in a dense network of relations. And in a knotted world of vibrant matter, to harm one section of the web may very well be to harm oneself. Such an enlightened or expanded notion of self-interest *is good for humans*. As I will argue further in chapter 8, a vital materialism does not reject self-interest as a motivation for ethical behavior, though it does seek to cultivate a broader definition of self and of interest.

Thing-Power V: Thing-Power and Adorno's Nonidentity

But perhaps the very idea of thing-power or vibrant matter claims too much: to know more than it is possible to know. Or, to put the criticism in Theodor Adorno's terms, does it exemplify the violent hubris of Western philosophy, a tradition that has consistently failed to mind the gap between concept and reality, object and thing? For Adorno this gap is ineradicable, and the most that can be said with confidence about the thing is that it eludes capture by the concept, that there is always a "nonidentity" between it and any representation. And yet, as I shall argue, even Adorno continues to seek a way to access—however darkly, crudely, or fleetingly—this out-side. One can detect a trace of this longing in the following quotation from *Negative Dialectics*: "What we may call the thing itself is not positively and immediately at hand. He who wants to know it must think more, not less."[37] Adorno clearly rejects the possibility of any direct, sensuous apprehension ("the thing itself is not positively and immediately at hand"), but he does not reject all modes of encounter, for there is one mode, "thinking more, not less," that holds promise. In this section I will explore some of the affinities between Adorno's nonidentity and my thing-power and, more generally, between his "specific materialism" (ND, 203) and a vital materialism.

Nonidentity is the name Adorno gives to that which is not subject to knowledge but is instead "heterogeneous" to all concepts. This elusive force is not, however, wholly outside human experience, for Adorno describes nonidentity as a presence that acts upon us: we knowers are haunted, he says, by a painful, nagging feeling that something's being forgotten or left out. This discomfiting sense of the inadequacy of representation remains no matter how refined or analytically precise one's concepts become. "Negative dialectics" is the method Adorno designs to teach us how to *accentuate* this discomforting experience and how to give it a meaning. When practiced correctly, negative dialectics will render the static buzz of nonidentity into a powerful reminder that "objects do not go into their concepts without leaving a remainder" and thus that life will always exceed our knowledge and control. The ethical project par excellence, as Adorno sees it, is to keep remembering this and to learn how to accept it. Only then can we stop raging against a world that refuses to offer us the "reconcilement" that we, according to Adorno, crave (ND, 5).[38]

For the vital materialist, however, the starting point of ethics is less the acceptance of the impossibility of "reconcilement" and more the recognition of human participation in a shared, vital materiality. We *are* vital materiality and we are surrounded by it, though we do not always see it that way. The ethical task at hand here is to cultivate the ability to discern nonhuman vitality, to become perceptually open to it. In a parallel manner, Adorno's "specific materialism" also recommends a set of practical techniques for training oneself to better detect and accept nonidentity. Negative dialectics is, in other words, the pedagogy inside Adorno's materialism.

This pedagogy includes intellectual as well as aesthetic exercises. The intellectual practice consists in the attempt to make the very process of conceptualization an explicit object of thought. The goal here is to become more cognizant that conceptualization automatically obscures the inadequacy of its concepts. Adorno believes that critical reflection

can expose this cloaking mechanism and that the exposure will inten-
sify the felt presence of nonidentity. The treatment is homeopathic: we
must develop a *concept* of nonidentity to cure the hubris of conceptualization. The treatment can work because, however distorting, concepts
still "refer to nonconceptualities." This is "because concepts on their
part are moments of the reality that requires their formation" (ND, 12).
Concepts can never provide a clear view of things in themselves, but
the "discriminating man," who "in the matter and its concept can distinguish even the infinitesimal, that which escapes the concept" (ND, 45),
can do a better job of gesturing toward them. Note that the discriminating man (adept at negative dialectics) both subjects his conceptualizations to second-order reflection and pays close *aesthetic* attention to
the object's "qualitative moments" (ND, 43), for these open a window
onto nonidentity.

A second technique of the pedagogy is to exercise one's utopian
imagination. The negative dialectician should imaginatively re-create
what has been obscured by the distortion of conceptualization: "The
means employed in negative dialectics for the penetration of its hard-
ened objects is possibility—the possibility of which their reality has
cheated the objects and which is nonetheless visible in each one" (ND,
52). Nonidentity resides in those denied possibilities, in the invisible
field that surrounds and infuses the world of objects.

A third technique is to admit a "playful element" into one's thinking
and to be willing to play the fool. The negative dialectician "knows how
far he remains from" knowing nonidentity, "and yet he must always talk
as if he had it entirely. This brings him to the point of clowning. He must
not deny his clownish traits, least of all since they alone can give him
hope for what is denied him" (ND, 14).

The self-criticism of conceptualization, a sensory attentiveness to
the qualitative singularities of the object, the exercise of an unrealistic
imagination, and the courage of a clown: by means of such practices
one might replace the "rage" against nonidentity with a respect for it,
a respect that chastens our will to mastery. That rage is for Adorno the
driving force behind interhuman acts of cruelty and violence. Adorno
goes even further to suggest that negative dialectics can transmute the
anguish of nonidentity into a will to ameliorative political action: the
thing thwarts our desire for conceptual and practical mastery and this

refusal angers us; but it also offers us an ethical injunction, according to which "suffering ought not to be, . . . things should be different. Woe speaks: 'Go.' Hence the convergence of specific materialism with criticism, with social change in practice" (*ND*, 202–3).[39]

Adorno founds his ethics on an intellectual and aesthetic attentiveness that, though it will always fail to see its object clearly, nevertheless has salutary effects on the bodies straining to see. Adorno willingly plays the fool by questing after what I would call thing-power, but which he calls "the preponderance of the object" (*ND*, 183). Humans encounter a world in which nonhuman materialities have power, a power that the "bourgeois I," with its pretensions to autonomy, denies.[40] It is at this point that Adorno identifies negative dialectics as a materialism: it is only "by passing to the object's preponderance that dialectics is rendered materialistic" (*ND*, 192).

Adorno dares to affirm something like thing-power, but he does not want to play the fool for *too* long. He is quick — too quick from the point of view of the vital materialist — to remind the reader that objects are always "entwined" with human subjectivity and that he has no desire "to place the object on the orphaned royal throne once occupied by the subject. On that throne the object would be nothing but an idol" (*ND*, 181). Adorno is reluctant to say too much about nonhuman vitality, for the more said, the more it recedes from view. Nevertheless, Adorno does try to attend somehow to this reclusive reality, by means of a negative dialectics. Negative dialectics has an affinity with negative theology: negative dialectics honors nonidentity as one would honor an unknowable god; Adorno's "specific materialism" includes the possibility that there is divinity behind or within the reality that withdraws. Adorno rejects any naive picture of transcendence, such as that of a loving God who designed the world ("metaphysics cannot rise again" [*ND*, 404] after Auschwitz), but the desire for transcendence cannot, he believes, be eliminated: "Nothing could be experienced as truly alive if something that transcends life were not promised also. . . . The transcendent is, and it is not" (*ND*, 375).[41] Adorno honors nonidentity as an *absent* absolute, as a messianic promise.[42]

Adorno struggles to describe a force that is *material* in its resistance to human concepts but *spiritual* insofar as it might be a dark promise of an absolute-to-come. A vital materialism is more thoroughly nontheistic in presentation: the out-side has no messianic promise.[43] But a philosophy of nonidentity and a vital materialism nevertheless share an urge to cultivate a more careful attentiveness to the out-side.

The Naive Ambition of Vital Materialism

Adorno reminds us that humans can experience the out-side only indirectly, only through vague, aporetic, or unstable images and impressions. But when he says that even distorting concepts still "refer to nonconceptualities, because concepts on their part are moments of the reality that requires their formation" (ND, 12), Adorno also acknowledges that human experience nevertheless includes encounters with an out-side that is active, forceful, and (quasi)independent. This out-side can operate at a distance from our bodies or it can operate as a foreign power internal to them, as when we feel the discomfort of nonidentity, hear the naysaying voice of Socrates's demon, or are moved by what Lucretius described as that "something in our breast" capable of fighting and resisting.[44] There is a strong tendency among modern, secular, well-educated humans to refer such signs back to a human agency conceived as its ultimate source. This impulse toward cultural, linguistic, or historical constructivism, which interprets any expression of thing-power as an effect of culture and the play of human powers, politicizes moralistic and oppressive appeals to "nature." And that is a good thing. But the constructivist response to the world also tends to obscure from view whatever thing-power there may be. There is thus something to be said for moments of methodological naiveté, for the postponement of a genealogical critique of objects.[45] This delay might render manifest a subsistent world of nonhuman vitality. To "render manifest" is both to receive and to participate in the shape given to that which is received. What is manifest arrives through humans but not entirely because of them.

Vital materialists will thus try to linger in those moments during which they find themselves fascinated by objects, taking them as clues to the material vitality that they share with them. This sense of a strange and incomplete commonality with the out-side may induce vital materialists to treat nonhumans—animals, plants, earth, even artifacts and commodities—more carefully, more strategically, more ecologically. But how to develop this capacity for naiveté? One tactic might be to revisit and become temporarily infected by discredited philosophies of nature, risking "the taint of superstition, animism, vitalism, anthropomorphism, and other premodern attitudes."[46] I will venture into vitalism in chapters 5 and 6, but let me here make a brief stop at the ancient atomism of Lucretius, the Roman devotee of Epicurus.

Lucretius tells of bodies falling in a void, bodies that are not lifeless stuff but matter on the go, entering and leaving assemblages, swerving into each other: "*At times quite undetermined and at undetermined spots they push a little from their path*: yet only just so much as you could call a change of trend. [For if they did not] . . . swerve, all things would fall downwards through the deep void like drops of rain, nor could collision come to be, nor a blow brought to pass for the primordia: so nature would never have brought anything into existence."[47] Louis Althusser described this as a "materialism of the encounter," according to which political events are born from chance meetings of atoms.[48] A primordial swerve says that the world is not determined, that an element of chanciness resides at the heart of things, but it also affirms that so-called inanimate things have a life, that deep within is an inexplicable vitality or energy, a moment of independence from and resistance to us and other bodies: a kind of thing-power.

The rhetoric of *De Rerum Natura* is realist, speaking in an authoritative voice, claiming to describe a nature that preexists and outlives us: here are the smallest constituent parts of being ("primordia") and here are the principles of association governing them.[49] It is easy to criticize this realism: Lucretius quests for the thing itself, but there is no there there—or, at least, no way for us to grasp or know it, for the thing is always already humanized; its object status arises at the very instant something comes into our awareness. Adorno levels this charge explicitly against Martin Heidegger's phenomenology, which Adorno interprets as a "realism" that "seeks to breach the walls which thought has built around itself, to pierce the interjected layer of subjective positions that have become a second nature." Heidegger's aim "to philosophize formlessly, so to speak, purely on the ground of things" (*ND*, 78)[50] is for Adorno futile, and it is productive of a violent "rage" against nonidentity.[51]

But Lucretius's poem—like Kafka's stories, Sullivan's travelogue, Vernadsky's speculations, and my account of the gutter of Cold Spring Lane—does offer this potential benefit: it can direct sensory, linguistic, and imaginative attention toward a material vitality. The advantage of such tales, with their ambitious naiveté, is that though they "disavow . . . the tropological work, the psychological work, and the phenomenological work entailed in the human production of materiality," they do so "in the name of *avowing* the force of questions that have been too . readily foreclosed by more familiar fetishizations: the fetishization of the subject, the image, the word."[52]

2

The Agency of Assemblages

Thing-power perhaps has the rhetorical advantage of calling to mind a childhood sense of the world as filled with all sorts of animate beings, some human, some not, some organic, some not. It draws attention to an efficacy of objects in excess of the human meanings, designs, or purposes they express or serve. Thing-power may thus be a good starting point for thinking beyond the life-matter binary, the dominant organizational principle of adult experience. The term's disadvantage, however, is that it also tends to overstate the thinginess or fixed stability of materiality, whereas my goal is to theorize a materiality that is as much force as entity, as much energy as matter, as much intensity as extension. Here the term *out-side* may prove more apt. Spinoza's stones, an absolute Wild, the oozing Meadowlands, the nimble Odradek, the moving deodand, a processual minerality, an incalculable nonidentity—none of these are passive objects or stable entities (though neither are they intentional subjects).[1] They allude instead to vibrant materials.

A second, related disadvantage of *thing-power* is its latent individualism, by which I mean the way in which the figure of "thing" lends itself to an atomistic rather than a congregational understanding of agency.

While the smallest or simplest body or bit may indeed express a vital impetus, conatus or *clinamen*, an actant never really acts alone. Its efficacy or agency always depends on the collaboration, cooperation, or interactive interference of many bodies and forces. A lot happens to the concept of agency once nonhuman things are figured less as social constructions and more as actors, and once humans themselves are assessed not as autonoms but as vital materialities.

In this chapter I will try to develop a theory of *distributive* agency by examining a real-life effect: a power blackout that affected 50 million people in North America in 2003. I will offer an analysis of the electrical power grid as an agentic assemblage. How does the agency of assemblages compare to more familiar theories of action, such as those centered around human will or intentionality, or around intersubjectivity, or around (human) social, economic, or discursive structures? And how would an understanding of agency as a confederation of human and nonhuman elements alter established notions of moral responsibility and political accountability?

Two philosophical concepts are important to my response to these questions: Spinoza's "affective" bodies and Gilles Deleuze and Félix Guattari's "assemblage." I will therefore offer a brief exposition of these concepts before I turn to an account of the power blackout that tries to take the out-side seriously and tries to remain faithful to the distributive quality of "agency."

Affective Bodies

Spinoza's conative bodies are also *associative* or (one could even say) *social* bodies, in the sense that each is, by its very nature as a body, continuously affecting and being affected by other bodies. Deleuze explicates this point: the power of a body to affect other bodies includes a "corresponding and inseparable" capacity to be affected; "there are two equally actual powers, that of acting, and that of suffering action, which vary inversely one to the other, but whose sum is both constant and constantly effective."[2] Spinoza's conative, encounter-prone body arises in the context of an ontological vision according to which all things are "modes" of a common "substance."[3] Any specific thing—"a shoe, a ship, a cabbage, a king" (to use Martin Lin's list)[4] or a glove, a rat, a cap, and the human narrator of their vitality (to use my list) — is neither subject nor object but a "mode" of what Spinoza calls "*Deus sive Natura*" (God or Nature).[5]

Spinoza also says that every mode is itself a mosaic or assemblage of many simple bodies, or, as Deleuze describes it, there are for Spinoza no "existing modes that are not actually composed of a very great number of extensive parts," parts that "come to it from elsewhere."[6] It is interesting that Lucretius, too, saw mosaicism as the way things essentially are: "It is right to have this truth . . . surely sealed and to keep it stored in your remembering mind, that there is not one of all the things, whose nature is seen before our face, which is built of one kind of primordia, nor anything which is not created of well-mingled seed." Lucretius links the degree of internal diversity to the degree of *power* possessed by the thing: "And whatever possesses within it more forces and powers, it thus shows that there are in it most kinds of primordia and diverse shapes."[7] Spinoza, as we shall see, makes a similar point.

For Spinoza, both simple bodies (which are perhaps better termed *protobodies*) and the complex or mosaicized modes they form are conative. In the case of the former, conatus is expressed as a stubbornness or inertial tendency to persist; in the case of a complex body or mode, conatus refers to the effort required to maintain the specific relation of "movement and rest" that obtains between its parts, a relation that defines the mode as what it is.[8] This maintenance is not a process of mere repetition of the same, for it entails continual invention: because each mode suffers the actions on it by other modes, actions that disrupt the relation of movement and rest characterizing each mode, every mode, if it is to persist, must seek new encounters to creatively compensate for the alterations or affections it suffers. What it means to be a "mode," then, is to form alliances and enter assemblages: it is to mod(e)ify and be modified by others. The process of modification is not under the control of any one mode — no mode is an agent in the hierarchical sense. Neither is the process without tension, for each mode vies with and against the (changing) affections of (a changing set of) other modes, all the while being subject to the element of chance or contingency intrinsic to any encounter.[9]

Conative substance turns itself into confederate bodies, that is, complex bodies that in turn congregate with each other in the pursuit of the enhancement of their power. Spinoza believes, for example, that the more kinds of bodies with which a body can affiliate, the better: "As the body is more capable of being affected in many ways and of affecting external bodies . . . so the mind is more capable of thinking."[10]

The key idea I want to take from Spinoza's rich and contestable philosophy, an idea I will put to work for a vital materialism, is this: bodies enhance their power *in* or *as a heterogeneous assemblage*. What this suggests for the concept of *agency* is that the efficacy or effectivity to which that term has traditionally referred becomes distributed across an ontologically heterogeneous field, rather than being a capacity localized in a human body or in a collective produced (only) by human efforts. The sentences of this book also emerged from the confederate agency of many striving macro- and microactants: from "my" memories, intentions, contentions, intestinal bacteria, eyeglasses, and blood sugar, as well as from the plastic computer keyboard, the bird song from the open window, or the air or particulates in the room, to name only a few of the participants. What is at work here on the page is an animal-vegetable-mineral-sonority cluster with a particular degree and duration of power. What is at work here is what Deleuze and Guattari call an assemblage.

What Is an Assemblage?

At the end of the twentieth century, the arena in which stuff happens — what the military calls the "theater of operations" — seemed to many people to have expanded dramatically. "Globalization" had occurred and the earth itself had become a space of events. The parts of this giant whole were both intimately interconnected and highly conflictual. This fact — of the coexistence of mutual dependency with friction and violence between parts — called for new conceptualizations of the part-whole relation. Organicist models, in which each member obediently serves the whole, were clearly out. A host of new ways to name the kind of relation obtaining between the parts of a volatile but somehow functioning whole were offered: network, meshwork, Empire.[11] My term of choice to describe this event-space and its style of structuration is, following Deleuze and Guattari, *assemblage*.

Assemblages are ad hoc groupings of diverse elements, of vibrant materials of all sorts. Assemblages are living, throbbing confederations that are able to function despite the persistent presence of energies that confound them from within. They have uneven topographies, because some of the points at which the various affects and bodies cross paths are more heavily trafficked than others, and so power is not distributed equally across its surface. Assemblages are not governed by any central head: no one materiality or type of material has sufficient competence to determine consistently the trajectory or impact of the group. The effects generated by an assemblage are, rather, emergent properties, emergent in that their ability to make something happen (a newly inflected materialism, a blackout, a hurricane, a war on terror) is distinct from the sum of the vital force of each materiality considered alone. Each member and proto-member of the assemblage has a certain vital force, but there is also an effectivity proper to the grouping as such: an agency *of* the assemblage. And precisely because each member-actant maintains an energetic pulse slightly "off" from that of the assemblage, an assemblage is never a stolid block but an open-ended collective, a "non-totalizable sum."[12] An assemblage thus not only has a distinctive history of formation but a finite life span.[13]

The electrical power grid offers a good example of an assemblage. It is a material cluster of charged parts that have indeed affiliated, remaining in sufficient proximity and coordination to produce distinctive effects. The elements of the assemblage work together, although their coordination does not rise to the level of an organism. Rather, its jelling endures alongside energies and factions that fly out from it and disturb it from within. And, most important for my purposes, the elements of this assemblage, while they include humans and their (social, legal, linguistic) constructions, also include some very active and powerful nonhumans: electrons, trees, wind, fire, electromagnetic fields.

The image of affective bodies forming assemblages will enable me to highlight some of the limitations in human-centered theories of action and to investigate some of the practical implications, for social-science inquiry and for public culture, of a theory of action and responsibility that crosses the human-nonhuman divide.

The Blackout

The *International Herald Tribune*, on the day after the blackout, reported that "the vast but shadowy web of transmission lines, power generating plants and substations known as the grid is the biggest gizmo ever built. . . . on Thursday [14 August 2003], the grid's heart fluttered. . . . complicated beyond full understanding, even by experts—[the grid] lives and occasionally dies by its own mysterious rules."[14] To say that the grid's "heart fluttered" or that it "lives and dies by its own rules" is to anthropomorphize. But anthropomorphizing has, as I shall argue in chapter 8, its virtues. Here it works to gesture toward the inadequacy of understanding the grid simply as a machine or a tool, as, that is, a series of fixed parts organized from without that serves an external purpose.

To the vital materialist, the electrical grid is better understood as a volatile mix of coal, sweat, electromagnetic fields, computer programs, electron streams, profit motives, heat, lifestyles, nuclear fuel, plastic, fantasies of mastery, static, legislation, water, economic theory, wire, and wood—to name just some of the actants. There is always some friction among the parts, but for several days in August 2003 in the United States and Canada the dissonance was so great that cooperation became impossible. The North American blackout was the end point of a cascade—of voltage collapses, self-protective withdrawals from the grid, and human decisions and omissions. The grid includes various valves and circuit breakers that disconnect parts from the assemblage whenever they are threatened by excessive heat. Generating plants, for example, shut down just before they are about to go into "full excitation,"[15] and they do the same when the "system voltage has become too low to provide power to the generator's own auxiliary equipment, such as fans, coal pulverizers, and pumps."[16] What seems to have happened on that August day was that several initially unrelated generator withdrawals in Ohio and Michigan caused the electron flow pattern to change over the transmission lines, which led, after a series of events including one brush fire that burnt a transmission line and then several wire-tree encounters, to a successive overloading of other lines and a vortex of disconnects. One generating plant after another separated from the grid, placing more and more stress on the remaining participants. In a one-minute period, "twenty generators (loaded to 2174 MW) tripped off line along Lake Erie."[17]

Investigators still do not understand why the cascade ever stopped itself, after affecting 50 million people over approximately twenty-four thousand square kilometers and shutting down over one hundred power plants, including twenty-two nuclear reactors.[18] The U.S.-Canada Power

Outage Task Force report was more confident about how the cascade began, insisting on a variety of agential loci.[19] These included *electricity*, with its internal differentiation into "active" and "reactive" power (more on this later); the *power plants*, understaffed by humans but overprotective in their mechanisms; *transmission wires*, which tolerate only so much heat before they refuse to transmit the electron flow; a *brush fire* in Ohio; Enron *FirstEnergy* and other energy-trading corporations, who, by legal and illegal means, had been milking the grid without maintaining its infrastructure; *consumers*, whose demand for electricity grows and is encouraged to grow by the government without concern for consequences; and the *Federal Energy Regulatory Commission*, whose Energy Policy Act of 1992 deregulated the grid, separated the generation of electricity from its transmission and distribution, and advanced the privatization of electricity. Let me say a bit more about the first and the last of these conative bodies in the assemblage.

First, the nonhuman: electricity. Electricity is a stream of electrons moving in a current, which is measured in amperes; the force of that current (the pressure pushing it through the wires) is measured in volts. In a system like the North American grid, electrical current and voltage are constantly oscillating like a pair of waves.[20] When the two waves are in phase with each other (rising and falling at exactly the same time), one has so-called active power, or the type of power used most heavily by lamps, blow-dryers, and other appliances. But some devices (such as the electric motors in refrigerators and air conditioners) rely also on so-called reactive power, where the waves are not in sync. Reactive power, though it lends no help in physically rotating a motor, is vital to the active power that accompanies it, for reactive power maintains the voltage (electricity pressure) needed to sustain the electromagnetic field required by the system as a whole. If too many devices demand reactive power, then a deficit is created. One of the causes of the blackout was a deficit of reactive power. To understand how the deficit occurred, we need to consider the other actants, including the Federal Energy Regulatory Commission.

In 1992 the commission gained U.S. congressional approval for legislation that separated the production of electricity from its distribution: companies could now buy electricity from a power plant in one part of the country and sell it to utilities in geographically distant locations.

This greatly increased the long-distance trading of electric power—and greatly increased the load on transmission wires. But here is the rub: "As transmission lines become more heavily loaded, they consume more of the reactive power needed to maintain proper transmission voltage."[21] Reactive power does not travel well, dissipating over distance, so it is best if generated close to where it will be used.[22] Power plants are technically quite capable of producing extra amounts of reactive power, but they lack the financial incentive to do so, for reactive-power production *reduces* the amount of salable power produced. What is more, under the new regulations, transmission companies cannot compel generating plants to produce the necessary amounts of reactive power.[23]

Reactive power, vital to the whole grid, proved a commodity without profit and thus came in short supply. Here emerged what Garrett Hardin has called a tragedy of the commons. Though rational for each user of reactive power to increase its demand for the free commodity, the aggregate effect is irrational in that it destroys the wellspring: in a world of finite resources, "freedom in a commons brings ruin to all."[24] The reactive power deficit was an effect unanticipated by human advocates of the regulations that created a huge, continent-wide market in energy trading. Their actions produced unintended consequences; or, to put the point in a vital materialist vocabulary, they were subject to the "slight surprise of action." The phrase is Bruno Latour's, and it refers to an effectivity proper to the action itself, arising only in the doing and thus in principle independent of any aim, tendency, or characteristic of the actants: "There is no object, no subject. . . . But there are events. I never *act*; I am always slightly surprised by what I do."[25]

Neither, says Latour, is the slight surprise of action confined to human action: "That which acts through me is also surprised by what I do, by the chance to mutate, to change, . . . to bifurcate."[26] In the case at hand, electricity was also an actant, and its strivings also produced aleatory effects. For example, "in the case of a power shipment from the Pacific Northwest to Utah, 33% of the shipment flows through Southern California and 30% flows through Arizona—far from any conceivable contract path."[27] And in August of 2003, after "the transmission lines along the southern shore of Lake Erie disconnected, the power that had been flowing along that path" dramatically and surprisingly changed its behavior: it "*immediately reversed direction and began flowing in a giant loop counterclockwise* from Pennsylvania to New York to Ontario and into Michigan."²⁸ Seeking to minimize the company's role in the black-out, a spokesman for FirstEnergy, the Ohio-based company whose East-lake power plant was an early actant in the cascade and an early target of blame, said that any analysis needed to "take into account large un-planned south-to-north power movements that were part of a phenome-non known as loop flows, which occur when power takes a route from producer to buyer different from the intended path."²⁹ Electricity, or the stream of vital materialities called electrons, is always on the move, always going somewhere, though where this will be is not entirely pre-dictable. Electricity sometimes goes where we send it, and sometimes it chooses its path on the spot, in response to the other bodies it encoun-ters and the surprising opportunities for actions and interactions that they afford.

In this selective account of the blackout, agency, conceived now as something distributed along a continuum, extrudes from multiple sites or many loci—from a quirky electron flow and a spontaneous fire to members of Congress who have a neoliberal faith in market self-regulation. How does this view compare to other conceptions of what an agent is and can do?

The Willing Subject and the Intersubjective Field

I have been suggesting that there is not so much a doer (an agent) be-hind the deed (the blackout) as a doing and an effecting by a human-nonhuman assemblage. This federation of actants is a creature that the concept of moral responsibility fits only loosely and to which the charge of blame will not quite stick. A certain looseness and slipperiness, often unnoticed, also characterizes more human-centered notions of agency. Augustine, for example, linked moral agency to free will, but the human will is, as Augustine reveals in his *Confessions*, divided against itself after the Fall: the will wills even as another part of the will fights that willing. Moreover, willing agents can act freely only in support of evil: never are they able by themselves to enact the good, for that always requires the intervention of divine grace, a force beyond human control. Agency, then, is not such a clear idea or a self-sufficient power in Augustine.³⁰

Neither is it in Immanuel Kant. He aspired to define agency in terms of the autonomous will of the person who submits to the moral law (whose form is inscribed in human reason). But, as William Connolly has explored, Kant, too, eventually found the will to be divided against itself, this time by an innate "propensity" for evil, wherein the will obeys maxims that derive from the inclinations.[31] It is not merely that the will fights against the pressure of an unwilled "sensibility": the propensity for evil lives inside the will itself. Human agency again appears as a vexed concept, though its snarls and dilemmas are easy to skate over when the alternatives are reduced to either a free human agency or passive, deterministic matter.

Some neo-Kantian accounts of agency emphasize intentionality (the power to formulate and enact aims) more than the moral will, but here the question is whether other forces in the world approximate some of the characteristics of intentional or purposive behavior on the part of humans.[32] An acknowledgment of something like this, of a kind of thing-power, may be at work in the "agency-versus-structure" debate in the social sciences, according to which structures are described as powerful entities that work with and against human purposes. But the category of "structure" is ultimately unable to give the force of things its due: a structure can act only negatively, as a constraint on human agency, or passively, as an enabling background or context for it. Active action or agency belongs to humans alone: "All agree that agency refers to the intentional choices made by men and women as they take action to realize their goals," even though "these actors are socially constituted beings embedded in sociocultural and ecological surroundings that both define their goals and constrain their actions."[33] Actors are "socially constituted," but the "constitutive" or productive power of structures derives from the human wills or intentions within them. There is no agency proper to assemblages, only the effervescence of the agency of individuals acting alone or in concert with each other. Structures, surroundings, and contexts make a difference to outcomes, but they are not quite vibrant matter.

The same point applies, I think, to the phenomenological theory of agency set forth by Maurice Merleau-Ponty. His *Phenomenology of Perception* was designed to avoid placing too much weight on human will, intentionality, or reason. It focused instead on the embodied character of human action, through its concept of motor intentionality,[34] and on the agentic contributions made by an intersubjective field.[35] Diana Coole, taking up Merleau-Ponty's task, replaces the discrete agent and its "residual individualism" with a "spectrum" of "agentic capacities" housed sometimes in individual persons, sometimes in human physiological processes or motor intentionality, and sometimes in human social structures or the "interworld": "At one pole [of the spectrum of agentic capacities] I envisage pre-personal, non-cognitive bodily processes; at the other, transpersonal, intersubjective processes that instantiate an interworld. Between them are singularities: phenomena with a relatively individual or collective identity."[36]

Coole's attempt to dislodge agency from its exclusive mooring in the individual, rational subject provides an important touchstone for my attempt to extend the spectrum even further — beyond human bodies and intersubjective fields to vital materialities and the human-nonhuman assemblages they form. For though Coole's spectrum gives no special privilege to the human individual, it recognizes only *human* powers: human biological and neurological processes, human personalities, human social practices and institutions. Coole limits the spectrum in this way because she is interested in a specifically political kind of agency, and for her politics is an exclusively human affair. Here I disagree, and as I will argue in chapter 7, a case can be made for including nonhumans in the demos. The prevention of future blackouts, for example, will depend on a host of cooperative efforts: Congress will have to summon the courage to fight industry demands at odds with a more common good, but reactive power will also have to do its part, on condition that it is not asked to travel too far. A vital materialism attempts a more radical displacement of the human subject than phenomenology has done, though Merleau-Ponty himself seemed to be moving in this direction in his unfinished *Visible and Unvisible*.

That text begins to undo the conceit that humanity is the sole or ultimate wellspring of agency. So does Latour's *Aramis*, which shows how the cars, electricity, and magnets of an experimental Parisian mass transit system acted positively (and not just as a constraint) alongside the activities of human and intersubjective bodies, words, and regulations.[37] Latour's later work continues to call for people to imagine other roles for things besides that of carriers of necessity, or "plastic" vehicles for "human ingenuity," or "a simple white screen to support the differentiation of society."[38]

The vital materialist must admit that different materialities, composed of different sets of protobodies, will express different powers. Humans, for example, can experience themselves as forming intentions and as standing apart from their actions to reflect on the latter. But even here it may be relevant to note the extent to which intentional reflexivity is also a product of the interplay of human and nonhuman forces. Bernard Stiegler does just this in his study of how tool-use engendered a being with an inside, with, that is, a psychological landscape of interiority. Stiegler contends that conscious reflection in (proto)humans first emerged with the use of stone tools because the materiality of the tool acted as an external marker of a past need, as an "archive" of its function. The stone tool (its texture, color, weight), in calling attention to its projected and recollected use, produced the first hollow of reflection.[39] Humanity and nonhumanity have always performed an intricate dance with each other. There was never a time when human agency was anything other than an interfolding network of humanity and nonhumanity; today this mingling has become harder to ignore.

Efficacy, Trajectory, Causality

Theodor Adorno claimed that it was not possible to "unseal" or parse a concept into its constituent parts: one could only "circle" around a concept, perhaps until one gets dizzy or arrives at the point at which nonidentity with the real can no longer be ignored. What also happens as one circles around a concept is that a set of related terms comes into view, as a swarm of affiliates. In the case of agency, these include (among others) efficacy, trajectory, and causality.[40]

Efficacy points to the creativity of agency, to a capacity to make something new appear or occur. In the tradition that defines agency as *moral* capacity, such new effects are understood as having arisen in the wake of an advance plan or an intention, for agency "involves not mere motion, but willed or intended motion, where motion can only be willed or intended by a *subject*."[41] A theory of distributive agency, in contrast, does not posit a subject as the root cause of an effect. There are instead always a swarm of vitalities at play. The task becomes to identify the contours of the swarm and the kind of relations that obtain between its bits. To figure the generative source of effects as a swarm is to see human intentions as always in competition and confederation with many other strivings, for an intention is like a pebble thrown into a pond, or an electrical current sent through a wire or neural network: it vibrates and merges with other currents, to affect and be affected. This understanding of agency does not deny the existence of that thrust called intentionality, but it does see it as less definitive of outcomes. It loosens the connections between efficacy and the moral subject, bringing efficacy closer to the idea of the power to make a difference that calls for response. And this power, I contend along with Spinoza and others, is a power possessed by nonhuman bodies too.

In addition to being tied to the idea of efficacy, agency is also bound up with the idea of a trajectory, a directionality or movement *away* from somewhere even if the toward-which it moves is obscure or even absent. Moral philosophy has figured this trajection as a purposiveness or a goal-directedness linked to a (human or divine) mind capable of choice and intention, but Jacques Derrida offers an alternative to this consciousness-centered thinking by figuring trajectory as "messianicity." Messianicity is the open-ended *promissory* quality of a claim, image, or entity. This unspecified promise is for Derrida the very condition of possibility of phenomenality: things in the world appear to us at all only because they tantalize and hold us in suspense, alluding to a fullness that is elsewhere, to a future that, apparently, is on its way. For Derrida this promissory note is never and can never be redeemed: the "straining forward toward the event" never finds relief. To be alive is to be waiting "for someone or something that, in order to happen . . . must exceed and surprise every determinate anticipation."[42] In naming the unfulfillable promise as the condition of the appearance of anything, Derrida provides a way for the vital materialist to affirm the existence of a certain trajectory or drive to assemblages without insinuating intentionality or purposiveness.

A third element in the agentic swarm is perhaps the most vague of all: causality. If agency is distributive or confederate, then instances of efficient causality, with its chain of simple bodies acting as the sole impetus for the next effect, will be impossibly rare. Is George W. Bush the efficient cause of the American invasion of Iraq? Is Osama bin Laden?

If one extends the time frame of the action beyond that of even an instant, billiard-ball causality falters. Alongside and inside singular human agents there exists a heterogenous series of actants with partial, overlapping, and conflicting degrees of power and effectivity.

Here causality is more emergent than efficient, more fractal than linear. Instead of an effect obedient to a determinant, one finds circuits in which effect and cause alternate position and redound on each other. If efficient causality seeks to rank the actants involved, treating some as external causes and others as dependent effects, emergent causality places the focus on the process as itself an actant, as itself in possession of degrees of agentic capacity. According to Connolly,

> emergent causality is causal . . . in that a movement at [one] . . . level has effects at another level. But it is emergent in that, first, the character of the . . . activity is not knowable in . . . detail prior to effects that emerge at the second level. [Moreover,] . . . the new effects become *infused* into the very . . . organization of the second level . . . such . . . that the cause cannot be said to be fully different from the effect engendered. . . . [Third,] . . . a series of . . . feedback loops operate between first and second levels to generate the stabilized result. The new emergent is shaped not only by external forces that become infused into it but *also by its own previously under-tapped capacities for reception and self-organization.*[43]

This sense of a melting of cause and effect is also expressed in the ordinary usage of the term *agent*, which can refer both to a human subject who is the sole and original author of an effect (as in "moral agent") and also to someone or something that is the mere vehicle or passive conduit for the will of another (as in "literary agent" or "insurance agent").

If ordinary language intuits the existence of a nonlinear, nonhierarchical, non–subject-centered mode of agency, Hannah Arendt makes the point explicitly by distinguishing between "cause" and "origin" in her discussion of totalitarianism. A cause is a singular, stable, and masterful initiator of effects, while an origin is a complex, mobile, and heteronomous enjoiner of forces: "The elements of totalitarianism form its origins if by origins we do not understand 'causes.' Causality, i.e., the factor of determination of a process of events in which always one event causes and can be explained by another, is probably an altogether alien and falsifying category in the realm of the historical and political sciences. Elements by themselves probably never cause anything. They become origins of events if and when they crystallize into fixed and definite forms. Then, and only then, can we trace their history backwards. The event illuminates its own past, but it can never be deduced from it."⁴⁴

For Arendt, it is impossible to discern in advance the cause of totalitarianism. Instead, like all political phenomena, its sources can only be revealed retroactively. These sources are necessarily multiple, made up of elements unaffiliated before the "crystallization" process began. In fact, what makes the event happen is precisely the contingent coming together of a set of elements. Here Arendt's view is consonant with a distributive notion of agency. But if we look at what spurs such crystallizations for her, we see her revert to a more traditional, subject-centered notion. Whereas the theorist of distributive agency would answer that anything could touch off the crystallization process (a sound, a last straw, a shoe, a blackout, a human intention), Arendt concludes that while the "significance" of an event can exceed "the intentions which eventually cause the crystallization," intentions are nevertheless the key to the event. Once again, human intentionality is positioned as the most important of all agential factors, the bearer of an exceptional kind of power.⁴⁵

Shi

Why speak of the *agency* of assemblages, and not, more modestly, of their capacity to form a "culture," or to "self-organize," or to "participate" in effects? Because the rubric of material agency is likely to be a stronger counter to human exceptionalism, to, that is, the human tendency to understate the degree to which people, animals, artifacts, technologies, and elemental forces share powers and operate in dissonant conjunction with each other. No one really knows what human agency is, or what humans are doing when they are said to perform as agents. In the face of every analysis, human agency remains something of a mystery. If we do not know just how it is that human agency operates, how can we be so sure that the processes through which nonhumans make their mark are qualitatively different?

An assemblage owes its agentic capacity to the vitality of the materialities that constitute it. Something like this congregational agency is called *shi* in the Chinese tradition. *Shi* helps to "illuminate something that is usually difficult to capture in discourse: namely, the kind of potential that originates not in human initiative but instead results from the very disposition of things."[46] *Shi* is the style, energy, propensity, trajectory, or élan inherent to a specific arrangement of things. Originally a word used in military strategy, *shi* emerged in the description of a good general who must be able to read and then ride the *shi* of a configuration of moods, winds, historical trends, and armaments: *shi* names the dynamic force emanating from a spatio-temporal configuration rather than from any particular element within it.

Again, the *shi* of an assemblage is vibratory; it is the mood or style of an open whole in which both the membership changes over time and the members themselves undergo internal alteration. Each member "possesses autonomous emergent properties which are thus capable of independent variation and therefore of being out of phase with one another in time."[47] When a member-actant, in the midst of a process of self-alteration, becomes out of sync with its (previous) self, when, if you like, it is in a reactive-power state,[48] it can form new sets of relations in the assemblage and be drawn toward a different set of allies. The members of an open whole never melt into a collective body, but instead maintain an energy potentially at odds with the *shi*. Deleuze invented the notion of "adsorbsion" to describe this kind of part-whole relationship: adsorbsion is a gathering of elements in a way that both forms a coalition and yet preserves something of the agential impetus of each element.[49] It is because of the creative activity *within* actants that the agency of assemblages is not best described in terms of social structures, a locution that designates a stolid whole whose efficacy resides only in its conditioning recalcitrance or capacity to obstruct.

The *shi* of a milieu can be obvious or subtle. It can operate at the very threshold of human perception or more violently. A coffee house or a school house is a mobile configuration of people, insects, odors, ink, electrical flows, air currents, caffeine, tables, chairs, fluids, and sounds. Their *shi* might at one time consist in the mild and ephemeral effluence of good vibes, and at another in a more dramatic force capable of engendering a philosophical or political movement, as it did in the cafés of Jean-Paul Sartre's and Simone de Beauvoir's Paris and in the Islamist schools in Pakistan in the late twentieth century.

Political Responsibility and the Agency of Assemblages

The electrical grid, by blacking out, lit up quite a lot: the shabby condition of the public-utilities infrastructure, the law-abidingness of New York City residents living in the dark, the disproportionate and accelerating consumption of energy by North Americans, and the element of unpredictability marking assemblages composed of intersecting and resonating elements. Thus spoke the grid. One might even say that it exhibited a communicative interest. It will be objected that such communication is possible only through the intermediary of humans. But is this really an objection, given that even linguistic communication necessarily entails intermediaries? My speech, for example, depends on the graphite in my pencil, millions of persons, dead and alive, in my Indo-European language group, not to mention the electricity in my brain and my laptop. (The human brain, properly wired, can light up a fifteen-watt bulb.) Humans and nonhumans alike depend on a "fabulously complex" set of speech prostheses.[50]

Noortje Marres rightly notes that "it is often hard to grasp just what the sources of agency are that make a particular event happen" and that this "ungraspability may be an [essential] aspect of agency."[51] But it is a safe bet to begin with the presumption that the locus of political responsibility is a human-nonhuman assemblage. On close-enough inspection, the productive power that has engendered an effect will turn out to be a confederacy, and the human actants within it will themselves turn out to be confederations of tools, microbes, minerals, sounds, and other "foreign" materialities. Human intentionality can emerge as agentic only by way of such a distribution. The agency of assemblages is not the strong, autonomous kind of agency to which Augustine and Kant (or an omnipotent God) aspired; this is because the relationship between tendencies and outcomes or between trajectories and effects is imagined as more porous, tenuous, and thus indirect.

Coole's account of a spectrum of agentic capacities, like the kind of agency that is subjected to structural constraints, does not recognize the agency of human-nonhuman assemblages. And this is in part because of the difficulty of theorizing agency apart from the belief that humans are *special* in the sense of existing, at least in part, outside of the order of material nature. To affirm a vitality distributed along a continuum of ontological types and to identify the human-nonhuman assemblage as a locus of agency is to unsettle this belief. But must a distributive, composite notion of agency thereby abandon the attempt to hold individuals responsible for their actions or hold officials accountable to the public? The directors of the FirstEnergy corporation were all too eager to reach this conclusion in the task force report: no one really is to blame. Though it is unlikely that the energy traders shared my vital materialism, I, too, find it hard to assign the strongest or most punitive version of moral responsibility to them. Autonomy and strong responsibility seem to me to be empirically false, and thus their invocation seems tinged with injustice. In emphasizing the ensemble nature of action and the interconnections between persons and things, a theory of vibrant matter presents individuals as simply incapable of bearing *full* responsibility for their effects.

The notion of a confederate agency does attenuate the blame game, but it does not thereby abandon the project of identifying (what Arendt called) the sources of harmful effects. To the contrary, such a notion broadens the range of places to look for sources. Look to long-term strings of events: to selfish intentions, to energy policy offering lucrative opportunities for energy trading while generating a tragedy of the commons, and to a psychic resistance to acknowledging a link between American energy use, American imperialism, and anti-Americanism; but look also to the stubborn directionality of a high-consumption social infrastructure, to unstable electron flows, to conative wildfires, to exurban housing pressures, and to the assemblages they form. In each item on the list, humans and their intentions participate, but they are not the sole or always the most profound actant in the assemblage.

Though it would give me pleasure to assert that deregulation and corporate greed are the real culprits in the blackout, the most I can honestly affirm is that corporations are one of the sites at which human efforts at reform can be applied, that corporate regulation is one place where intentions might initiate a cascade of effects. Perhaps the ethical responsibility of an individual human now resides in one's response to the assemblages in which one finds oneself participating: Do I attempt to extricate myself from assemblages whose trajectory is likely to do harm? Do I enter into the proximity of assemblages whose conglomerate effectivity tends toward the enactment of nobler ends? Agency is, I believe, distributed across a mosaic, but it is also possible to say something about the kind of striving that may be exercised by a human within the assemblage. This exertion is perhaps best understood on the model of riding a bicycle on a gravel road. One can throw one's weight this way or that, inflect the bike in one direction or toward one trajectory of motion. But the rider is but one actant operative in the moving whole.

In a world of distributed agency, a hesitant attitude toward assigning singular blame becomes a presumptive virtue. Of course, sometimes moral outrage, akin to what Plato called *thumos*, is indispensable to a democratic and just politics. In the years leading up to the publication of this book, these were some of the things that called me to outrage: the doctrine of preemptive war, the violation of human rights and of the Geneva Accords at Guantánamo Bay, the torture of prisoners in Iraq and in accordance with a policy of so-called extraordinary rendition, the restriction of protesters at President Bush's public appearances to a "free speech zone" out of the view of television cameras, the U.S. military's policy of not keeping a count of Iraqi civilian deaths. Outrage will not and should not disappear, but a politics devoted too exclusively to moral condemnation and not enough to a cultivated discernment of the web of agentic capacities can do little good. A moralized politics of good and evil, of singular agents who must be made to pay for their sins (be they bin Laden, Saddam Hussein, or Bush) becomes unethical to the degree that it legitimates vengeance and elevates violence to the tool of first resort. An understanding of agency as distributive and confederate thus reinvokes the need to detach ethics from moralism and to produce guides to action appropriate to a world of vital, crosscutting forces.

These claims are contestable, and other actants, enmeshed in other assemblages, will offer different diagnoses of the political and its problems. It is ultimately a matter of political judgment what is more needed today: should we acknowledge the distributive quality of agency to address the power of human-nonhuman assemblages and to resist a politics of blame? Or should we persist with a strategic understatement of material agency in the hopes of enhancing the accountability of specific humans?

3

Edible Matter

It is not controversial to say that trash, gadgets, electricity, and fire are relevant to politics, or to say that though such things do not qualify as political stakeholders, they form the milieu of human action or serve as means or impediments to it. But do the categories of context, tool, and constraint capture the full range of powers possessed by nonhuman bodies? In this chapter I will focus on one subset of those bodies, the kind that you can eat. I will treat food as conative bodies vying alongside and within an other complex body (a person's "own" body). To the roles of context, tool, and constraint (or background, resource, and limit) I will add the role of actant. Food will appear as actant inside and alongside intention-forming, morality-(dis)obeying, language-using, reflexivity-wielding, and culture-making human beings, and as an inducer-producer of salient, public effects. We can call the assemblage formed by these human and nonhuman bodies "American consumption" and name as one of its effects the "crisis of obesity."

My case for food as a participant in this assemblage has two prongs. The first seeks support in scientific studies of the effects of dietary fat on human moods and cognitive dispositions (and not simply its effects on the size or volume of the body). The second revisits the robust nineteenth-century discussions of the moral and political efficacy of diet. Here I will focus on motifs from the work of Friedrich Nietzsche and Henry David Thoreau, according to which eating constitutes a series of mutual transformations between human and nonhuman materials. I conclude with some thoughts about how an enhanced alertness to edible matter can contribute to a theory of vital materiality, a theory in competition with matter as "homogeneous, unorganized and quiescent stuff."[1]

The Efficacy of Fat

In 1917 the English physiologist W. M. Bayliss wrote that "it may be taken for granted that every one is sincerely desirous of avoiding unnecessary consumption of food."[2] This assumption seems no longer to hold in many parts of the developed world. In a recent Roper Report, for example, 70 percent of the Americans surveyed said that they ate "pretty much whatever they want," which means, on an average day, fifty-two teaspoons of sugar and corn sweeteners,[3] more than one half of a pound of meat,[4] and one-fifth of a pound of butter and oils.[5] Overall, what Americans want is to eat between five hundred and eight hundred more calories a day than they did in 1950.[6]

That would explain why the bodies of Americans are larger and heavier than ever before. Here we stumble on a banal instance of what Michel Foucault might have called the "productive power" of food: once ingested, once, that is, food coacts with the hand that places it in one's mouth, with the metabolic agencies of intestines, pancreas, kidneys, with cultural practices of physical exercise, and so on, food can generate new human tissue. In the case of some foods, say potato chips, it seems appropriate to regard the hand's actions as only quasi- or semiintentional, for the chips themselves seem to call forth, or provoke and stoke, the manual labor. To eat chips is to enter into an assemblage in which the I is not necessarily the most decisive operator. Chips challenge the idea, implicit in the Roper survey, that what people "want" is a personal preference entirely of their own making.

That food can make people larger is a fact so ordinary and obvious that it is difficult to perceive it as an example of a nonhuman agency at work. The case becomes a bit stronger, perhaps, when we learn of hitherto unrecognized powers of dietary fats, in particular their ability to make a qualitative as well as quantitative difference. Several recent studies suggest that fat (not the fat in potato chips, but the omega-3 fatty acids prevalent in some wild fish) can make prisoners less prone to violent acts, inattentive schoolchildren better able to focus, and bipolar persons less depressed. A widely cited 2002 "double-blind, placebo-controlled, randomised trial of nutritional supplements on 231 young adult prisoners, comparing disciplinary offences before and during supplementation" shows a 35 percent reduction of offences among British prisoners given omega-3 fatty acids.[7] A similarly designed study of dietary supplementation with fatty acids in children with "difficulties in learning, behavior, and psychosocial adjustment" finds "significant improvement" in reading, spelling, and behavior.[8] A journal of neuropsycho pharmacology reports that a thirty-year-old pregnant woman with chronic schizophrenia showed a "dramatic improvement in both positive and negative symptoms of schizophrenia" in response to an open trial of omega-3 supplementation.[9] The "60-fold variation across countries in the annual prevalence of major depression is strongly inversely correlated with national fish consumption. . . . For bipolar affective disorder, . . . prevalence rates rise precipitously below an apparent annual fish intake threshold of approximately 75 lbs. per person, with prevalence rates of . . . 0.04% in Taiwan (81.6 lb per person) and 6.5% in Germany (27.6 lb per person)." (Americans in 2000 ate about 15 lb per person.)[10] Other fats seem to have negative cognitive effects: high levels of hydrogenated fats in the diet of "middle-aged rats" dulls memory and leads "to the production of inflammatory substances in the brain."[11]

Results such as these are always subject to further research and to various interpretations, but they lend support to the idea that certain lipids promote particular human moods or affective states. This effectivity ought not to be imagined as a mechanical causality, nor do I want to suggest that we will someday arrive at a nutritional science that can demonstrate that specific fats are the cause of a quantifiable and invariant set of cognitive or behavioral effects. It is more likely that an emergent causality is at work here: particular fats, acting in different ways in different bodies, and with different intensities even within the same body at different times, may produce patterns of effects, though not in ways that are fully predictable. This is because a small change in the eater-eaten complex may issue in a significant disruption of its pattern or function.[12] The assemblage in which persons and fats are participants is perhaps better figured as a nonlinear system: "In a linear system, the ultimate effect of the combined action of two different causes is merely the [addition] . . . of the effects of each cause taken individually. But in a nonlinear system adding a small cause to one that is already present can induce dramatic effects that have no common measure of the amplitude of the cause."[13] In nonlinear assemblages, "effects" resonate with and against their "causes," such that the impact of any added element (omega-3 fatty acid) or set of elements (high fish diet) cannot be grasped at a glance. Instead, the agency of the added element(s) is only "slowly brought to light as the assemblage stabilizes itself through the mutual accommodation of its heterogeneous components."[14]

A particular element can be so contingently well placed in an assemblage that its power to alter the direction or function of the whole is unusually great. As noted in chapter 1, Gilles Deleuze's and Félix Guattari's term for such a particularly efficacious element is an "operator." As an example they cite a piece of grass used by a finch both to make a nest and for its courtship dance. The grass stem "acts as a component of passage between the territorial assemblage and the courtship assemblage. . . . The grass stem is a deterritorialized component. . . . It is neither an archaism nor a transitional or part-object. It is an operator, a vector. It is an *assemblage converter*."[15]

A particular edible can also act as an "assemblage converter," an idea similar to what Michel Serres calls a "thermal exciter." For Serres, a thermal exciter does not effect a revolutionary transformation in the assemblage it enters. Instead, it makes it "change state differentially. It inclines it. It makes the equilibrium of the energetic distribution fluctuate. It does it. It irritates it. It inflames it. Often this inclination has no effect. But it can produce gigantic ones by chain reactions or reproduction."[16]

To take seriously the efficacy of nonhuman fat is, then, not only to shift one's idea about what counts as an actor but also to focus one's attention away from individuals and onto actants in assemblages. The problem of obesity would thus have to index not only the large humans and their economic-cultural prostheses (agribusiness, snack-food vending machines, insulin injections, bariatric surgery, serving sizes, systems of food marketing and distribution, microwave ovens) but also the strivings and trajectories of fats as they weaken or enhance the power of human wills, habits, and ideas.

Nietzsche, Warrior Food, and Wagnerian Music

Most evidence of the active power of foodstuffs (a potential activated when the foodstuff congregates with a power-enhancing set of other vital materialities) comes by way of the physical or biological sciences, as in the studies cited above. When the social sciences and humanities take up the question of food, they tend to focus on human acts, on, for example, the sociocultural rituals through which meaningful food objects are produced, the rhetoric of culinary self-expression, or the aesthetic-commercial techniques through which desire for a new food product is induced. With the exception of the cookbook author or restaurant reviewer who features the color, texture, and aroma of ingredients, food writing seldom attends to the force of materiality. As David Goodman puts it in his critique of agro-food studies in sociology, it is all too rare to find an acknowledgment of food as an "ontologically real and active, lively presence."[17]

In the nineteenth century, however, it was fairly easy to find a philosopher who believed that food had the power to shape the dispositions of persons and nations. These thinkers examined the lived experience of eating and saw a profound reciprocity between eater and eaten. Nietzsche, for example, claimed (without the benefit of randomized, double-blind experiments) that psychological, cognitive, aesthetic, and moral complexions were altered and reformed by what was ingested. He pointed to "an incorrect diet (the alcoholism of the Middle Ages; the absurdity of the vegetarians)" as one source of "the deep depression, the leaden exhaustion, the black melancholy of the physiologically inhibited."[18] He believed that "the reason why . . . individuals have different feelings and tastes is usually to be found in some oddity of their life style, nutrition, or digestion, perhaps a deficit or excess of inorganic salts in their blood and brain."[19] He offered these "hints" from his morality: "No meals between meals, no coffee: coffee spreads darkness. *Tea* . . . is very unwholesome and sicklies one o'er the whole day if it is too weak by a single degree."[20] The "strong and savory sayings" and "new desires" of Zarathustra were nourished not with "flatulent vegetables" but with (an unnamed) "warrior food, with conquerer food."[21] (Perhaps raw meat?)

In these quotations Nietzsche attends to a kind of *material* agency, exhibited not only by drugs like alcohol and caffeine but by all foods. In the picture that emerges from his scattered references to foodstuffs, edible matter appears as a powerful agent, as stuff that modifies the human matter with which it comes into contact. (Here Nietzsche's thinking may resonate with a Spinozist model of conative bodies that must engage each other if their power is to be enhanced.)

The efficacy of a food will vary, Nietzsche notes, depending on the other foods in the diet, the particular human body that takes them in, and the culture or nation in which the diet is consumed. He discusses, for example, a popular diet book of his day, Luigi Cornaro's *La vita sobria* (*Art of Living Long*). Cornaro (1464–1566) lived to the age of 102 eating only twelve ounces of solid food ("bread, the yolk of an egg, a little meat, and some soup"[22]) and fourteen ounces of wine a day ("waters, in whatever way they may be doctored or prepared, have not the virtue of wine, and fail to relieve me"[23]). Nietzsche complains that though Cornaro "recommends his meagre diet as a recipe for a long and happy life — a virtuous one, too," such a diet will be able to enhance the vitality of only *some* bodies. One diet does not fit all, says Nietzsche. For someone like Cornaro, with "an extraordinarily slow metabolism," a sparse diet will have good effects, but "a scholar of *our* day, with his rapid consumption of nervous energy, would kill himself with Cornaro's regimen."[24]

The effectivity of a foodstuff varies from body to body, but what is even more interesting about Nietzsche's discussion of Cornaro is his suggestion that the effectivity of the "same" food in the "same" body will vary over time as actants enter and leave the scene. "Warrior food," if it is to produce warriors, must join forces with a whole host of other actants. Nietzsche gestures toward the agency of the food-person-sound-nation assemblage in his discussion of anti-Semitism's hold on Bismarck's Germany: he names beer as a contributing source, but beer as part of a diet consisting also of German "newspapers, politics, . . . and

a productive power intrinsic to foodstuff, which enables edible matter to coarsen or refine the imagination or render a disposition more or less liable to ressentiment, depression, hyperactivity, dull-wittedness, or violence. They experience eating as the formation of an assemblage of human and nonhuman elements, all of which bear some agentic capacity. This capacity includes the negative power to resist or obstruct human projects, but it also includes the more active power to affect and create effects. On this model of eating, human and nonhuman bodies recorporealize in response to each other; both exercise formative power and both offer themselves as matter to be acted on. Eating appears as a series of mutual transformations in which the border between inside and outside becomes blurry: my meal both is and is not mine; you both are and are not what you eat.

Vagabond Matter

If the eaten is to become food, it must be digestible to the out-side it enters. Likewise, if the eater is to be nourished, it must accommodate itself to the internalized out-side. In the eating encounter, all bodies are shown to be but temporary congealments of a materiality that is a process of becoming, is hustle and flow punctuated by sedimentation and substance. Emma Roe's phenomenology of eating practices in Britain highlights how food bobs above and below the threshold of a distinct entity: a carrot as it first enters the eater's mouth is a full-blown entity, with a distinctive taste, color, odor, texture; once swallowed, however, its coherence gradually dissipates until, if one were to continue to observe it via a tiny camera inserted into the gut, the difference between carrot and eater vanishes altogether.[41] Maud Ellman also describes the various comings and goings of food:

> [Food's] disintegration in the stomach, its assimilation in the blood, its diaphoresis in the epidermis, its metempsychosis in the large intestine; its viscosity in okra, gumbo, oysters; its elasticity in jellies, its deliquescence in blancmanges; its tumescence in the throats of serpents, its slow erosion in the bellies of sharks; its odysseys through pastures, orchards, wheat fields, stock-yards, supermarkets, kitchens, pig troughs, rubbish dumps, disposals; the industries of sowing, hunting, cooking, milling, processing, and canning

it; the wizardry of its mutations, ballooning in bread, subsiding in souffles; raw and cooked, solid and melting, vegetable and mineral, fish, flesh, and fowl, encompassing the whole compendium of living substance.[42]

Edibles disclose, in short, what Deleuze and Guattari called a certain "vagabond" quality to materiality, a propensity for continuous variation that is elided by "all the stories of matter-form."[43] The activity of metabolization, whereby the outside and inside mingle and recombine, renders more plausible the idea of a vital materiality. It reveals the swarm of activity subsisting below and within formed bodies and recalcitrant things, a vitality obscured by our conceptual habit of dividing the world into inorganic matter and organic life.

How Food Matters

My final example of artful consumption is the slow food movement, founded in Italy in 1986 to contest the McDonaldization, environmental unsustainability, and petrocentrism of a globalized system of food production, marketing, and distribution. According to its manifesto, "Slow Food is dedicated to stewardship of the land and ecologically sound food production; to the revival of the kitchen and the table as centers of pleasure, culture, and community; to the invigoration and proliferation of regional, seasonal culinary traditions; to the creation of a collaborative, ecologically-oriented, and virtuous globalization; and to living a slower and more harmonious rhythm of life."[44]

What is distinctive about slow food, and what might enable it to become a particularly powerful assemblage, is its appeal both to the "granolas" and to the "foodies." It celebrates, in one fell swoop, ecological sustainability, cultural specificity, nutritional economy, aesthetic pleasure, and the skills needed to make meals from scratch. In grouping these images and practices together, in forming that particular congregation, slow food just might have a chance to reform the public that once coalesced under the banner of "environmentalism." Perhaps slow food's cocktail of concerns—tasty food, lean energy use, and love of the Earth—can awaken us from what Barbara Kingsolver describes as our "mass hallucinatory fantasy in which the megatons of waste we dump in our rivers and bays are not poisoning the water, the hydrocarbons we pump into the air are not changing the climate, overfishing is not depleting the oceans, fossil fuels will never run out, wars that kill masses of civilians are an appropriate way to keep our hands on what's left, we are not desperately overdrawn at the environmental bank, and, really, the kids are all right."[45]

The slow food program involves taking the time not only to prepare and savor the food, but also to reflect on the economic, labor, agricultural, and transportation events preceding its arrival to the market. In this way it endorses a commodity-chain approach to food that chronicles the "life-history" of a food product and traces "the links that connect people and places at different points along the chain."[46] This practice provides consumers with better insight into just what is going into their mouths: not only in terms of ingredients such as pesticides, animal hormones, fats, sugars, vitamins, minerals, and the like but also in terms of the suffering of food workers and the greed of agribusiness and its agents in Congress.[47] But the assemblage of slow food could be strengthened further, I think, if it broadened its focus beyond the activities of humans. It tends to perceive of food as a resource or means, and thus to perpetuate the idea that nonhuman materiality is essentially passive stuff, on one side of an ontological divide between life and matter. To the extent that we recognize the agency of food, we also reorient our own experience of eating. What would happen if slow food were to incorporate a greater sense of the active vitality of foodstuff? If I am right that an image of inert matter helps animate our current practice of aggressively wasteful and planet-endangering consumption, then a materiality experienced as a lively force with agentic capacity could animate a more ecologically sustainable public.

In contrast to this picture of food as a tool to "be taken possession of if life is to continue," I have construed food as itself an actant in an agentic assemblage that includes among its members my metabolism, cognition, and moral sensibility. Human intentionality is surely an important element of the public that is emerging around the idea of diet, obesity, and food security, but it is not the only actor or necessarily the key operator in it. Food, as a self-altering, dissipative materiality, is also a player. It enters into what we become. It is one of the many agencies operative in the moods, cognitive dispositions, and moral sensibilities that we bring to bear as we engage the questions of what to eat, how to get it, and when to stop.

4

A Life of Metal

In a short story by Franz Kafka called "A Report to an Academy," the urbane but hirsute Rotpeter speaks before a rapt audience of humans: "Honored members of the Academy! You have done me the honor of inviting me to give you an account of the life I formerly led as an ape. . . . What I have to tell [will] . . . indicate the line an erstwhile ape has had to follow in entering and establishing himself in the world of men." Through an accelerated program of evolution, Rotpeter apes his way into the human life world: he learns to smoke a pipe and drink some schnapps, and then, elated by these achievements and "because I could not help it, because my senses were reeling," calls out "a brief and unmistakable 'Hallo!' breaking into human speech, and with this outburst broke into the human community, and felt its echo: 'Listen, he's talking.'" [1]

Rotpeter gives an account of his "life": the term here refers to a biological condition consistent with the capacity for emotion, sociality, and reflection. This is a life, Kafka makes clear, that apes share with men, for the difference between them is only that between points on a single

"line." Since Kafka's time, the gap between human and animal has nar-
rowed even further, as one after another of the traits or talents thought
to be unique to humanity are found to exist also in nonhuman animals.[2]
It is no longer so controversial to say that animals have a biosocial, communicative, or even conceptual life. But can nonorganic bodies also
have a life? Can materiality itself be vital?

In the previous chapters, the vitality of matter referred to the conative
drive or motility of simple or protobodies, to the tendency of forces to
form agentic assemblages, or to the ability of plants and animal matter
to induce effects in the human bodies that eat them. In this chapter I
turn my attention explicitly to the figure of life to see just how far it can
be pulled away from its mooring in the physiological and organic. Does
life only make sense as one side of a life-matter binary, or is there such
a thing as a mineral or metallic life, or a life of the it in "it rains"? I think
that there is, and that there are good ecological and biotechnological
reasons for us to get better acquainted with it.[3]

A Life

In a short essay by Gilles Deleuze called "Immanence: A Life," we are
introduced to the concept of "a" life. As the indefinite article suggests,
this is an indeterminate vitality, a "pure a-subjective current."[4] A life is
visible only fleetingly, for it is "a pure event freed . . . from the subjectivity and objectivity of what happens."[5] A life inhabits that uncanny
nontime existing between the various moments of biographical or morphological time. When it pokes into the scene, we catch a glimpse of the
virtual subsisting in Rotpeter's life world. Deleuze cites as an example
of this impersonal vitality very small children who, though not yet individuals, are "singularities" in that each, according to the contingencies
of their encounters, expresses just *this* smile, or gesture, or grimace.
These little ones "are traversed by an immanent life that is pure power
and even beatitude. . . . The indefinites of a life."[6] The pure power of
a life can manifest as beatitude, or as an unspeakable, sheer violence,
and I would amend Deleuze's term here to acknowledge the dark side
of "*a* life." Veena Das, in her ethnography of people's attempts to piece
their lives back together in the wake of "world-annihilating" violence

(e.g., the mass killings after the assassination of Indira Gandhi), notes a certain "frozen-slide quality of the . . . non-narrations" of such violence. This is when words become "numbed" or seem to have lost "touch with life," by which Das means that they have lost touch with a cultural life world.[7] Could it be that in losing touch with the life world, these utterances thereby express "a life"? But now a life no longer looks so appealing, and here Das's work suggests to me that the eruption of a life ought to be described less exclusively through metaphors of overflow and vitality. Sometimes a life is experienced less as beatitude and more as terror, less as the plentitude of the virtual and more as a radically meaningless void.

A life thus names a restless activeness, a destructive-creative force-presence that does not coincide fully with any specific body. A life tears the fabric of the actual without ever coming fully "out" in a person, place, or thing. A life points to what *A Thousand Plateaus* describes as "matter-*movement*" or "matter-*energy*," a "matter in variation that enters assemblages and leaves them."[8] A life is a vitality proper not to any individual but to "pure immanence," or that protean swarm that is not actual though it is real: "A life contains only virtuals. It is made of virtualities."[9] A life is "a-subjective": Deleuze elsewhere laments the way French novelists tend to reduce life to "something personal," whereas the genuine writer strives to become a "great Alive" who is "only too weak for the life which runs in him or for the affects which pass in him."[10] We can hear in that quotation an echo of Friedrich Nietzsche's distinctive brand of vitalism, expressed, for example, in *Will to Power*: "Do you know what Life is to me? A monster of energy . . . that does not expend itself but only transforms itself. . . . [A] play of forces and waves of forces, at the same time one and many . . . ; a sea of forces flowing and rushing together, eternally changing" (entry 1067).[11]

The Dead Weight of Adamantine Chains

In a play by Aeschylus called *Prometheus Bound*, the chains that bind Prometheus are as dead, immobile, and actual as a life is vibratory, liquid, and virtual. In the first scene, Kratos (Might) calls on Hephaestus (the metallurgist) to secure these chains:

This is the world's limit that we have come to;

this is the Scythian country, an untrodden desolation.

Hephaestus, it is you that must heed the commands the father laid upon
you

to nail this malefactor to the high craggy rocks

in fetters unbreakable of adamantine chain.[12]

Hephaestus, friend to Prometheus, reluctantly cedes to Kratos, just as Prometheus must yield to metal, for the chains are indeed *adamantine*, from the Greek *adamantinos*: of the *hardest* metal, like iron or steel. The "malefactor" struggles mightily against them, but his flesh is no match for the hard and impassive metal, an absolute no.

The association of metal with passivity or a dead thingness persists: the "adamantine chain" is one of a long line of tropes that will come to include the iron cage, brass tacks, steely glares, iron wills, solid gold hits. Who would choose *metal* as the symbol of vitality? Deleuze and Félix Guattari: in a short section of the "Nomadology" plateau, they name metal as the exemplar of a vital materiality; it is metal that best reveals this quivering effervescence; it is metal, bursting with a life, that gives rise to "the prodigious idea of Nonorganic Life."[13]

I follow Deleuze and Guattari in experimenting with the "prodigious" idea that activity is the "vague essence" of matter.[14] But just what kind of activity is this? Thomas Hobbes long ago insisted that life was but matter in motion, that there was "a continual relinquishing of one place, and acquiring of another" by bodies.[15] Is this the "material vitality" of which Deleuze and Guattari speak? Not quite, for whereas Hobbes focused attention on the activity of formed bodies as they move through a void of space, Deleuze and Guattari highlight an activeness that is not quite bodily and not quite spatial, because a body-in-space is only one of its possible modalities. This activity is better imagined through terms such as quivering, evanescence, or an indefinite or nonpurposive suspense. This vibratory vitality precedes, or subsists within, or is simply otherwise than, formed bodies. *A Thousand Plateau* is full of quickening, effervescent proto- and no-bodies—of becomings-animals, of Bodies without Organs—which are best described, in Spinozist terms, as "a set of speeds and slownesses between unformed particles [with] . . . the individuality of a day, a season, a year, a life."[16] This is the activity of intensities rather than of things with extension in space, the "pure pro-

ductivity" of "virtual" matter or "matter-energy."[17] Deleuze and Guattari
believe that such a "material vitalism . . . doubtless exists everywhere
but is ordinarily hidden or covered, rendered unrecognizable by the
hylomorphic model."[18]

The "hylomorphic" model (a term they borrow from the French philosopher of technology, Gilbert Simondon) is an explanatory model of
how bodies change or develop. According to it a presumably passive, unorganized, or raw matter can be given organic "form" only by the agency
of something that is not itself material. The hylomorphic model is thus a
kind of vitalism, positing some nonmaterial supplement with the power
to transform mere matter into embodied life. Leon Kass, discussed in
chapter 3, offered a hylomorphic account of eating: metabolism, as the
mechanical movements of mere matter, cannot explain the "life" of the
organism, for that requires "some immaterial 'thing' that unites and in-
forms" the organism.[19] Kass acknowledges that this spiritual force is
"absolutely dependent upon material" ("One never finds the form of
lion separated from its leonine flesh"), but it has a reality that is both
independent of and deeper and truer than flesh. Thus it is, says Kass,
that the "*organism persists, though its materials do not.*"[20]

According to a hylomorphic model, any "formative" power must be
external to a brute, mechanical matter. The model can neither posit nor
discern the presence of what John Marks calls the "implicit topological
forms" inside materiality. These topological tendencies do not merely
put up a passive resistance to the activities of external agents but they
actively endeavor to express themselves: they are conative without being
quite "bodied." The hylomorphic model is ignorant of what woodwork-
ers and metallurgists know quite well: there exist "variable intensive affects" and "incipient qualities" of matter that "external forms [can only]
bring out and facilitate."[21] Instead of a formative power detachable from
matter, artisans (and mechanics, cooks, builders, cleaners, and anyone
else intimate with things) encounter a creative materiality with incipient tendencies and propensities, which are variably enacted depending
on the other forces, affects, or bodies with which they come into close
contact.

In sum, when Deleuze and Guattari speak of a material vitality, they
do not mean simply to draw attention to a "Hobbesian" movement of
bodies in space. Neither are they making the familiar point about the *his-*

toricity of objects, about the way the form and meaning of things change as they age and detach from a social whole or become embedded in new relations with new things. (This is what the "social lives of objects" tradition in anthropology, sociology, and science studies does.) What Deleuze and Guattari set their sights on is something else: a vibratory effluescence that persists before and after any arrangement in space: the peculiar "motility" of an intensity. Or what nonrepresentational geographers like Alan Latham and Derek McCormack call the "processually emergent" quality of matter-energy, or what the philosopher Brian Massumi describes as the "pressing crowd of incipiencies and tendencies" that *is* matter.[22] The aim here is to rattle the adamantine chain that has bound materiality to inert substance and that has placed the organic across a chasm from the inorganic. The aim is to articulate the elusive idea of a materiality that is *itself* heterogeneous, itself a differential of intensities, itself *a* life. In this strange, *vital* materialism, there is no point of pure stillness, no indivisible atom that is not itself aquiver with virtual force.

Michel Foucault may also have been trying to mark this kind of activeness when he spoke of an "incorporeal" dimension of bodies, a quaking tension unrepresentable within a philosophical frame of bodies-in-space and unthinkable when matter is conceived as extension. In "Theatrum Philosophicum" Foucault introduces the idea of the incorporeal by recalling the Epicurean idea of simulacra, those one-layer-thin sheets of atoms continually being shed from the thicker and slower compound bodies of objects. These filmy sheaves, and not the full object in the round, are the stimuli to human perception, for it is these mobile floaters that hit our sense apparatus to give notice of the presence of an outside. Simulacra, says Foucault, are a strange kind of matter: they are all surface and no depth; "emissions" that rise like "the wisps of a fog"; a materiality that "dissipate[s] the density of matter."[23] Foucault names this the incorporeal because it is not quite a discrete body or substantial corpus. But also because this mobile activity remains *immanent* to the material world, remains *in*-corporeality.[24]

How can this ontological imaginary square with our everyday encounters with what greet us as stable bodies? Here, the vital materialist can invoke a theory of relativity (of sorts): the stones, tables, technologies, words, and edibles that confront us as fixed are mobile, internally heterogeneous materials whose rate of speed and pace of change are *slow* compared to the duration and velocity of the human bodies participating in and perceiving them. "Objects" appear as such because their becoming proceeds at a speed or a level below the threshold of human discernment. It is hard indeed to keep one's mind wrapped around a materiality that is not reducible to extension in space, difficult to dwell with the notion of an incorporeality or a differential of intensities. This is because to live, humans need to interpret the world reductively as a series of fixed objects, a need reflected in the rhetorical role assigned to the word *material*. As noun or adjective *material* denotes some stable or rock-bottom reality, something adamantine. To invoke "material interests" is, for example, to position oneself as a realist compared to those who trade in empty abstractions or naive hopes.[25] Historical materialism also relies on the trope of fixity: Ben Anderson notes a long "tradition of structuralist and historical materialist work that articulates 'the material' as a founding pre-discursive space standing before, and determining, 'in the last instance', a realm of culture."[26]

A Life of Metal

Aeschylus presented Prometheus's chains as fixed matter. The chains are strong because their metal is uniform and homogeneous, devoid of any internal differences (variations in texture, ductility, rates of decay, etc.) that Prometheus might have exploited to break it apart. The chains are impregnable, we are told, because their matter does not vary across its own surface or depth.

It seems, however, that this is not a good empirical account of the microstructure of metals, which consists in irregularly shaped crystals that do not form a seamless whole. The historian of science Cyril Smith offers this description:

> Metals, like nearly all other inorganic substances, are polycrystalline in nature, that is, they consist of hosts of very tiny crystals packed together to fill space. The shape of these crystals is not that of the beautiful [gem stone] . . . , but [they] have curved surfaces because each crystal interferes with its neighbor's growth, and the interface determines the shape more than does the internal structure. . . . If grains are separated from each other, they will

be seen to have few flat surfaces and many curved ones. They are not plane-faced polyhedra and they differ in size and shape: the only uniformity lies in the angles at which the faces meet each other to form the edges. On the average, each grain has about fourteen faces, with an average of five and one-seventh sides.[27]

The crystal grains of, say, iron come in a large variety of sizes and shapes, depending on "the space-filling pressures of their neighbors."[28] Though the atoms within each individual grain are "arranged in regular array on a space lattice,"[29] there are also "*imperfections* in the array,"[30] most notably the presence of loose atoms at the "interfaces" of grains. These atoms "belong" to none of the grains,[31] and they render the boundaries of each grain porous and quivering: a grain of iron is *not* "some kind of an enveloped entity," as is "a grain of wheat."[32] This means that the crystalline structure of metal is full of holes or "intercrystalline spaces."[33] These "vacancies" can be "as important as the atom" in determining properties of a particular metal.[34] It is the variegated topology of a metal sheet or rod that metallurgists exploit when, for example, they use heat to produce an alloy or to turn iron into steel.

A metallic *vitality*, a (impersonal) life, can be seen in the quivering of these free atoms at the edges between the grains of the polycrystalline edifice. Manuel De Landa points to another instance of a life of metal in the "complex dynamics of spreading cracks." These cracks, too, are a function of "certain defects . . . within the component crystals"; they are "line defects." The line of travel of these cracks is not deterministic but expressive of an emergent causality, whereby grains respond on the spot and in real time to the idiosyncratic movements of their neighbors, and then to their neighbors' response to their response, and so on, in feedback spirals.[35]

The dynamics of spreading cracks may be an example of what Deleuze and Guattari call the "nomadism" of matter. Playing on the notion of metal as a conductor of electricity, they say that metal "conducts" (ushers) itself through a series of self-transformations, which is not a sequential movement from one fixed point to another, but a tumbling of continuous variations with fuzzy borders. What is more, this tumbling is a function not only of the actions applied to metal *by* metallurgists but of the protean activeness of the metal itself: "[In] the Sumerian empire, there are a dozen varieties of copper inventoried with different names according to their places of origin and degrees of refining. This forms . . . a continuous melody of copper, and the artisan will say: that's what I need. But regardless of the breaks operated by the artisan, there is no fixed order for alloys, variety of alloys, continuous variability of alloys."[36]

Deleuze and Guattari, following Henri Bergson and anticipating more recent work in contemporary complexity theory, posit a mode of becoming that is both material and creative, rather than mechanical and equilibrium maintaining. Though much of the time the process of material composition is regular and predictable, sometimes the arraignment of various intensities produces unpredictably mobile fault lines or energetic currents. Deleuze and Guattari may gesture toward this dimension of free play of a life with their oxymoronic invocation of a material "*esprit de corps.*"[37]

Sometimes, of course, Aeschylus is right: metallic materiality can act as an absolute no, as when lead refuses the current of electricity or when the links of an iron chain are stronger than the muscles of a man. But Cyril and other Smiths know that this is only part of the story of the life of metal.

A Life of Men

I have so far been speaking of metal as if it existed independently of other materials. But metal is always metallurgical, always an alloy of the endeavors of many bodies, always something worked on by geological, biological, and often human agencies. And human metalworkers are themselves emergent effects of the vital materiality they work. "We are," says Vladimir Ivanovich Vernadsky, "walking, talking minerals."[38] This theme, of the "it" inside the "I," is one to which I shall return at the end of the book. Indeed, Smith's central thesis in *A History of Metallography* is that it was the human metalworkers' intense intimacy with their material that enabled *them*, rather than (the less hands-on) scientists, to be the ones to first discover the polycrystalline structure of nonorganic matter. The desire of the craftsperson to see what a metal can *do*, rather than the desire of the scientist to know what a metal *is*, enabled the former to discern *a* life in metal and thus, eventually, to collaborate more productively with it.[39]

Over the past decade or so, many political theorists, geographers, art historians, philosophers, sociologists, dancers, literary theorists, and others have explored the contributions made by affect to public culture, whereby affect refers to how moods and aesthetic sensibilities influence ethics and politics as much as do words, arguments, and reasons. While I agree that human affect is a key player, in this book the focus is on an affect that is not only not fully susceptible to rational analysis or linguistic representation but that is also not specific to humans, organisms, or even to bodies: the affect of technologies, winds, vegetables, minerals. Social science has for a long time acknowledged that however "cultural" an assemblage (e.g., capitalism, the military-industrial complex, gender) may be, it still can resist and elude cultural control. Social constructs are widely understood as having a negative "life" of their own. The figure of *a life* pushes this point. First, a life is not only a negative recalcitrance but a positive, active virtuality: a quivering protoblob of creative élan. Second, a life draws attention not to a lifeworld of human designs or their accidental, accumulated effects, but to an interstitial field of non-personal, ahuman forces, flows, tendencies, and trajectories.

The project, then, is to theorize a kind of geoaffect or material vitality, a theory born of a methodological commitment to avoid anthropocentrism and biocentrism—or perhaps it is more accurate to say that it is born of an irrational love of matter. Here another "prodigious idea" comes to mind: Mario Perniola's "the sex appeal of the inorganic." Perniola posits the existence in humans of a "neutral sexuality, an abstract and endless excitation, . . . with no concern for beauty, age, and in general, form." This neutral sexuality draws human bodies to apparently dead things—to objects, stones, bits of matter. Humans, inexplicably, are "excited" by what we otherwise believe to be "altogether inadequate stimuli."[40] The "sex appeal" of the inorganic, like a life, is another way to give voice to what I think of as a shimmering, potentially violent vitality intrinsic to matter.

Vitalists, too, have insisted on the presence of some kind of energetic, free agency whose spontaneity cannot be captured by the figure of bodies or by a mechanistic model of nature. But if for vitalists like Bergson and Hans Driesch, matter seemed to require a not-quite-material supplement, an *élan vital* or entelechy, to become animate and mobile, for Deleuze and Guattari it is clear that materiality needs no animating accessory. It is figured as *itself* the "active principle."

5

Neither Vitalism nor Mechanism

In the previous chapters I have experimented with narrating events (encounters with litter, electricity, foods, metal) in ways that present nonhuman materialities as bona fide participants rather than as recalcitrant objects, social constructs, or instrumentalities. What would happen to our thinking about nature if we experienced materialities as actants, and how would the direction of public policy shift if it attended more carefully to their trajectories and powers? I am looking for a materialism in which matter is figured as a vitality at work both inside and outside of selves, and is a force to be reckoned with without being purposive in any strong sense.

Such a vital materialism would run parallel to a historical materialism focused more exclusively on economic and social structures of human power. It would be part ad hoc invention and part a gathering of elements from a previous tradition of thinking inhabited by Epicurus, Lucretius, Thomas Hobbes, Baruch Spinoza, Denis Diderot, Friedrich Nietzsche, Henry David Thoreau, and others. In that tradition, the distinction between life and matter, or organic and inorganic, or human and nonhuman, or man and god, is not always the most important or salient difference to recognize.

A vital materialism today would also do well, I think, to reengage the so-called vitalists, especially those who, in the early twentieth century, called themselves "critical" or "modern" vitalists.[1] Henri Bergson and Hans Driesch, for example, distinguished themselves from those "naive" vitalists who posited a spiritual force or soul that was immune to any scientific or experimental inquiry. The critical vitalists also opposed the mechanistic model of nature assumed by the "materialists" of their day. Nature was not, for Bergson and Driesch, a machine, and matter was not in principle calculable: something always escaped quantification, prediction, and control. They named that something *élan vital* (Bergson) and entelechy (Driesch). Their efforts to remain *scientific* while acknowledging some *incalculability* to things is for me exemplary.

In this chapter I try to show how Driesch and Bergson, in their attempts to give philosophical voice to the vitality of things, came very close to articulating a vital materialism. But they stopped short: they could not imagine a *materialism* adequate to the vitality they discerned in natural processes. (Instead, they dreamed of a not-quite-material life force.) Their vitalisms nevertheless fascinate me, in part because we share a common foe in mechanistic or deterministic materialism, and in part because the fabulously vital materiality of which I dream is so close to their vitalism.

Critical Vitalism

Just before the First World War, there was in the United States a new sense of the universe as lively and incalculable, as "a world of incessant and unforeseeable change and possibility, a world always about to be."[2] There was, in short, an outbreak of vitalism. Central to this vitalism, a revival fueled by Bergson's *L'évolution créatrice* (1907; published as *Creative Evolution* in 1910) and Driesch's popular Gifford lectures titled *The Science and Philosophy of the Organism* (1907–8), was the idea that life was irreducible to a mechanical or deterministic matter. There must exist a life principle that (sometimes) animated matter, which was not itself material even though it took on existence only when in relation to matter. "The concept of *nature* must be enlarged," Driesch wrote, so that it "consists of one completely spatial and one only partly spatial portion."[3] The vital force, or that "only partly spatial portion" of nature, provided the impetus for morphological changes in the embryo. But the critical vitalists also thought it was responsible for the progressive development of personality and history: insofar as seeds, embryos, personalities, and cultures were all *organic* wholes, there was an isomorphism between physical, psychological, and civilizational orders.

There was some disagreement among the critical vitalists about just how to depict the vital force: Bergson's *élan vital*, for example, competed with Driesch's entelechy. But on the question of what matter was, they agreed with each other as well as with their materialist opponents: matter was unfree, mechanistic, and deterministic (though "dynamic" in the sense of capable of undergoing regular changes of state). Whereas the vitalists lifted instances of "life" outside the reach of this mechanical world, the materialists insisted that every entity or force, however complex, "organic," or subtle, was ultimately or in principle explicable in mechanical or, as they called it, "physico-chemical" terms.

Bergson and Driesch each identified a not-wholly-calculable, not-quite-material impetus — a vital force or principle of life — as responsible for such growth. Perhaps one of the reasons they enjoyed great popularity in America (Bergson's lecture at Columbia University in 1913 occasioned one of the first traffic jams in New York) was because they were received as defenders of freedom, of a certain open-endedness to life, in the face of a modern science whose pragmatic successes were threatening to confirm the picture of the universe as a godless machine.[4]

The star of this chapter is the fascinating but little known vitalism of Driesch, though I will also attend to the vitalism of his more famous contemporary, Bergson. I will focus on the different figures of vital force (that life principle infusing an otherwise passive matter) put forward by each. And because Immanuel Kant's thinking about life and matter was so influential to both of them,[5] I will also explore Kant's flirtation (in *Critique of Judgment*) with the idea of a *Bildungstrieb* (formative drive) that made the difference between inert matter and organic life. Following Kant, Driesch and Bergson took pains to tie their answer to the question "what is life?" to insights provided by the experimental science of their day. And though the biophilosophies of Driesch and Bergson both complicated Kant's strong life/matter binary, neither fully sheds Kant's image of inert matter. The association of matter with passivity still haunts us today, I think, weakening our discernment of the force of things. But it might be only a small step from the creative agency of a vital force to a materiality conceived as itself this creative agent.

Bildungstrieb

In *Critique of Judgment*, Kant famously insisted that matter as such can have no "spontaneity":[6] "We cannot even think of living matter as possible. (The concept of it involves a contradiction, since the essential character of matter is lifelessness, *inertia*)" (*Judgment*, sec. 73, #394); we must not "endow matter, as mere matter, with a property [viz., the property of life . . .] that conflicts with its nature" (*Judgment*, sec. 65, #374; brackets in original).

Kant's insistence on an unbridgeable chasm between life and "crude matter" (*Judgment*, sec. 81, #424) raises for him the difficult question of how then to represent the close conjoining of life and matter in the case of organisms. An organism is that kind of being which we can "cognize . . . as possible only as a natural purpose," or as "a *self-organizing* being" (*Judgment*, sec. 65, #374) that is "both cause and effect of itself" (*Judgment*, sec. 65, #372).[7] Kant addresses the problem in part by invoking a special "formative drive," or *Bildungstrieb*, which attaches itself to and enlivens dead matter.[8]

Bildungstrieb names the inscrutable self-organizational power present in organisms but not in mere aggregates of matter. It is an "ability" distinguishable from "the commonly present, merely mechanistic power of formation" (*Judgment*, sec. 81, #424).[9] Some such "principle of original organization" must be posited, Kant reasons, for "to speak of *autocracy* of matter in products that our understanding can grasp only as purposes is to use a word without meaning" (*Judgment*, sec. 80, #421). *Bildungstrieb*, one of the marvelous concepts that populate Kant's philosophical landscape, names a nonmaterial, teleological drive that imparts to matter its functional coherence, its "organic" quality (wherein each part of the whole is both cause and effect of the others). *Bildungstrieb* is what

impels an undifferentiated, crude mass of matter to become an organized articulation of cooperating parts, the highest version of which is
"Man."[10]

Kant is careful to distinguish his *Bildungstrieb* from a disembodied
soul: "We must [not] supplement matter with an alien principle (soul),
conjoined to it" (*Judgment*, sec. 65, #375). A soul is something said to be
able to exist *without* a body present, whereas *Bildungstrieb* has existence
only inside a body, only in conjunction with the mechanical activities
of matter, with, that is, those activities driven by Newtonian (rather
than vital) forces. Kant was careful to associate *Bildungstrieb* very closely
with matter without erasing the difference between them. The dependence of *Bildungstrieb* on matter is, in Kant's view, what distinguishes
his own position from that of the naive vitalists of his time. The concept of *Bildungstrieb* would *not* banish the organism from the system of
corporeal nature; it did *not* violate one of Kant's core methodological
procedures, that is, "to explain all products and events of nature, even
the most purposive ones, in mechanical terms as far as we possibly can
(we cannot tell what are the limits of our ability for this way of investi-
gating)" (*Judgment*, sec. 78, #415). As we shall see, Bergson and Driesch,
too, distinguished their figures of vital force from religious notions of
the soul; they also rejected the idea that the vital force could have any
existence apart from the bodies in which it operated.

Kant borrowed the concept of *Bildungstrieb* from Johann Friedrich
Blumenbach, a member of the medical faculty at Göttingen. In August
1790 (just after the publication of *Critique of Judgment*), Kant wrote
to Blumenbach to thank him for his "excellent work on the formative
force [*Bildungstrieb*]. . . . [In it], you unite two principles — the physical-
mechanical and the sheerly teleological mode of explanation of organized nature. These are modes which one would not have thought
capable of being united. In this you have quite closely approached the
idea with which I have been chiefly occupied — but an idea that required
such confirmation [as you provide] through facts."[11] Kant endorsed Blumenbach's *Bildungstrieb* only as a regulative principle; it "would allow
the biologist to pursue the study of organisms *as if* they had developed
under the aegis of a directive, vital force, while yet restricting the researcher to explaining organic activity by appeal only to mechanistic
laws."[12] Blumenbach, especially early in his work, may have thought of

Bildungstrieb in a more empirical (or even experiential) sense, as when he speaks of it as the "inborn, life-long active drive" that "exists in all living creatures, from men to maggots and from cedar trees to mold."[13] Nevertheless, Blumenbach consistently insisted (in a way that pleased Kant) that the operations of *Bildungstrieb* could never become fully transparent to us. Kant writes approvingly in *Critique of Judgment* of Blumenbach's acknowledgment of the fundamentally "inscrutable" nature of *Bildungstrieb*, a causality necessarily obscure to us.[14] For Blumenbach as well as for Kant—and later for Driesch—the formative drive can be known only indirectly, only by examining its effects, that is, the specific organisms it had composed. (My vital materialism posits the causality of *both* inorganic and organic matter to be, to some extent, inscrutable to us, and also that a mechanistic model is inadequate to both.)

As Kant saw it, one virtue of *Bildungstrieb* as a concept was that it provided a way to affirm the *uniqueness* of the phenomenon of organic growth, which was simultaneously a mechanical and a teleological process. Organisms were mechanical in that they were governed by Newtonian forces that applied to *all* physical systems, but they also had to be seen as systems of purposes, and as such required a different principle of exposition. Blumenbach modeled his *Bildungstrieb* on the idea of a Newtonian force of gravity; he sought to do "for organic bodies what Newton had accomplished for inert matter."[15]

Blumenbach, like Kant, rejected the idea that inorganic matter could "spontaneously" give rise to organic life (hence the need to posit a nonmaterial *Bildungstrieb* in the first place), and both men also sought to associate the vital force very, very closely with matter. Blumenbach notes, for example, that repaired parts of a damaged organism are *never* quite as large as the originals, a fact due, he reasoned, to the necessary correspondence between the intensity of the *Trieb* (drive) and the volume of the material. This was empirical evidence of the extreme familiarity of *Bildungstrieb* with the matter to which it was bound.[16]

Blumenbach focused on the constraint imposed on the formative force by the spatiality of matter, and so did Kant. But Kant pointed also to a constraint *internal* to *Bildungstrieb*: the formative drive includes within it and thus is partially determined by implicit or *virtual* "purposive predispositions [*Anlagen*] imparted to the stock" (*Judgment*, sec. 81, #423).[17] These predispositions direct the natural organism toward a

set of ends, thus linking its becoming to a stable order of Creation. One
could say that the moment of *natura naturans* (*Bildungstrieb*) is balanced
by the moment of *natura naturata* (*Anlagen*). My point here is that Kant's
Bildungstrieb is not radically open-ended in the effects it could produce:
tied both to materiality and to *Anlagen*, it could not produce new beings
never seen before or those not already virtually preformed in the stock
from which the organism sprang (*Judgment*, sec. 81, #423).

Kant's invocation of *Bildungstrieb* reveals much about his notion
of materiality: it is a dull, mechanistic stuff in need of a supplement
(which is neither material nor soul) to become active. *Bildungstrieb* is
also an *impersonal* agency that comes automatically with an organically
organized body; it is indifferently distributed to all organisms. But lest
the idea of *Bildungstrieb* suggest that humans were *determined* by a purposive drive, Kant was careful to add that in the organism "Man," the
Bildungstrieb coexisted alongside a will that is (or we must assume to be)
free. Kant sought to make the case not only for a qualitative gap between
inorganic matter and organic life but also for a quantum leap between
humans and all other organisms.[18]

In addition to the appeal to a *Bildungstrieb*, further evidence of Kant's
flirtation with vitalism can be seen in his response to the materialism
of the Epicureans, who rejected the idea of matter as inert and who,
by extension, depicted the difference between human and nonhuman
(and between organism and machine) as a matter of degree rather than
kind, as more a case of different compositions of differently textured
and shaped materials. The Epicureans did not see the atomic swerve
(*clinamen*) as added or heterogeneous to matter, but as a lively impetus
intrinsic to materiality per se. Lucretius, for example, has no need to
import a *Bildungstrieb* or some other supplement into his physics, for his
universe consists not of dead matter and living beings but of swerving
atoms forming turbulent and productive flows.[19] (Here, the vital materialist sides with the Epicureans.)

Kant condemns Epicureanism as unscientific: without the heuristic
principle of purposiveness (expressed in *Bildungstrieb* but absent in Epicureanism), we would have to regard the exquisite, organic relationship between, say, a bird's anatomy and its flight as merely accidental.
We would, in other words, have to entertain the possibility that nature
"could have structured itself differently in a thousand ways without hit-
ting on precisely the [organic] unity" of a bird. But to regard the bird's

organic unity as a randomly generated fortuity would be to lack an "a priori . . . basis for that unity," which for Kant would mean to lack a *scientific* explanation (*Judgment*, sec. 61, #360).

Kant liked *Bildungstrieb* because it enabled him to combine teleological with mechanistic explanations. What interests me about it is that it gestures toward an impersonal, ahistorical agency, an impetus that "drives" men on. *Bildungstrieb* has an agentic power irreducible to the purposive energies invested in it by humans. For Kant, of course, any such drive would have to be thought of as having a divine source. Contra Kant, I think it is both possible and desirable to experiment with the idea of an impersonal agency integral to materiality as such, a vitality distinct from human or divine purposiveness.

In invoking a lively *Bildungstrieb* operative within the otherwise lifeless materiality of an organism, Kant sets the stage for the reflections on life and matter pursued by Bergson and Driesch. Driesch, to whom I will turn first, insisted that life was qualitatively different from matter and that, because mechanistic explanation is inadequate to biological forms, we must assume the presence of a nonmaterial impetus, of a vital force, *Trieb* — or what Driesch names as entelechy.

Entelechy

Driesch was an independently wealthy embryologist. He was also one of the first non-Jews to be stripped of his professorship by the Nazis because he objected to their use of his vitalism to justify a German conquest of "less vital" peoples. The question of the relationship between belief in vital force and political violence recurs today as one notes the conjoining of the evangelical Christian notion of a "culture of life" with a doctrine of preemptive war. (This is a topic taken up in the following chapter.)

In lectures at the University of Aberdeen in 1907–8, Driesch affirmed Kant's image of matter as in need of some supplement if it was to become active, organized, and capable of change in a structured but not fully determined way. I say "structured but not fully determined" because Driesch, again following Kant, imagined the vital principle not as an open-ended impetus but as shaped by certain predispositions intrinsic to the seed or embryo. Driesch also echoed Kant's claim that the vital principle would never become fully transparent to us and could be known only as an invisible presence performing the tasks in fact performed within the organism but which no mechanical matter could ever possibly perform by itself. Entelechy is born in the negative spaces of the machine model of nature, in the "gaps" in the "chain of strictly physico-chemical or mechanical events." Driesch rejects a Spinozist theory of "psycho-physical parallelism" precisely because Spinozism, as Driesch understands it, holds "that the physical side of [the] . . . duality forms a continuous chain of strictly physico-chemical or mechanical events without any gap in it."[20]

Because Driesch endorses Kant's critique of "dogmatic metaphysics," it is very important to him that his "proof" of vitalism be understood as a *negative* one: "All *proofs* of vitalism i.e. all reasonings by which it is shown that not even the machine-theory covers the field of biological phenomena, can only be indirect proofs: they can only make it clear that mechanical or singular causality is not sufficient for an explanation of what happens."[21] Driesch's case for entelechy also employs transcendental arguments: X *must* be operative, given the indisputable reality of y. For example, to demonstrate that the vital principle cannot be "physico-chemical" in nature, he starts from the observation that in morphogenesis (the process by which a fertilized egg becomes an adult organism), "manifoldness in space is produced where no manifoldness was." Though at first glance it might seem that this manifoldness in space emerged directly from the spatially uniform, undifferentiated egg, theoretical reason reveals this to be impossible: a *spatial* manifold cannot have a *spatial* unity as its source. Thus it must be that *some other kind* of "manifold" is present "previous to morphogenesis." Lacking an "extensive character," this prior manifold, the basis of the organism's later differentiation, *must* be an "'intensive manifoldness,'"[22] that is, "an agent acting manifoldly without being in itself manifold in space."[23] "That is to say, [it is] . . . composite, though not in space."[24] We thus have a first definition of entelechy: it is the *intensive* manifold out of which emerges the extensive manifoldness of the mature organism.

In addition to providing negative and indirect proof of entelechy, Driesch's case for vitalism also appeals to his positive and direct interventions in the laboratory. Indeed, what had initially provoked Driesch to posit the "autonomy of life" was not theoretical reason but experiments on cell division in the sea urchin. It was a calculated intrusion into the mechanism of sea urchins that uncovered for Driesch the fact that life was inexplicable if conceived exclusively as a mechanism. That entelechy was nonmaterial, nonspatial, and nonmechanical did not, however, mean that it was a psyche or spirit: "The contrary of *mechanical* is merely *non-mechanical*, and not 'psychical.'"[25] For Driesch as for Kant the vital principle must be conceived as neither mechanical body nor ethereal soul.

The goal of Driesch's laboratory work, and the reason for his strict adherence to the protocols of empirical science, was not simply to gain a more subtle understanding of the dynamic chemical and physical properties of the organism but also to better discern what *animated* the machine: "Why then occurs all that folding, and bending . . . , and all the other processes we have described? There must be something that *drives them out*, so to say."[26] Driesch names that something, that driving force, entelechy. Neither a substance nor an energy (though active only in relation to them), entelechy is "the non-mechanical agent responsible for the phenomena of life."[27] Like Kant, Driesch borrows his term of art: he takes *entelechy* from Aristotle, retaining its sense of a self-moving and self-altering power but rejecting its peculiarly Aristotelian teleology.[28]

In addition to animating matter, entelechy is also what "arranges" or composes artistically the bodies of organisms. To see how entelechy performs its "forming" task, *nonmechanically*, we need to take a closer look at morphogenesis, the mode of becoming that Driesch says is unique to organisms. Morphogenesis refers both to the process by which a blastocyst moves from a less to a more differentiated form (ontogenesis), and to the process by which a mature organism re-forms itself in response to damage or disease (restitution).[29] Inorganic systems are of course capable of *change*, but only life, says Driesch, can *morph*: a crystal formation can diminish or increase in mass, but it cannot become qualitatively more complex and it cannot restore itself by replacing or repairing parts such that the "same" whole endures.[30] The parts of a plant, unlike the mineral and chemical elements of a mountain, are *members*: when a change occurs in one, the others are not only thereby affected but affected in such a way as to provoke a *coordinated* response. To further sharpen the contrast between machines and organisms, Driesch notes that whereas a phonograph "receives vibrations of the air and gives off vibrations of the air" and so "previous stimulus and later reaction are of the *same* nature," in an organism the "impressions on its sensory organs," for example sounds, can issue in conversations, which belong to an "absolutely *different* class of phenomena."[31]

Neither can inorganic systems (as mere matter) *learn* from their experiences, says Driesch, for that entails not only "the mere recollection of what has happened, but . . . also the ability to use *freely* in another field of occurring the elements of former happening for newly combined *individualised* specificities of the future which are *wholes*."[32] Driesch describes this free activity as following "a curious principle, which may be called . . . *individual correspondence*. That is to say: any real action is an *individual* 'answer' to an individual stimulus."[33] Such individualized action tailored specifically to the situation at hand constitutes what he terms the "directing" action of entelechy.

Elsewhere Driesch describes this directing power inside the organism as a kind of gatekeeping function: entelechy decides which of the many formative possibilities inside the emergent organism become actual. In (what will come to be known as) the stem cells of the sea urchin, for example, there is "an enormous number of possibilities of happening in the form of difference of 'potential'" in each cell.[34] But if "something else *can* be formed than actually is formed, why then does there happen in each case just what happens and nothing else?" Again Driesch reasons that there *must* be some agent responsible for the singular specificity of the outcome, some decisive agent guarding the entrance to actuality:

> According to our hypothesis, . . . in each of the *n* cells the *same* great number of possibilities of becoming is physico-chemically prepared, but checked, so to say, by entelechy. Development of the system now depends, according to our assumption, upon the fact that entelechy *relaxes its suspensory power* and thus . . . in cell *a* one thing is allowed to occur, in cell *b* another, and in cell *c* something else; but what now actually occurs in *a* might also have occurred in *b* or *c*; for *each one* out of an enormous number of possibilities *may* occur in each cell. Thus, by the regulatory *relaxing* action of entelechy in a system in which an enormous variety of possible events had been suspended by it, it may happen that an *equal distribution* of *possibilities* is transformed into an *unequal distribution* of *actual effects*.[35]

Note that Driesch here again describes the power of entelechy to determine the trajectory of organic growth in negative terms: it acts by selectively "relaxing" its "suspensory power." This capacity for (nega-tive) choice operates in a context of multiple possibilities, and so the actual path of organic growth is not determined in a rigid, mechanical way. Likewise, neither are the individual movements of an adult organ-ism fully determined or mechanically caused by the stimuli of their en-vironment: outside events do affect the individual, but they create only "*a general stock* of *possibilities* for further acting and have *not* determined all further reactions quite in detail."[36] There is thus an "*indefiniteness* of correspondence between specific cause and specific effect."[37] Neverthe-less, the organism's ability to respond perspicuously and inventively to an event (its capacity for "individual correspondence") is not *radically* free: entelechy, like *Bildungstrieb*, is incapable of producing that which is *utterly* new, for its intelligent responsiveness remains under the guid-ance of compacted intensities (which Driesch calls "a general stock of possibilities" and Kant calls "purposive dispositions," or *Anlagen*).

Driesch affirms a qualitative difference between entelechy-infused life and inorganic matter: entelechy (as a *self-directing* activeness) is what distinguishes a crystal from an embryo, a parking lot from a lawn, me from my corpse. But Driesch is less certain about a qualitative dif-ference between human and other forms of life. On the one hand, the directing power of entelechy (unlike its "formative power," which is dis-tributed equally across all organisms) operates inside humans with a special intensity. But, on the other hand, Driesch also claims that some analog of knowing and willing exists in all organic processes.[38] He does not know just what this analog is, but though it "may seem very strange" that the most perspicuous means toward the end of maintaining the organic whole are "known and *found*" by every organism, "it is a *fact*."[39] Kant positioned humans as noumenal as well as phenomenal, as natu-ral bodies but also as above or outside the order of nature. This human exceptionalism is less pronounced in Driesch.[40]

Close attention to morphogenesis reveals to Driesch a mode of be-coming distinctive to "life": it is change that organizes and sustains a complex whole even amid changing circumstances. Might these organic wholes be complex *machines*? If so, there would be no need to invoke a vital principle like entelechy to explain morphogenesis. Driesch takes up the question explicitly and finds all mechanistic accounts of mor-phogenesis inadequate. Here is why: an organism is a working whole

capable of innovative action—it repairs injured parts, re-creates sev-
ered ones, and adapts old parts to perform new roles—all to maintain
the normal functioning of the whole and to preserve its identity. In contrast, a machine (as a mere aggregation of physico-chemical elements)
"*does not remain itself, if you take from it whatever you please.*"[41] Because
machines cannot self-repair, one must again conclude that there must
be at work in the organism some nonmaterial agent that provides "the
specific and real stimulus which calls forth the restoring processes."[42]

Neither does the machine analogy hold, says Driesch, for individual
organs of an organism. An ovary, for example, emerges from a single,
totipotent cell ("Anlage") that "has been divided and re-divided innumerable times,"[43] but "*how could a machine . . . be divided innumerable
times and yet remain what it was?*"[44] Driesch's experimental evidence for
this involves the hydroid polyp Tubularia, whose cut segments, however
small, will regenerate the whole organism. According to the mecha-
nists, each segment would have to contain a machine, each of which,
when cut in two, would continue to function as a half-size but complete
machine. Mikhail Bakhtin, an early critic of Driesch's work, aptly describes the conclusions Driesch draws from his experiments on Tubularia: "What kind of machine is this which we can divide to our heart's
content and which always preserves its normal functions? A number of
highly complex, large and small machines with the same function must
be contained within our two cm segment. . . . Moreover, these machines
overlap one another: parts of one correspond to completely different
parts of another. Such a mechanism contradicts the very concept of a
mechanism. Thus, the machine theory (in Driesch's opinion) leads to
the absurd."[45]

In describing entelechy as the invisible but "real stimulus" for the
movement of morphing, Driesch also considers the question of whether
entelechy might be conceived as "energy," and thus as a special kind
of physico-chemical entity. Again he answers no, rejecting the idea of
"vital energy" as oxymoronic, for life is *unquantifiable* and all energies
remain for him quantities: "In asserting . . . phenomena to be of the
energetical order, we state that there can be a *more or less* of them. . . .
But entelechy *lacks all the characteristics of quantity*: entelechy *is order of
relation* and absolutely *nothing* else."[46]

Driesch consistently emphasizes the intensely intimate relationship between entelechy and the regular, observable operations of matter. Entelechy can only make use of "the possibilities of becoming" that are "physico-chemically prepared," for "life is unknown to us except in association with bodies";[47] entelechy always "uses material means in each individual morphogenesis";[48] entelechy cannot make sulphuric acid if no hydrogen is present, but it can "*suspend* for as long a period as it wants any one of all the reactions which are *possible* with such compounds as are present, and which would happen without *entelechy*."[49] These formulations display Driesch's struggle to make the life-matter relationship as close as it can possibly be without going all the way to a (mechanistic) materialism and also resisting a metaphysics of "soul."

What intrigues me perhaps the most about entelechy is, as in the case of *Bildungstrieb*, the way in which it is a figure of impersonal agency. Like the Homeric Greek notion of *psuche*,[50] entelechy does not vary from person to person; it is not a unique soul, but neither does it vary across organisms. It is, rather, the immanent vitality flowing across all living bodies. This makes entelechy more resistant than soul to the strongest or most punitive notions of personal moral responsibility. Entelechy coordinates parts on behalf of a whole in response to event and does so without following a rigid plan; it answers events innovatively and perspicuously, deciding on the spot and in real time which of the many possible courses of development will in fact happen. The agentic capacity of entelechy is not a disembodied soul, for it is constrained by the materiality that it must inhabit and by the preformed possibilities contained therein. But despite this heteronomy, entelechy has real efficacy: it animates, arranges, and directs the bodies of the living, even under changing conditions. It is "an effective extra-spatial intensively manifold constituent of nature."[51]

Driesch's invention of entelechy as a creative causality is propelled by his assumption that materiality is stuff so passive and dull that it could not possibly have done the tricky work of organizing and maintaining morphing wholes. Sometimes this matter is infused with entelechy and becomes life, and sometimes it is not and coagulates into inorganic machines. Driesch thought he had to figure entelechy as nonmaterial because his notion of materiality was yoked to the notion of a mechanistic, deterministic machine. In 1926 Bakhtin wrote an interesting rebuttal to Driesch, arguing that he failed to imagine the possibility of "a relentlessly self-constructing, developing machine [which] . . . builds itself not from pre-prepared parts, but from self-constructing ones." Such a machine, were it to be damaged, would indeed be capable of a self-repair, a restitution prompted and guided by subtle and interactive physico-chemical signals, and thus would have no need for entelechy.[52]

Bakhtin points out that Driesch's vitalism depends on his critique of materialism, and that critique depends on equating materiality with mechanical causality, with an image of machine as a "totally prefabricated" and "fixed and immovable" assemblage.[53] Bakhtin recommends that we rethink what a machine can be, rather than reject the physico-materialist explanation per se.[54] Driesch will not entertain the possibility of a creatively self-organizing or intelligently adaptive machine, no more than he will allow entelechy to be assimilated to the category of energy, because machines and energies are concepts that simply cannot stretch to include as much freedom and spontaneity (i.e., that "*indefiniteness* of correspondence between specific cause and specific effect") as Driesch senses to be operative in the world. What ultimately distinguishes Bahktin from Driesch, then, is the question of whether or not natural creativity is even in principle calculable. Driesch says no, Bahktin seems to say yes. Here I side with Driesch.

Bergson and *Élan Vital*

Bergson's vitalism is also based on the distinction between life and matter, though Bergson openly acknowledges that these categories fix what really are but "tendencies" of a cosmic flow. Life and matter are strivings that exist only in conjunction and competition with each other; they are not permanent conditions but "nascent changes of direction."[55] Life names a certain *propensity* for "the utmost possible" activeness, a bias in favor of mobile and morphing states. Likewise, matter must be understood as a *leaning* toward passivity, a tendency in favor of stable formations. Bergson, like Driesch, associates matter with extension, but again he complicates things by cautioning against imagining matter as *completely* extended in space, for pure spatiality would "consist in a perfect externality of parts in their relation to one another," whereas in fact "there is no material point that does not act on every other material point." It is thus more precise to say that "matter *extends* itself in space without being absolutely *extended* therein." In other words, matter is a *tendency* toward spatialization.[56]

Attracted to the route of least resistance, the material tendency is a lazy preference for inertia, and it is in this sense that Bergson, too, participates in the tradition of imagining matter as inert (CE, 128–29). But for Bergson we *necessarily* turn a spatializing tendency into a world of fixed entities. This distortion is necessary and useful because humans must regard the world instrumentally if they are to survive in it: there is an "inevitable propensity of our mind" to view the world as if it consisted not of an ever-changing flow of time but of a calculable set of things.

Bergson shares with Driesch the view that life is not susceptible to quantification, though Bergson ascribes life's immunity to "mathematical treatment" to its nature as a moving flow. Bergson is here speaking of mathematics qua geometry. In contrast, "infinitesmal calculus" is pro-life. It is "precisely an effort to substitute for the *ready-made* what is in process of *becoming*" (CE, 20). Life "splays" itself out in new forms that are not even conceivable before they exist, says Bergson, and were they to be quantified and measured, it would already be too late, for life will have moved on.

As is the case with entelechy, the idea of *élan vital* arises in the wake of a critique of mechanism. Noting the existence of eyes in organisms as physiologically dissimilar as a mollusk and a man, Bergson concludes that "this production of the same effect by two different accumulations of an enormous number of small causes is contrary to the principles of mechanistic philosophy." And, as in Driesch, the phenomenon of restitution suggests to Bergson the need to invoke a nonmechanical vital agent: "[In the] *Salamandra maculata*, if the lens be removed and the iris left, the regeneration of the lens takes place at the upper part of the iris; but if this upper part . . . be taken away, the regeneration takes place in the inner . . . layer of the remaining region. Thus, parts differently situated, differently constituted, meant normally for different functions, are capable of performing the same duties and even of manufacturing . . . the same pieces of the machine. . . . Whether we will or no, we must appeal to *some inner directing principle* in order to account for this convergence of effects" (CE, 75–76; my emphasis).

Élan vital, like entelechy, is this "inner directing principle." Recall that entelechy, in addition to "arranging" matter, also has the power to "impel" restitution and "drive out" physico-chemical processes.[57] Bergson underscores this sparking, instigating quality even more: *élan vital* is "the tremendous internal push of life," "the primitive impetus of the whole," the "impulse which thrusts life into the world, which made it divide into vegetables and animals, which shunted the animal on to suppleness of form, and which, at a certain moment, in the animal kingdom threatened with torpor, secured that, on some points at least, it should rouse itself up and move forward" (CE, 132). The task of *élan vital* is to shake awake that lazy bones of matter and insert into it a measure of surprise: "At the root of life there is an effort to engraft on to the necessity of physical forces the largest possible amount of *indetermination*" (CE, 114). *Élan vital*, "traversing the bodies it has organized one after another, passing from generation to generation," never sleeps (CE, 26).

Like entelechy, *élan vital* is not itself simple or homogeneous. Driesch speaks of entelechy as an "intensive manifold," while Bergson describes a process of self-diversification of the vital impetus "in the form of a sheaf" (CE, 99). *Élan vital* self-dirempts as it flows, dispensing itself "without losing anything of its force, rather intensifying in proportion to its advance" (CE, 26).[58] This peculiar kind of self-division, by which the vital impulse gains strength as it distributes itself, helps explain what Bergson means when he says that "*life does not proceed by the association and addition of elements, but by dissociation and division*" (CE, 89).

Driesch's entelechy is directional in the sense of pursuing the general goal of arranging and then preserving organic wholes. The specific means employed for this task vary because they are chosen in "individual correspondence" to the circumstances at hand. Bergson repeats Driesch's claim that the means used by vital force are contingent on the specifics of their enactment, but this contingency proves more radical for Bergson. The means available to *élan vital* do not preexist (even as latent "possibilities") the moment of their deployment, but rather emerge in tandem with their effects. Bergson thus contests Driesch's claim that the aim of the vital impulse is to *maintain the whole*: for Bergson any whole that would be maintained is not "given" but always in transition, on the way in or out. Again, what *élan vital* does—its distinctive activity—is to increase the *instability* of material formations, to "insert some *indetermination* into matter. Indeterminate, *i.e.* unforsee-able, are the forms it creates in the course of its evolution" (CE, 126). *Élan vital* brings new events into existence and makes each form over-flow its present (CE, 103). Driesch, too, hinted at the idea that the vital force is *creative* (but not that it is a *flow*) in his discussion of individual correspondence, but the theme is more pronounced in Bergson's vital-ism, according to which life is "a perpetual efflorescence of novelty" and "unceasing creation" (CE, 23).[59] Driesch attributed a kind of inventive-ness to the organism's (or even the organ's) responses to each uniquely configured event, but entelechy's agency does not seem to include the creation of the radically new.

It would be misleading to call *élan vital*'s injection of indetermination a telos. Yes, *élan vital* is an effort *in a direction*—how could efforts be otherwise?—but it is not the realization of a plan. Deleuze says that for Bergson "there is no 'goal,' because these directions . . . are themselves created 'along with' the act that runs through them."[60] *Élan vital* is drive without design, a searching that is a "groping":[61] "It would be futile to try to assign to life an end. . . . To speak of an end is to think of a pre-existing model which has only to be realized. It is to suppose, therefore, that all is given, and that the future can be read in the present. . . . Life, on the contrary. . . . is undoubtedly creative, *i.e.* productive of effects in which it expands and transcends its own being. These effects were therefore not given in it in advance, and so it could not take them for ends" (CE, 51–52).

For both Bergson and Driesch vitality can only operate within the constraints of persistent and powerful physico-chemical propensities. "Even in its most perfect works," such as unprecedented works of art, *élan vital* "is at the mercy of the materiality which it has had to assume" (CE, 127). It also can only "make the best of a pre-existing energy which it finds at its disposal."[62] Like Driesch, Bergson refuses to assimilate vitality to "energy" and rather sees the latter as a resistant means used by the former. But more than Driesch, Bergson emphasizes that some of the obstacles to the production of harmonious wholes are *internal* to *élan vital* itself, a function of its own unharmonious manifoldness. The vital impetus *is* a splaying out, a rendering of itself more indeterminate, and this means that some lines of the spray will conflict or counteract others. As self-dispensing, *élan vital* is profoundly at odds with itself:

"Always seeking to transcend itself," it "always remains inadequate to the work it would fain produce" (CE, 126).

For Bergson, the universe that results from the self-dispensing flow of *élan vital* is a nonharmonious whole, albeit an "indivisible continuity."[63] Nature "admits of much discord because each species, each individual even, retains only a certain impetus from the universal vital impulsion and tends to use this energy in its own interest. . . . harmony is rather behind us than before. It is due to an identity of impulsion and not to a common aspiration" (CE, 50–51). Driesch also did not affirm a *simple* model of harmony: he, too, insisted that there is internal alteration *within* parts as they develop, as well as changes in the relationship *between* parts: "It is far from being true that the development of each embryonic part depends on the existence or development of every other one. On the contrary, it is a very important . . . feature of organogenesis that it occurs in . . . lines of processes which may start from a common root, but which are absolutely independent of one another in their manner of differentiation. . . . Suppose a part, A, shows that phenomenon of self-differentiation: this means that the further development of A is not dependent on certain others parts, B, C, and D; it does *not* mean at all that . . . there might not be formative actions among the constituents of A itself."[64]

Driesch and Bergson both believed that nature, irreducible to matter as extension in space, also included a dynamic intensity or animating impetus. Neither *élan vital* nor entelechy is *reducible* to the material and energetic forces that each inhabits and must enlist; both are *agents* in the sense of engaging in actions that are more than reflexes, instincts, or prefigured responses to stimuli; both have the generative power to produce, organize, and enliven matter, though Driesch emphasizes the arranging and directing powers of the vital agent and Bergson accents its sparking and innovating capacities. In general, entelechy is less free ranging in operation than *élan vital*, not quite the "ceaseless upspringing of something new, which has no sooner arisen to make the present than it has already fallen back into the past" (CE, 47). The agency of entelechy is, from my point of view, also too self-contained: its power to makes things happen by itself is overstated (despite Driesch's acknowledgment of its "dependency" on matter). The figure of entelechy, however, does nicely capture the pulsing, conative dimension of agency, but such a pulse must be engaged in a system of pulses, in an assemblage that links them and forms circuits of intensities.

Driesch was an experimental embryologist first and only later became a philosopher, and it is Bergson who offers a more detailed philosophy of becoming as "creative evolution." But Driesch's greater identification with and immersion in the techniques of experimental science may offer the advantage of better protection against the temptation in vitalism to *spiritualize* the vital agent. As an example of a vitalism that surrenders to this temptation, I turn in the next chapter to another figuration of vital force, the "soul" invoked by American advocates of the "culture of life." This vitalism hooked up with an evangelical Christianity, stem cells, American weaponry, and the territory of Iraq (and other actants), forming an assemblage with violent effectivity. My aim in the next chapter is to discern how some of these links were established, and to thereby shed some light on the complicated relationship between images of matter and visions of politics.

6

Stem Cells and the Culture of Life

When, at the turn of the twentieth century, Hans Driesch and Henri
Bergson defended their notions of vital force, they were participating in
a debate that also engaged a larger public. In response to new discover-
ies in cellular biology and in embryology, the American public had become fascinated with the question of developmental growth: just how
did change happen inside plants, animals, psyches, cultures, or other
self-sustaining wholes? The ensuing debate was simultaneously moral
and scientific: the vitalist-mechanist controversy combined discourses
of freedom and life with studies of morphology and matter.

In the early twenty-first century, Americans were again participating
in debates of this hybrid kind, debates also premised on a fundamental
distinction between life and matter. One powerful voice in these debates—over abortion, artificial life support, and embryonic stem cell
research—was the "culture of life" position advocated by evangelical
Christians and Roman Catholics, including President George W. Bush.
This position is, I will contend, a latter-day vitalism. The culture-of-
life movement echoes a claim made by Immanuel Kant, Driesch, and

Bergson: there exists a vital force inside the biological organism that is irreducible to matter because it is a free and undetermined agency. Like the vitalists who preceded them, defenders of the culture of life believe there to be something profoundly inadequate about a mechanistic metaphysic.

But not all vitalisms are alike. For Bush and other evangelicals, the vital force is a divine spirit that animates the matter of the embryo; they affirm what Kant, Driesch, and Bergson each rejected as a vitalism of soul. Driesch especially took pains to distinguish his entelechy from religious notions of a disembodied spirit. Persuaded by Kant's critique of dogmatic philosophy, he gave methodological priority to naturalistic explanation: Driesch sought to make the laboratory the final court of appeal with regard to questions of embryonic development. And because Driesch sought to avoid scientific as well as religious dogmatism, he emphasized that the verdicts of the lab were subject to revision as new data emerged.

Driesch believed that empirical experimentation in the lab on non-human systems would shed light on truths that applied also to human systems. The "formative" power (entelechy) was present in sea urchin embryos, human embryos, the larger organic whole called history (that "suprapersonal process which [is] . . . *unique and not yet finished in* [its] *uniqueness*"), and even perhaps in inorganic systems: "There is the material world as the world of chance, but there is also a world of form or order that manifests itself in certain areas of the material world, namely, in the biological individual, and probably, in another way, in phylogeny and history also; there *may* even be formlike constellations in what we call the Inorganic."[1]

Driesch was a secularist in that he tried to bracket his religious convictions when engaging in public reasoning. But this is not to say that he believed science to be irrelevant to public morality. Quite to the contrary, when the Nazis invoked entelechy to support their claim that some forms of life were more vital than others — by the mid-1930s entelechy had become a kind of "*Fuhrer* de l'organisme"[2] — Driesch objected vehemently. The science of critical vitalism, he said, led to the conclusion that entelechial vitality is present in *all* human organisms. As the historian Anne Harrington notes, for Driesch, entelechy "recognized no state boundaries," and thus "the only biological 'whole' to which one could rightfully belong was 'humanity.' He opposed . . . the militaristic actions of nation against nation . . . [as] '*the most terrible of all sins*' against the vitalistic principles of life, holistic cooperation and higher development."[3]

Two different vitalisms (one soul-based, one not), two different politics (one hawkish, one pacifist). I do not think that there is any *direct* relationship between, on the one hand, a set of ontological assumptions about life or matter and, on the other hand, a politics; no particular ethics or politics follow inevitably from a metaphysics. But the hierarchical logic of God-Man-Nature implied in a vitalism of soul easily transitions into a political image of a hierarchy of social classes or even civilizations. I will suggest below that something like this seems to have happened with the culture of life. Unlike that evangelical vitalism, the "critical," "modern," or "scientific" vitalism of Driesch pairs an *affirmation* of non-material agencies (entelechies) at work in nature with an *agnosticism* about the existence of any supernatural agency. Driesch's first loyalty was to the method of experimental science, and what that method revealed to him was the vitalistic nature of all being: no one group has the natural right to rule or dispose of the others.

Driesch rejected the notion of a soul; he strove to replace faith-based claims with experimental hypotheses, and he associated the idea of vital force with a liberal pacisfism. Culture-of-life vitalism does none of these things. In the next section I will contrast that latter-day vitalism to the critical vitalism of Driesch, with a focus on the political valence of each.

Stem Cells

In May of 2005, the president of the United States appeared on the steps of the White House with babies and toddlers born from test-tube embryos, embryos produced as extras for couples using fertility technologies. Inhabiting the role of baby-kissing politician, Bush cooed at the children who would have been preemptively killed had the embryos from which they sprang been used for embryonic stem cell research. The *New York Times* described stem cell research as an "important 'culture of life' issue" for conservative Christians and the president, and it noted that the theatricality of the White House event "demonstrated just how far Mr. Bush is willing to assert himself on policy that goes to what he considers the moral heart of his presidency. . . . Tom De-Lay of Texas managed the opposition to the bill, also casting it in stark moral terms. 'An embryo is a person, a distinct internally directed, self-integrating human organism.'"[4]

In April of 2007, at a National Catholic Prayer Breakfast concurrent with Supreme Court deliberations over the constitutionality of a law banning late-term abortions, Bush reiterated his commitment to life: "We must continue to work for a culture of life where the strong protect the weak, and where we recognize in every human life the image of our Creator."[5] Three days later, and four years into a preemptive war that killed (as of August 2007) 3,689 American soldiers and estimated to have preempted the lives of between tens of thousands and hundreds of thousands of Iraqis,[6] Bush opposed any timetable for the withdrawal of U.S. troops and described the invasion and occupation as a "vital war," ostensibly consistent with "the culture of life."[7] I will return to this dual celebration of life and violence later in the chapter.

Stem cell is a neologism for a bit of matter believed to be pluripotent, that is, able to become any of the various kinds of cells or tissues of the mature, differentiated organism. The hope is that a better understanding of pluripotency will enable scientists to, for example, induce the production of new nerve cells in damaged spinal cords or new brain tissue in people with Alzheimer's disease. A stem cell, while pluripotent, is not, however, "totipotent," or able by itself to give rise to a fully differentiated organism.[8] The procedure offensive to advocates of the culture of life consists in extracting cells from the blastula stage of the fertilized egg, when the egg is changing from a solid mass of cells into a hollow ball of cells. The blastocyst may then continue on to the "gastrula" stage, where it differentiates into three germ layers, whose cells, "channeled into their respective fate paths," are no longer pluripotent.[9] Bush and others oppose embryonic stem cell research because the extraction halts the morphological process at the gastrula stage. DeLay described it as "the dismemberment of living, distinct human beings for the purposes of medical experimentation."[10]

When human stem cells are taken from embryos, the embryos are destroyed. Stem cells can also be taken or grown from umbilical-cord blood, adult human bone marrow, fertilized embryos too old to be capable of developing further, and, as of the time of this writing, human skin cells.[11] The Bush administration did not object to these sources of stem cells, perhaps because if blood, marrow, skin, and decayed embryos are dead matter rather than life, their use poses no threat to the culture of life.

A Natural Order of Rank

The culture of life was the central theme of Pope John Paul II's 1995 "Evangelium Vitae" before it was adopted by non-Catholic evangelicals in the United States to refer to a cluster of theological beliefs linked to a set of public policies.[12] The policies are easy to name: the culture of life has been invoked to support legislation to keep a feeding tube inserted into a woman whose brain function had ceased, to restrict access by minors to abortion and to outlaw certain modes of abortion, as well as to oppose federal funding for embryonic stem cell research. The theological beliefs within the culture of life are less clearly articulated, but the following four claims seem central:

1. *Life is radically different from matter.* Life is organized, active, self-propelled, and, in diverse registers of the term, "free." Matter is intrinsically passive and predetermined in its operation. Life may be, and usually is encountered as, embodied; and when it is, it operates alongside physicochemical entities and processes. But life is irreducible to the sum of those entities and processes. Life is detachable from embodiment.

2. *Human life is qualitatively different from all other life.* Like other organisms, humans are endowed with a life force, but unlike all others, this force is "a unique life-principle or soul."[13] According to the president of the Culture of Life Foundation, "If society loses the sense of the essential distinction of human life from animal life and material things, whether in theory or in the practice of attempting to clone a human embryo, it has lost its stature as a human society. It has lost the compass of humanness and is, instead, laying the foundation for the replacement of a human living with biological chaos."[14] The ensouled human organism is a quantum leap above other organisms.

3. *Human uniqueness expresses a divine intention.* Human exception-alism is not a contingent event, an accident of evolution, or a function of the distinctive material composition of the human body. It results, rather, from an omnipotent being ("the Almighty") who implants a divine spark or soul into each human individual.

4. *The world is a divinely created order and that order has the shape of a fixed hierarchy.* Humans are not only organic, unique, and ensouled but they also occupy the top of the ontological hierarchy, in a position *superior* to everything else on earth.

The first belief, that life is irreducible to matter, resonates with what Driesch said was the core belief of any vitalism, that is, that the develop-mental processes of the organism are *not* "the result of a special *con-stellation of factors known already* to the sciences of the inorganic," but are rather "the result of an *autonomy* peculiar" to life.[15] Insofar as this autonomy is conceived as a soul whose existence is not dependent on being in relationship to matter, it also qualifies as what Driesch called "old vitalism." This vitalism, in contrast to "modern" or "critical" vital-ism, fails to avail itself of the benefit of scientific insight into nature. For Driesch the lab and the reasoning scientist were the privileged point of access to the life principle, and it was always "essential to reflect once more with an open mind on the actual biological data."[16] Critical vital-ism offered falsifiable hypotheses rather than dogma that only immoral-ists would be moved to contest.

Advocates of the culture of life affirm science and its products, in par-ticular weaponry, insofar as it advances the power of the United States. But no science could contravene the theological verities of ensoulment, human exceptionalism, and the qualitative hierarchy of Creation. To DeLay, for example, no revelation from molecular chemistry or com-plexity theory about the self-organizing capacity of *inorganic* systems could disprove his conviction that matter is inert and only life is free and open ended. And no data concerning the differential plasticity of cells at the blastula and gastrula stages could possibly alter the conclu-sion that the fertilized egg is a person ensouled by the Almighty.[17] For DeLay and other soul vitalists, the vital force is a personal rather than, as for Driesch and Bergson, an impersonal agency. To use the terms de-veloped in chapter 4, it is the life of a unique subject rather than *a* life.

Soul vitalism is, in short, more anthropocentric and hierarchical than critical vitalism. Its cosmos is a morally ranked Creation at the top of which God has placed his most vital creature, Man. Man is the most vital in the sense of being the most animate or alive and thus powerful, and also in the sense of possessing the greatest degree of freedom or capacity to act in ways that cannot be reduced to their situational or environmental determinants. Organic life, it is asserted, is not only higher in rank than inorganic matter but radically or qualitatively different from it. Likewise, *human* life is not only higher in rank than nonhuman organisms but qualitatively different from it, that is, ensouled. Life is special, but we as humans are the most special. This same logic continues at the level of different peoples: for Bush and his associates, although all humans are imbued with soul, not all of these souls are equally activated, vital, or free. Soul vitalism calls on those peoples who are "strong" to "protect the weak," even if it also reminds them to "recognize in every human life the image of our Creator."[18] This paternalistic care is conjoined to a doctrine of vital war and to other manifestations of a not-so-hidden attraction to violence, such as the ardent defense of torture, guns, and all things military (the civilian presidency became, at the insistence of Bush, defined primarily as the job of a commander in chief).

How can love of life coexist with love of violence? How was this strange link between care and conquest forged? It seems that the idea of a hierarchy of natural species was extended, or bled, into the idea that peoples are also ranked according to degrees of freedom. That, at least, would be one explanation for how, for those inside the culture of life, the invasion of Iraq constitutes an act of caring for the weak that offers them the gifts of vitality and freedom. That explanation, however, focuses rather exclusively on human actants, on the interplay of different human beliefs and practices. A richer account would treat the culture of life as an assemblage of human and nonhuman actants. In it, the human belief in a cosmic hierarchy presided over by an Almighty patriarch, the human feeling of pity for the weak, and the human pleasure taken in acts of aggression and violence would congregate and join forces with pluripotent stem cells, ultrasound images of unborn fetuses, the impersonal momentum of American empire, and the spectacular fires and explosions in Iraq.

Evangelical advocates of the sanctity of life celebrate preemptive war;

Nazis invoked entelechy to make their case that the German nation had to fulfill its vital destiny and wage a vital war. Is there something intrinsic to vitalism, to faith in the autonomy of life, that allies itself with violence? The counterexample of Driesch suggests otherwise. I am not sure just what it was about Driesch's brand of vitalism that fostered his generous politics, but a good candidate is his practical work in the laboratory: his hands-on, face-to-face, repeated encounters with sea urchins, seawater, sulfuric acid, and various pieces of glass and metal equipment. Such attentiveness to nonhuman matter and its powers is likely to erode any notion of a preformed or static hierarchy of nature.

Driesch fought to dissociate his theory of organic wholes from those for whom vitality was unevenly distributed across peoples. Driesch ultimately defended not only the entelechial equality of all people but also the possibility that this vitality is shared by *all* things. He suggests the latter at the end of his *The History and Theory of Vitalism*, where he surprises the reader by rejecting the very life-matter binary on which he had founded his argument. The universe, he ultimately concludes, is not dead matter sometimes supplemented with organic life, but one big organism, "*a something in evolution. All natural becoming is like one great embryology.*" Every thing is entelechial, life-ly, vitalistic. Driesch ends his defense of vitalism by "destroying" "the [very] difference between 'mechanism' and 'Vitalism,' . . . which we have established so carefully."[19] It is at this point, I would say, that Driesch begins to transition from vitalism to a vital materialism.

Vitality and Freedom

Mikhail Bakhtin, a mechanistic materialist, criticized Driesch's claim that the blastomere contained multiple intensities, only one of which, after being chosen by entelechy, became actual. For Bakhtin it was simply not true that there existed several possible paths: each act of morphogenesis only takes place under a singular set of conditions, and so there exists only *one* possible outcome, the one determined precisely by the physicochemical situation at hand. Driesch's "talk of several potentials and possibilities serves only one purpose: it allows for the presupposition that they are all equally possible . . . and that therefore it is possible to *choose* one of them freely. Freedom of choice . . . is the ground of all of Driesch's constructions."[20]

The link between vitalism and violence is, I think, contingent. But I agree with Bakhtin that what is essential to vitalism is an affirmation of free activity: a freedom imagined by evangelical Christians as free will and by the critical vitalists as the less personal force of *élan vital* or entelechy. Whether it is the freedom of a certain "*indefiniteness* of correspondence between specific cause and specific effect,"[21] the freedom of a "ceaseless upspringing of something new,"[22] or the freedom to invade the territory of those who hate freedom because they "love terror,"[23] vitalism recurs because it defends a world that is not predetermined but open, a land of opportunity for creativity, surprise, and choice. Freedom is an appealing idea: note that what generated all the excitement about stem cells is their pluripotentiality, or open-ended freedom to become any of the various kinds of cells or tissues of the mature, differentiated organism.

Analogous to *Bildungstrieb*, entelechy, *élan vital*, and soul is the notion of the out-side. This material vitality is resistant to calculation, hovering in what Georges Canguilhem called "des enclaves d'indetermination, des zones de dissidence, des foyers d'héresie."[24] The various figures of free vitality stand as reminders to secular modernists that while we can surely intervene in the material world, we are not in charge of it, for there are "foreign" powers about.

Though the controversy about embryonic stem cell research in the United States is often depicted as a struggle between religious people and scientific people (or, as the *Times* article cited earlier implies, as a clash between those for whom morality trumps medical progress and those for whom the reverse it true), I have presented it as the return of a vitalism-materialism debate. Vitalism has repeatedly risen from the ashes of scientific critiques of it. As Francis Sumner put it in a 1916 review of Driesch's *The History and Theory of Vitalism*, "Vitalism will not down. A consideration of recent literature drives us to this conclusion. One of the most widely read philosophical works of the past few decades (Bergson's *Creative Evolution*) is primarily a defense of this doctrine. The writings of Driesch, both in German and in English, have followed one another with marvelous rapidity and forced themselves upon the attention of even the most unswerving mechanist."[25]

But vitalism is the reaction formation to mechanistic materialism. There is, of course, a rich tradition of another materialism, one in which atoms swerve, bodies are driven by conatus, and "unformed elements and materials dance."[26] From the perspective of this tradition, mechanical materialism underestimates the complex, emergent causality of materiality, a materiality figured by Louis Althusser as a "process that has no subject."[27] The machine model of nature, with its figure of inert matter, is no longer even scientific. It has been challenged by systems theory, complexity theory, chaos theory, fluid dynamics, as well as by the many earlier biophilosophies of flow that Michel Serres has chronicled in *The Birth of Physics*.[28] It is also challenged, as we shall see, by the National Institutes of Health's report on stem cells. Yet the popular image of materialism as mechanistic endures, perhaps because the scientific community tends to emphasize how human ingenuity can result in greater control over nature more than the element of freedom in matter. And perhaps *that* is because to highlight the limits of human power and the indeterminate vitality of matter would bring science into too close an alliance with theology, such as the latter-day vitalism of Bush.

Diving into Matter

The National Institutes of Health 2001 report on stem cells made two claims that surprised me. The first was that no one yet knows whether "embryonic stem cells" exist as such in human embryos in the womb, that is, whether they have a presence *before* they are extracted from blastocysts and placed in a new, laboratory-generated milieu. Though "most scientists now agree that *adult* stem cells exist in many tissues of the human body (*in vivo*) . . . , it is less certain that embryonic stem cells exist as such in the embryo. Instead, embryonic stem cells . . . *develop in tissue culture* after they are *derived* from the inner cell mass of the early embryo."[29] The second startling claim was that it is also uncertain whether even the embryonic stem cells produced in the lab are in fact "homogeneous and undifferentiated," even though they appear to be and their promise of pluripotency is premised on that state of pure, quivering indeterminacy.

My response to these points was surprise, even alarm. What? Embry-

onic stem cells might not even *exist* in the body and their laboratory ava-
tars might not even *be* an exemplar of undifferentiated pluripotency?
My reaction revealed the extent to which I also had been thinking of my
body as a physiological mechanism with fixed and determinate parts,
including stem cells. I had absorbed the machine model of nature, and
if I was not careful it would, as a default, limit my ability to perceive the
vitality of things. In contrast, the National Institutes of Health affirmed
Bergson's view that "materiality" is a flow, an indivisible continuum of
becomings whose protean elements are not only exquisitely imbricated
in a flowing environment but also *are* that very flow. Extensive and intensive forms swirl around and become an open and living whole, a
"whole that is not given," as Bergson would say.[30] If it turns out that
there are no "embryonic stem cells" in vivo, this may be because an embryo is *not* a collection of discrete parts, perhaps not even of protoparts
or preformed possibilities, and that it is only in the closed system *of the
lab* that what Bergson called the "indivisible continuity" of life allows
itself to be sliced and diced into "embryonic stem cells." The human
technological ability to create differentiation in cells is not an explanation of why they differentiate on their own. We can trigger this process,
but we do not know what its own trigger is. (Driesch would name that
internal trigger entelechy.)

My foray into Kant, Driesch, Bergson, and the culture of life was propelled by the desire to understand the appeal of the life-matter binary
and its correlate, the machine model of nature, as well as to put forward
another materialism, one that acknowledges an indeterminate vitality
in the world without slipping back into a vitalism of nonmaterial agents.
Ralph Waldo Emerson wrote in his journal in 1848: "I have no longer
any taste for these refinements you call life, but shall dive again into
brute matter."[31] The vital materialist, too, goes diving there—and finds
matter not so brute at all.

Johann Gottfried von Herder, objecting to what he saw as Kant's theo-
logically induced blindness to the pulsing vitality of matter, sought to
put "an end to all the objectionable expressions of how God, according
to this or that system, may work on and through dead matter. It is not
dead but lives. For in it and conforming to its outer and inner organs, a
thousand living, manifold forces are at work. The more we learn about
matter, the more forces we discover in it, so that the empty concep-

tion of a dead extension completely disappears."[32] The vital materialist affirms a figure of matter as an active principle, and a universe of this lively materiality that is always in various states of congealment and diffusion, materialities that are active and creative without needing to be experienced or conceived as partaking in divinity or purposiveness. Driesch and Bergson share with me a picture of the universe in which becoming continually vies with being, but for them becomings include a moment of transcendence in the form of *élan vital* or entelechy. Despite their respect for the complexity of physicochemical processes, they could not quite imagine a materialism adequate to the flowering of life. But the critical vitalists came very close, and I locate my vital materialism in their wake.

7

Political Ecologies

In this chapter I have two goals. The first is easier than the second: I retell a couple of worm stories, first heard from Charles Darwin and Bruno Latour, to show how worms are "like" us. Here, as elsewhere in the book, I find in a non- or not-quite-human body evidence of the vitality of matter. Worms, or electricity, or various gadgets, or fats, or metals, or stem cells are actants, or what Darwin calls "small agencies," that, when in the right confederation with other physical and physio-logical bodies, can make big things happen. The second goal is to con-front the hard question of the *political* capacity of actants. Even if a con-vincing case is made for worms as active members of, say, the ecosystem of a rainforest, can worms be considered members of a *public*? What is the difference between an ecosystem and a political system? Are they analogs? Two names for the same system at different scales? What is the difference between an actant and a political actor? Is there a clear difference? Does an action count as *political* by virtue of its having taken place "in" a public? Are there nonhuman members of a public? What, in sum, are the implications of a (meta)physics of vibrant materiality for political theory?

After the worm stories, I try to explore these very difficult questions by engaging two theories of democracy. I will focus on their different understandings of what a public is, how a public is formed and de-formed, and what counts as a political act. I choose the first theory, by John Dewey, because in it the analogy between an ecosystem and a political system is fairly strong and the gap between action and political action relatively small. Key here is Dewey's notion of the generative field that he calls "conjoint action." Conjoint action is the agency be-hind the emergence of a public; a public's agency or capacity to produce effects is also a function of conjoint action. Dewey's theory leaves open the possibility that some of the acts of conjoint action originate in non-human (natural and technological) bodies. I choose the second theory, that of Jacques Rancière, because it emphasizes the extent to which the political constitutes a distinctive realm of action and thus outlines why a polity ought not to be considered an ecology. On Rancière's account, the public is constituted by bodies with uniquely human capabilities, talents, and skills, and political action is something that only they can do. Both models are instructive, and together they help us begin to dis-cern the politics of vital materialism.

The "Small Agency" of Worms

Darwin watched English worms: many, many of them for many, many hours. He watched how they moved, where they went, and what they did, and, most of all, he watched how they made topsoil or "vegetable mould": after digesting "earthly matter," they would deposit the castings at the mouth of their burrows, thus continually bringing to the surface a refined layer of vegetable mold. It is, writes Darwin, "a marvellous re-flection that the whole of the . . . mould over any . . . expanse has passed, and will again pass, every few years through the bodies of worms."[1] But the claim with which Darwin ends his *Formation of Vegetable Mould through the Actions of Worms with Observations on Their Habits* (1881) is not about biology or agronomy but about history: "Worms have played a more important part in the history of the world than most persons would at first assume" (*Mould*, 305). How do worms make history? They make it by making vegetable mold, which makes possible "seedlings of all kinds," which makes possible an earth hospitable to humans, which makes possible the cultural artifacts, rituals, plans, and endeavors of human history (*Mould*, 309). Worms also "make history" by preserving the artifacts that humans make: worms protect "for an indefinitely long period every object, not liable to decay, which is dropped on the surface of the land, by burying it beneath their castings," a service for which "archaeologists ought to be grateful to worms" (*Mould*, 308).

Darwin claims that worms inaugurate human culture and then, working alongside people and their endeavors, help preserve what people and worms together have made. Darwin does not claim that worms intend to have this effect so beneficial to humankind, or that any divine intention is at work through them. Rather, that the exertions of worms contribute to human history and culture is the unplanned result of worms acting in conjunction and competition with other (biological, bacterial, chemical, human) agents. Darwin describes the activities of worms as one of many "small agencies" whose "accumulated effects" turn out to be quite big.[2] It would be consistent with Darwin to say that worms participate in heterogeneous assemblages in which agency has no single locus, no mastermind, but is distributed across a swarm of various and variegated vibrant materialities.[3]

Worms do not intend to enable human culture, but worms do, according to Darwin, pursue what appear to be prospective endeavors. His close observations of worms led him to conclude that worm actions are *not* the result of "an unvarying inherited impulse" (*Mould*, 64–65), but are intelligent improvisations. For example, in "plugging up the mouths of their burrows" with leaves, worms "act in nearly the same manner as would a man" — that is, they make apparently free, or at least unpredictable, decisions based on the available materials. Though they usually seize leaves (to be dragged to their burrows) by their pointed ends, "they do not act in the same unvarying manner in all cases," but adjust their technique to the particular situation and its set of possibilities: Which leaves are available? Is the ground wet or dry? What other creatures are around? (*Mould*, 312). Further evidence of a certain freedom to their acts is the phenomenon of a worm *overriding* a normal physiological response, as when a worm fails to recoil and retreat to its burrow when exposed to a bright light. Darwin notes that this overruling occurs when a worm is focused closely on a task, such as eating, dragging leaves, or mating:

When a worm is suddenly illuminated and dashes like a rabbit into its burrow . . . we are at first led to look at the action as a reflex one. The irritation
of the cerebral ganglia appears to cause certain muscles to contract in an
inevitable manner, independently of the will or consciousness . . . , as if it
were an automaton. But [this is contested by] . . . the fact that a worm when
in any way employed and in the intervals of such employment, whatever
set of muscles and ganglia may then have been brought into play, is often
regardless of light. . . . With the higher animals, when close attention to
some object leads to the disregard of the impressions which other objects
must be producing on them, we attribute this to their attention being then
absorbed; and attention implies the presence of a mind. (*Mould*, 23–24)

Darwin's worms pay attention, and they respond appropriately to unprecedented situations, displaying what Hans Driesch called the power
of "individual correspondence." Their actions are neither an expression
of divine purpose nor reducible to an unvarying mechanical instinct.
Let us call the assemblage in which these wiggling actants participate
not (as in Baruch Spinoza) God or Nature, but History or Nature, or, to
be more precise, British History or England's Nature. This assemblage
is an ecology in the sense that it is an interconnected series of parts, but
it is not a fixed order of parts, for the order is always being reworked in
accordance with a certain "freedom of choice" exercised by its actants.

In *Pandora's Hope*, Latour tells a story about Amazonian rather than
English worms, and again we see that worms play a more important
part in the history of (that part of) the world than most persons would
at first suppose. The story begins with the puzzling presence, about ten
meters into the rainforest, of trees typical only of the savanna. The soil
under these trees is "more clayey than the savanna but less so than the
forest." How was the border between savanna and forest breached? Did
"the forest cast its own soil before it to create conditions favorable to
its expansion," or is the savanna "degrading the woodland humus as it
prepares to invade the forest"?[4] This question presumes a kind of vegetal agency in a natural system understood not as a mechanical order of
fixed laws but as the scene of not-fully-predictable encounters between
multiple kinds of actants. Savanna vegetation, forest trees, soil, soil
microorganisms, and humans native and exotic to the rainforest are all
responding, in real time and without predetermined outcome, to each
other and to the collective force of the shifting configurations that form.

The task at hand for humans is to find a more horizontal representation of the relation between human and nonhuman actants in order to be more faithful to the style of action pursued by each.

Latour and the scientists he is observing eventually conclude that, for reasons unknown to the humans, worms had gathered at the border and produced a lot of aluminum, which transformed the silica of the sandy soil into the clay more amenable to forest trees, and so it was the forest that was advancing into the savanna.[5] It is difficult to pinpoint just who or what was the key operator or "assemblage converter" here:[6] The worms? Their diet? The aluminum excrement? Had the human inhabitants of the rainforest done something to make the worms migrate? These various materialities do not exercise exactly the same kind of agency, but neither is it easy to arrange them into a hierarchy, for in some times and places, the "small agency" of the lowly worm makes more of a difference than the grand agency of humans.

We consider it a political act, for example, when people distribute themselves into racially and economically segregated neighborhoods, even if, in doing so, they are following a cultural trend and do not explicitly intend, endorse, or even consider the impact of their movements on, say, municipal finances, crime rates, or transportation policy. There are many affinities between the act of persons dragging their belongings to their new homes in the suburbs and the acts of worms dragging leaves to their burrows or migrating to a savanna-forest border.

A Note on Anthropomorphism

Darwin and Latour help make a case for worms as vibrant material actants whose difference from us may be smaller than we thought. And without worms or aluminum (or edibles or stem cells) and their conative endeavors, it would be difficult if not impossible for humans to exercise our exquisite wills or intentions. It seems both that worms are "like" us and that (to use a Kantian formulation) we must posit a certain nonhuman agency as the condition of possibility of human agency. Or are these claims fatally dependent on anthropomorphization?

Anthropomorphizing, the interpretation of what is not human or personal in terms of human or personal characteristics, is clearly a part of the story, but it is less clear how fatal it is. According to George Levine, "Darwin's extraordinary curiosity about the talents of worms has to do with his inveterate anthropomorphism," which was "absolutely central to his larger theoretical project."[7] Darwin anthropomorphized his worms: he saw in them an intelligence and a willfulness that he recognized as related to his own. But the narcissism of this gaze backfired, for it also prompted Darwin to pay close attention to the mundane activities of worms, and what came to the fore through paying attention was their own, distinctive, material complexity. He was able to detect what natural historians call the "jizz" of a worm, which the geographer Jamie Lorimer describes as "the unique combination of properties . . . that allows its ready identification and differentiation from others."[8] In a vital materialism, an anthropomorphic element in perception can uncover a whole world of resonances and resemblances—sounds and sights that echo and bounce far more than would be possible were the universe to have a hierarchical structure. We at first may see only a world in our own image, but what appears next is a swarm of "talented" and vibrant materialities (including the seeing self).

A touch of anthropomorphism, then, can catalyze a sensibility that finds a world filled not with ontologically distinct categories of beings (subjects and objects) but with variously composed materialities that form confederations. In revealing similarities across categorical divides and lighting up structural parallels between material forms in "nature" and those in "culture," anthropomorphism can reveal isomorphisms. A good example of this is the sensibility expressed in the *Great Treatise on Supreme Sound*, a fourteenth-century handbook for musicians. It describes the various sounds of the lute in terms of a movement style expressed by an animal and instructs the lute player to mimic that movement style: to make a staccato sound, the player should try to reproduce with his finger the motion of "an emaciated crow perched on a bare tree or pecking at the snow in hope of finding something to eat"; to make the characteristic sound that comes when the index, middle, and third fingers grip two strings at once, the lutist is to render his hand in the image of "the nonchalant flick of a carp's tail"; to produce a "floating sound," fingers should imitate the series of movements made by a "white butterfly fluttering at flower level" who "lingers but does not stay."[9] In the twentieth century, complexity theory also focused on isomorphic resonances. Clusters of neurons in a human brain, groupings of buildings in a city, and colonies of slime molds all have been shown to follow similar organizational rules; each is an instance of what Steven Johnson has called "organized complexity."[10]

The Public and Its Problems

What, if anything, does the claim that worms and trees and aluminum are participants in an ecosystem say about political participation? The answer depends in part on whether a political system itself constitutes a kind of ecosystem. Dewey's notion of a public suggests that it does. I turn now to him and to the advantages and limits of modeling politics as an ecology. If Darwin highlights the power of choice in worms to contest the idea that worms are moved only by animal instinct or bodily affect, Dewey closes the gap between human and nonhuman from the other direction: he highlights the affective, bodily nature of human responses.

In *The Public and Its Problems*, Dewey presents a public as a confederation of bodies, bodies pulled together not so much by choice (a public is not exactly a voluntary association) as by a shared experience of harm that, over time, coalesces into a "problem." Dewey makes it clear that a public does not preexist its particular problem but emerges in response to it.[11] A public is a contingent and temporary formation existing alongside many other publics, protopublics, and residual or postpublics. Problems come and go, and so, too, do publics: at any given moment, many different publics are in the process of crystallizing and dissolving.[12]

When diverse bodies suddenly draw near and form a public, they have been provoked to do so by a problem, that is, by the "indirect, serious and enduring" consequences of "conjoint action."[13] Problems are effects of the phenomenon of conjoint action. Like the conjoint action of Darwin's worms, the conjoint action of Dewey's citizens is not under the control of any rational plan or deliberate intention. No efficient cause of the problems it generates can really be pinpointed. What is more, there is no action that is *not* conjoint, that does not, in other words, immediately become enmeshed in a web of connections. For Dewey, any action is always a trans-action, and any act is really but an initiative that gives birth to a cascade of legitimate and bastard progeny. This is because an act can only take place in a field already crowded with other endeavors and their consequences, a crowd with which the new entrant immediately interacts, overlaps, interferes. The field of *political* action is thus for Dewey a kind of ecology. No one body owns its supposedly own initiatives, for initiatives instantly conjoin with an impersonal swarm of contemporaneous endeavors, each with its own duration and intensity, with endeavors that are losing or gaining momentum, rippling into and recombining with others. In Dewey's own terms, conjoint actions generate "multitudinous consequences," and each of these consequences "crosses the others" to generate its own problems, and thus its own publics or "group of persons especially affected."[14]

Dewey imagines a public as a set of bodies affected by a common problem generated by a pulsing swarm of activities. Let us bracket for the moment Dewey's claim that a public is a group of "*persons* especially affected" and leave aside the question of what *kinds* of bodies can do the "acts" that are conjoining, and focus instead on the way Dewey defines the members of a public in terms of their "affective" capacity. We would then get this (Spinozist) version of Dewey's theory of the public and of conjoint action: problems give rise to publics, publics are groups of bodies with the capacity to affect and be affected; problems are signals that the would-be or protomembers of a public had already encountered the indirect effects of other endeavoring bodies, effects that have decreased the capacity for action of the protomembers. A public is a cluster of bodies harmed by the actions of others or even by actions born from their own actions as these trans-act; harmed bodies draw near each other and seek to engage in new acts that will restore their power, protect against future harm, or compensate for damage done — in *that* consists their political action, which, fortunately or unfortunately, will also become conjoint action with a chain of indirect, unpredictable consequences.

Dewey presents the members of a public as having been *inducted* into rather than *volunteering* for it: each body finds itself thrown together with other harmed and squirming bodies. Dewey's political pragmatism, like the one expressed at the end of my discussion of the blackout in chapter 2, emphasizes consequences more than intentions and makes "responsibility" more a matter of responding to harms than of identifying objects of blame. Dewey's concept of conjoint action distributes responsibility to many different (human) actors. What is more, in naming a *problem* (rather than an act of will) as the driving force behind the formation of a public, Dewey (almost) acknowledges that a *political* action need not originate in human bodies at all. For is it not the case that some of the initiatives that conjoin and cause harm started from (or later became conjoined with) the vibrant bodies of animals, plants, metals, or machines?

In *Art as Experience*, Dewey comes close to saying that even human initiatives are not *exclusively* human; he flirts with a posthuman conception of action when he notes the porosity of the border between a human body and its out-side: "The epidermis is only in the most superficial way an indication of where an organism ends and its environment begins. There are things inside the body that are foreign to it, and there are things outside of it that belong to it de jure if not de facto; that must be taken possession of if life is to continue. The need that is manifest in the urgent impulsions that demand completion through what the environment—and it alone—can supply, is a dynamic acknowledgment of this dependence of the self for wholeness upon its surroundings."[15]

Of course, Dewey is not quite a vital materialist. His language quoted above ultimately relegates the nonhuman and the nonorganic to the role of "environment" rather than actor and affirms a profound "dependence" of humans on "surroundings," but not a true reciprocity between participants of various material compositions. And Dewey generally assumes that the acts in conjoint action are *human* endeavors. Such anthropocentrism is impossible to avoid completely: as Theodor Adorno said, we are (almost) blind to the gap between concept and thing, and we have a tendency, as did even Spinoza, to privilege *human* efforts even when acknowledging the presence of other kinds of conative bodies. A pragmatic approach to politics, which emphasizes problem solving, may call forth with particular vigor what Henri Bergson described as action-oriented perception. For are not human bodies the ones best equipped to analyze a problem and devise strategies for its solution? All kinds of bodies may be able to join forces, but a pragmatist would be quick to note that only *some* bodies can make this association into a *task* force. And yet there also persists a self-interested motivation for the presumption that all material bodies are potential members of the public into which one has been inducted. Such a presumption will enable me to discern more fully the extent of their power over me: How is this food or worm or aluminum contributing to a problem affecting me? How might these nonhumans contribute to its solution?

Latour pushes Dewey's theory of the public and its problems further in a vital materialist direction. He does so, first, by inventing the concept of an actant, which is an attempt, as is conjoint action, to pry some space between the idea of action and the idea of human intentionality. Second, Latour explicitly rejects the categories of "nature" and "culture" in favor of the "collective," which refers to an ecology of human and nonhuman elements.[16] A polity is one of these collectives. Third, Latour frames political action not as the enactment of choices but as the call-and-response between "propositions."[17] A proposition has no decisionistic power but is a lending of weight, an incentive toward, a pressure in the direction of one trajectory of action rather than another.[18] Any given response to a problem is less the result of "deliberation" than of the "fermentation" of the various propositions and energies of the affected bodies.[19] Finally, Latour distributes agentic capacity also to the "event." Policy directions and political moods are irreducible to the sum of the propositions of even an ontologically plural public, for there is always a slight surprise of action: "There are events. I never *act*; I am always slightly surprised by what I do. That which acts through me is also surprised by what I do, by the chance to mutate, to change, and to bifurcate."[20]

Dewey's account of a public as the product of conjoint action paints a picture of a political system that has much in common with a dynamic natural ecosystem. This, along with his claim that a member of a public is one "affected by the indirect consequences of transactions to such an extent that it is deemed necessary to have those consequences systematically cared for,"[21] paves the way for a theory of action that more explicitly accepts nonhuman bodies as members of a public, more explicitly attends to how they, too, participate in conjoint action, and more clearly discerns instances of harm to the (affective) bodies of animals, vegetables, minerals, and their ecocultures. These harms will surely provoke some "events" in response, but it is an open question whether they will provoke people to throw their weight toward a solution to them. Humans may notice the harm too late to intervene effectively, or their strategies of intervention may be ineffective, or they simply may deem it *unnecessary* "to systematically care for" a harm, as we regularly sacrifice some actants for the sake of ourselves. For while every public may very well be an ecosystem, not every ecosystem is democratic. And I cannot envision any polity so egalitarian that important human needs, such as health or survival, would not take priority.

Why not? Since I have challenged the uniqueness of humanity in several ways, why not conclude that we and they are equally entitled? Because I have not eliminated all differences between us but examined instead the affinities across these differences, affinities that enable the very assemblages explored in the present book. To put it bluntly, my conatus will not let me "horizontalize" the world completely. I also identify with members of my species, insofar as they are bodies most similar to mine. I so identify even as I seek to extend awareness of our interinvolvements and interdependencies. The political goal of a vital materialism is not the perfect equality of actants, but a polity with more channels of communication between members. (Latour calls this a more "vascularized" collective.[22])

There are many practical and conceptual obstacles here: How can communication proceed when many members are nonlinguistic? Can we theorize more closely the various forms of such communicative energies? How can humans learn to hear or enhance our receptivity for "propositions" not expressed in words? How to translate between them? What kinds of institutions and rituals of democracy would be appropriate? Latour suggests that we convene a "parliament of things," an idea that is as provocative as it is elusive.[23] Perhaps we can make better progress on this front by looking at a theory designed to open democracy to the voices of excluded *humans*. I turn to Rancière's theory of democracy as disruption.

Disruptions and the Demos

Compared to Dewey and Latour, Rancière is less concerned with how a public emerges than with the means by which its (apparent) coherence can be interrupted. In his influential *Disagreement*, he focuses on a potentially disruptive human force that exists within (though is not recognized by) the public. He calls this the force of the people or of the "demos." The democratic act par excellence occurs when the demos does something that exposes the arbitrariness of the dominant "partition of the sensible."[24] This is the partition that had been rendering some people visible as political actors while pushing others below the threshold of note. Politics, as Rancière frames it, consists not in acts that preserve a political order or respond to already articulated problems, but is "the name of a singular disruption of this order of distribution of bodies."[25]

These singular disruptions are neither intentional acts nor aleatory eruptions; Rancière locates them in the between-space of the staged event. The demos more or less spontaneously constructs "a polemical scene" within which what was formerly heard as noise by powerful persons begins to sound to them like "argumentative utterances."[26] Such scenes, however different in their cast of characters, always tell the same story: the story of "the equality of speaking beings."[27] The "mise-en-scènes that reconfigure the relations of the visible and the sayable" expose "the ultimate secret of any social order,"[28] that is, that "there is no natural principle of domination by one person over another."[29]

For Rancière, then, the political act consists in the exclamatory interjection of affective bodies as they enter a preexisting public, or, rather, as they reveal that they have been there all along as an unaccounted-for part. (Rancière would be helped here, I think, were he to adopt Dewey's insight about multiple, coexisting publics, rather than speak of a single demos with an overt and a latent set of members.) What difference does this interjection by formerly ignored bodies make, according to Rancière? It modifies the "partition of the perceptible" or the "regime of the visible,"[30] and this changes everything. As an example Rancière cites the interruption staged by the plebeians of the Roman (patrician) Republic:

> The plebs gatherd on the Aventine . . . do not set up a fortified camp in the manner of the Scythian slaves. They do what would have been unthinkable for the latter: they establish another order, another partition of the perceptible, by constituting themselves not as warriors equal to other warriors but as speaking beings sharing the same properties as those who deny them these. They thereby execute a series of speech acts that mimic those of the patricians: they pronounce imprecations and apotheoses; they delegate one

of their number to go and consult *their* oracles; they give themselves representatives by rebaptizing them. In a word, they conduct themselves like beings with names. Through transgression, they find that they too . . . are endowed with speech that does not simply express want, suffering, or rage, but intelligence.[31]

The plebs managed to repartition the regime of the sensible. Is this an exclusively human power? Though the metaphors of eruption or disruption that Rancière employs may suggest that the political act is "like" a force of nature, his description of the act increasingly takes on a linguistic cast ("disruption" becomes "interruption" and then "disagreement"). It is an "objection to a wrong," where a wrong is defined as the unequal treatment of beings who are equally endowed with a capacity for *human* speech. When asked in public whether he thought that an animal or a plant or a drug or a (nonlinguistic) sound could disrupt the police order, Rancière said no: he did not want to extend the concept of the political that far; nonhumans do not qualify as participants in a demos; the disruption effect must be accompanied by the desire to engage in reasoned discourse.[32]

Despite this reply, I think that even against his will, so to speak, Rancière's model contains inklings of and opportunities for a more (vital) materialist theory of democracy. Consider, for example, the way it imagines the being of the demos: not as a formed thing or fixed entity, but as an unruly activity or indeterminate wave of energy. The demos is, we read, "neither the sum of the population nor the disfavored element within," but an "excess" irreducible to the particular *bodies* involved.[33] This idea of a force that traverses bodies without itself being one resonates with Spinoza's conatus and Deleuze's notion of (the motility of) intensities, discussed in chapters 2 and 4, respectively. Does not the protean "excess" that Rancière invokes flow through nonhuman bodies? Might not this be what the *New York Times* was pointing to by saying that the grid "lives and dies by its own rules"? (Or what is intuited in phrases like "the war has a momentum of its own"?) Rancière implicitly raises this question: Is the power to disrupt really limited to human speakers?

A second opportunity for a more materialist theory of democracy arises when Rancière chooses to define what counts as political by what *effect* is generated: a political act not only disrupts, it disrupts in such a way as to change radically what people can "see": it repartitions the sensible; it overthrows the regime of the perceptible. Here again the political gate is opened enough for nonhumans (dead rats, bottle caps, gadgets, fire, electricity, berries, metal) to slip through, for they also have the power to startle and provoke a gestalt shift in perception: what was trash becomes things, what was an instrument becomes a participant, what was foodstuff becomes agent, what was adamantine becomes intensity. We see how an animal, plant, mineral, or artifact can sometimes catalyze a public, and we might then see how to devise more effective (experimental) tactics for enhancing or weakening that public. It feels dangerous to leave the gate open, for it renders many conceptual, moral, and psychological possessions exposed and vulnerable. It seems safer to figure eruptive events as "argumentative utterances."

It is, of course, quite normal for democratic theory to be anthropocentric and quite reasonable to tie political participation to some degree of linguistic or deliberative competence.[34] These tendencies have directed democratic theorists toward important problems: the uninformed voter and a scarcity of deliberative forums, the unequal access of different human groups to political power, the harm caused when we fail to discern not just established constituencies but also what William Connolly has described as those protean identities emerging from inarticulate "currents of experience."[35]

But what if we loosened the tie between participation and human language use, encountering the world as a swarm of vibrant materials entering and leaving agentic assemblages? We might then entertain a set of crazy and not-so-crazy questions: Did the typical American diet play any role in engendering the widespread susceptibility to the propaganda leading up to the invasion of Iraq? Do sand storms make a difference to the spread of so-called sectarian violence? Does mercury help enact autism? In what ways does the effect on sensibility of a video game exceed the intentions of its designers and users? Can a hurricane bring down a president? Can HIV mobilize homophobia or an evangelical revival? Can an avian virus jump from birds to humans and create havoc for systems of health care and international trade and travel?

Though Rancière objects to the "Platonic" prejudice against the demos, which positions commoners as defective versions of men in possession of logos, to imagine politics as a realm of human activity alone may also be a kind of prejudice: a prejudice against a (nonhuman) multitude misrecognized as context, constraint, or tool. A vital materialist theory of democracy seeks to transform the divide between speaking subjects and mute objects into a set of differential tendencies and variable capacities. I think this is also what Darwin and Latour were trying to do when they told their worm stories.

A Diet of Worms

As our ability to detect and translate the more subtle forms of animal behavior and communication has grown, so, too, has our willingness to attribute intelligence to it and to recast it from behavior to action. But to truly take worms seriously, we would not only have to revise our assessment of their activities but also need to question our larger faith in the uniqueness of humans and to reinvent concepts now attached to that faith.[36] Theories of democracy that assume a world of active subjects and passive objects begin to appear as thin descriptions at a time when the interactions between human, viral, animal, and technological bodies are becoming more and more intense. If human culture is inextricably enmeshed with vibrant, nonhuman agencies,[37] and if human intentionality can be agentic only if accompanied by a vast entourage of nonhumans,[38] then it seems that the appropriate unit of analysis for democratic theory is neither the individual human nor an exclusively human collective but the (ontologically heterogeneous) "public" coalescing around a problem.[39] We need not only to invent or reinvoke concepts like conatus, actant, assemblage, small agency, operator, disruption, and the like but also to devise new procedures, technologies, and regimes of perception that enable us to consult nonhumans more closely, or to listen and respond more carefully to their outbreaks, objections, testimonies, and propositions. For these offerings are profoundly important to the health of the political ecologies to which *we* belong.

Of course, to acknowledge nonhuman materialities as participants in a political ecology is not to claim that everything is always a participant, or that all participants are alike. Persons, worms, leaves, bacteria, metals, and hurricanes have different types and degrees of power, just as different persons have different types and degrees of power, different worms have different types and degrees of power, and so on, depending on the time, place, composition, and density of the formation. But surely the scope of democratization can be broadened to acknowledge more nonhumans in more ways, in something like the ways in which we have come to hear the political voices of other humans formerly on the outs: "Are you ready, and at the price of what sacrifice, to live the good life together? That this highest of moral and political questions could have been raised, for so many centuries, by so many bright minds, *for human only* without the nonhumans that make them up, will soon appear, I have no doubt, as extravagant as when the Founding Fathers denied slaves and women the vote."[40]

8

Vitality and Self-interest

In response to a series of practical problems, including Hurricane Katrina (August 2005), expensive gasoline, tornadoes in months and places where they had not normally occurred, the dead and tortured bodies from the invasions of Iraq and Afghanistan, and pathogens in spinach, hot peppers, chicken, and beef produced by long-distance factory farming, an American public seemed to be coalescing. Stirred from their "fatalistic passivity" by a series of harms, some members of this public began to note aloud — in the news, in schools, on the street — the self-destructive quality of the American way of life.[1] Environmentalism, invented in the 1970s, was making a comeback. This comeback was motivated in large part by self-interest, by a fear of the environmental "blowback" of human actions.[2]

Following John Dewey, I do not object to the self-interested character of this emergent public. But I do wonder whether environmentalism remains the best way to frame the problems, whether it is the most persuasive rubric for challenging the American equation of prosperity with wanton consumption, or for inducing, more generally, the political will to create more sustainable political economies in or adjacent to global

capitalism. Would a discursive shift from environmentalism to vital materialism enhance the prospects for a more sustainability-oriented public? That is an open, empirical question. In advance it is possible only
to say that the two concepts call to the fore different sets of affects and
invoke different histories of use, and thus are likely to catalyze different publics. It is difficult, for example, for a public convened by environmentalism to include animals, vegetables, or minerals as bona fide
members, for nonhumans are already named as a passive environment
or perhaps a recalcitrant context for human action. A more materialist
public would need to include more earthlings in the swarm of actants.
If environmentalists are selves who live on earth, vital materialists are
selves who live as earth, who are more alert to the capacities and limitations — the "jizz" — of the various materials that they are. If environmentalism leads to the call for the protection and wise management of an
ecosystem that surrounds us, a vital materialism suggests that the task
is to engage more strategically with a trenchant materiality that is us as
it vies with us in agentic assemblages.[3]

The discourse of environmentalism has certainly raised good political
questions. To name just a few: What is the relationship between environmental protection and capitalist markets? What are the strengths
and limitations of the Kyoto approach to global warming? How do hier-
archies of race, class, gender, and civilization complicate the project of
environmental protection? Might animals and plants be assigned legal
rights? Yet other questions have been occluded: How can humans become more attentive to the public activities, affects, and effects of nonhumans? What dangers do we risk if we continue to overlook the force
of things? What other affinities between us and them become apparent
if we construe both us and them as vibrant matter?

Freya Mathews, Bruno Latour, Donna Haraway, Gay Hawkins, Tim
Ingold, N. Katherine Hayles, Karen Barad, Sarah Whatmore, Nick Bingham, Félix Guattari, Don Ihde, and W. J. T. Mitchell have been making
the call for more sustainable, less noxious modes of production and
consumption in the name of a vigorous materiality rather than in the
name of the environment.[4] In the next section I will examine the contributions made by Guattari in this regard. But let me first name three
advantages, or possible advantages, of the discourse of encountering a
vital materiality over that of caring for an environment.

First, if the environment is defined as the substrate of human culture, *materiality* is a term that applies more evenly to humans and non-humans. I am a material configuration, the pigeons in the park are material compositions, the viruses, parasites, and heavy metals in my flesh and in pigeon flesh are materialities, as are neurochemicals, hurricane winds, E. coli, and the dust on the floor. Materiality is a rubric that tends to horizontalize the relations between humans, biota, and abiota. It draws human attention sideways, away from an ontologically ranked Great Chain of Being and toward a greater appreciation of the complex entanglements of humans and nonhumans. Here, the implicit moral imperative of Western thought—"Thou shall identify and defend what is special about Man"—loses some of its salience.

A second advantage hinges on the inflection of matter as vibrant, vital, energetic, lively, quivering, vibratory, evanescent, and effluescent (to recall some modifiers I have used throughout the book). In a world of lively matter, we see that biochemical and biochemical-social systems can sometimes unexpectedly bifurcate or choose developmental paths that could not have been foreseen, for they are governed by an emergent rather than a linear or deterministic causality. And once we see this, we will need an alternative both to the idea of nature as a purposive, harmonious process and to the idea of nature as a blind mechanism. A vital materialism interrupts both the teleological organicism of some ecologists and the machine image of nature governing many of their opponents.

A third advantage of the notion of "vital materiality" compared to "environment" is the one I will focus on in this chapter. Vital materiality better captures an "alien" quality of our own flesh, and in so doing reminds humans of the very *radical* character of the (fractious) kinship between the human and the nonhuman. My "own" body is material, and yet this vital materiality is not fully or exclusively human. My flesh is populated and constituted by different swarms of foreigners. The crook of my elbow, for example, is "a special ecosystem, a bountiful home to no fewer than six tribes of bacteria. . . . They are helping to moisturize the skin by processing the raw fats it produces. . . . The bacteria in the human microbiome collectively possess at least 100 times as many genes as the mere 20,000 or so in the human genome."[5] The *its* outnumber the *mes*. In a world of vibrant matter, it is thus not enough to say that we are "embodied." We are, rather, *an array of bodies*, many different kinds of them in a nested set of microbiomes. If more people marked this fact more of the time, if we were more attentive to the indispensable foreignness that we are, would we continue to produce and consume in the same violently reckless ways?

It is very hard to keep focused on the oxymoronic truism that the human is not exclusively human, that we are made up of its. But I think this truism, and the cultivated talent for remembering it, forms a key part of the newish self that needs to emerge, the self of a new self-interest. For what counts as self-interest shifts in a world of vital materialities. I turn next Guattari's *The Three Ecologies* and to the various rhetorical tactics and conceptual inventions he uses to express this truism and to remain present to it.

I as It: The Outside That's Within

Guattari's *The Three Ecologies*, written in 1986, begins with an appeal to self-interest. The problem we are facing, he says, is not simply "environmental" decay but a disease afflicting all three "ecological registers": the environmental, the social, and the mental.[6] The modern "period of intense techno-scientific transformations" has degraded both the impersonal environment and our own sociopsychic networks: air, water, and soil are contaminated as "kinship networks tend to be reduced to a bare minimum; domestic life is being poisoned by the gangrene of mass-media consumption; family and married life are frequently 'ossified' by a sort of standardization of behavior; and neighborhood relations are generally reduced to their meanest expression."[7] And so, warns Guattari, if we have a humanistic interest in a richer kinship, marital, or civic life, we had better pursue a more ecological sustainable relationship with nonhuman nature.

Guattari insists that the relationship between the three ecologies is extremely close; they are not really even "discrete domains" but only "interchangeable lenses or points of view." In fact, the three ecologies form a single whole, which Guattari calls Integrated World Capitalism (IWC). This complex assemblage works to manufacture the particular psychosocial self in the interest of which environmentalism is initially pursued. It does so by means of various "modules of subjectification,"[8] which include ideological as well as (Foucaultian) disciplinary components, all designed to organize bodily energies (including the "intensive" forces of the unconscious) into the form of the consumer-self. This consumer-self has an "interest" in environmentalism. But if the greening is to develop beyond the superficial level allowed by the consumeristic selves of IWC (beyond what Timothy W. Luke has persistently criticized as "green consumerism"[9]), then new modules of subjectification must be created and deployed. It is precisely because IWC works by appropriating bodily affect and channeling unconscious intensities that a greener self-culture-nature will require not only new "laws, decrees and bureaucratic programmes" but "new micropolitical and microsocial practices, new solidarities, a new gentleness, together with new aesthetic and new analytic practices regarding the formation of the unconscious."[10]

Guattari's claim that the ecological problem is as much a matter of culture- and psyche-formation as it is of watershed management and air quality protection has since been echoed by others.[11] What is especially intriguing, however, is his particular articulation of the impossible fact that humans are both "in" and "of" nature, both are and are not the outside. Guattari's rhetorical strategy here echoes that pursued by Roman Catholicism to express the mysterious unity of the three persons of God. There are three ecologies, says Guattari, or, as the Baltimore Catechism says, the Father, Son, and Holy Spirit are three persons "really distinct from one another." And yet, says Guattari, the three ecologies form a single whole, IWC, or, in the worlds of the catechism, "The Trinity is One."[12] We must, says Guattari, learn to think the three-in-one: to think "transversally" or fix our mind's eye on the interlacing of the mechanosphere, the social sphere, and the inwardness of subjectivity.[13]

Guattari first categorically distinguishes the human (or social and mental ecologies) from the nonhuman (mechanosphere or environmental ecology), but then he immediately calls this division into question and calls for a "transversal" mode of perception. In his contribution to a collection of "postenvironmentalist" essays, Latour describes this double move as a characteristically "modern" one. The modern, urban self on the one hand feels more and more *removed* from nature, as family farming becomes agribusiness, hands-on food preparation becomes the consumption of fast food, bloody wars are waged from high altitudes, fuel is consumed with little recognition of the violence of its extraction and distribution, and so on. These distances are encoded into the figure of nature as an abstract environment, or expressed as three separate ecologies. But on the other hand, continues Latour, the modern self feels increasingly *entangled*—cosmically, biotechnologically, medically, virally, pharmacologically—with nonhuman nature. Nature has always mixed it up with self and society, but Latour notes that lately this commingling has intensified and become harder to ignore. "Whereas at the time of ploughs we could only scratch the surface of the soil, we can now begin to fold ourselves into the molecular machinery of soil bacteria."[14] There is a cognitive dissonance between the everyday experience of this comingling and the rubric of an environment that we direct from above and outside.

Some people respond to the proliferation of entanglements between human and nonhuman materialities with a desire to reenforce the boundary between culture and nature, as Jürgen Habermas seems to do in *The Future of Human Nature*, or as American evangelicals do in their "culture of life" opposition to cloning or embryonic stem cell research. Another response is to accept the mingling and to seek to bring the conceptual vocabulary more in line with this condition: ecological thinking should become more dialectical, or dialogical, or phenomenological, or we should no longer speak of "nature" but only of "second nature." The idea of "second nature" emphasizes that what we used to call natural is actually the cultural determination of nature. But here the vital materialist points out that culture is *not* of our own making, infused as it is by biological, geological, and climatic forces. (There is, as I suggest in chapter 4, a life of metal as well as a life of men.) These impinge on us as much as we impinge on them. In other words, the fugitive disadvantage of the figure of "second nature" is the same as its apparent advantage: it highlights the agency of humans.[15]

Latour makes this same point when he notes that we are much better at admitting that humans infect nature than we are at admitting that nonhumanity infects culture, for the latter entails the blasphemous idea that nonhumans—trash, bacteria, stem cells, food, metal, technologies, weather—are actants more than objects. Latour argues for a pragmabased politics that explicitly acknowledges this commingling, and for (liberal democratic) public policies designed to "*follow through*" or attend to the problems for human flourishing caused by the intimacy of the human and the nonhuman.[16] Admit that humans have crawled or secreted themselves into every corner of the environment; admit that the environment is actually inside human bodies and minds, and then proceed politically, technologically, scientifically, in everyday life, with careful forbearance, as you might with unruly relatives to whom you are inextricably bound and with whom you will engage over a lifetime, like it or not. Give up the futile attempt to disentangle the human from the nonhuman. Seek instead to engage more civilly, strategically, and subtly with the nonhumans in the assemblages in which you, too, participate.

Like Latour, Guattari also calls for a politics that openly acknowledges the porosity of the borders between (what he categorizes as) subjectivity, society, and machines.[17] He, too, rejects any attempt to unstir the cream from the coffee—to disentangle the cultural from the natural. It makes no political sense, writes Guattari in 1986, to try to withdraw from nature, for the health of the planet is "increasingly reliant upon human intervention, and a time will come when vast programmes will need to be set up in order to regulate the relationship between oxygen, ozone and carbon dioxide in the Earth's atmosphere. . . . In the future, much more than the simple defense of nature will be required; we will have to launch an initiative if we are to repair the Amazonian 'lung,' for example."[18]

It is futile to seek a pure nature unpolluted by humanity, and it is foolish to define the self as something purely human. But how can I start to feel myself as not only human? Guattari's call for us to cultivate a "transversal" style of thinking gestures toward one of the ways we might develop this newish self. A vital materialism also recasts the self in the light of its intrinsically polluted nature and in so doing recasts what counts as self-interest. Let me turn next to an additional tactic in the struggle to remain present to the paradox of a self that is its own outside, is vibrant matter. It takes the form of an onto-story.

Natura Naturans

In lieu of an environment that surrounds human culture, or even a cosmos that cleaves into three ecologies, picture an ontological field without any unequivocal demarcations between human, animal, vegetable, or mineral. *All* forces and flows (materialities) are or can become lively, affective, and signaling. And so an affective, speaking human body is not *radically* different from the affective, signaling nonhumans with which it coexists, hosts, enjoys, serves, consumes, produces, and competes.

This field lacks primordial divisions, but it is not a uniform or flat topography. It is just that its differentiations are too protean and diverse to coincide exclusively with the philosophical categories of life, matter, mental, environmental. The consistency of the field is more uneven than that: portions congeal into bodies, but not in a way that makes any one type the privileged site of agency. The source of effects is, rather, always an ontologically diverse assemblage of energies and bodies, of simple and complex bodies, of the physical and the physiological.

In this onto-tale, everything is, in a sense, alive. This liveliness is not capped by an ultimate purpose or grasped and managed through a few simple and timeless (Kantian) categories. What I am calling vital materiality or vibrant matter is akin to what is expressed in one of the many historical senses of the word *nature*.[19] Though nature can refer to a stable substrate of brute matter, the term has also signaled generativity, fecundity, Isis or Aphrodite, or the "Spring" movement of Antonio Vivaldi's *Four Seasons*.[20] This creativity can be purposive or not. The contrast between nature as brute or purposive matter and nature as generativity is nicely captured by the distinction, key to Baruch Spinoza's *Ethics*, between *natura naturata* and *natura naturans*. *Natura naturata* is passive matter organized into an eternal order of Creation; *natura naturans* is the uncaused causality that ceaselessly generates new forms. When the English Romantics and American transcendentalists sought to refine their senses, they did so in part to be able to better detect *natura naturans*. This universal creativity requires a special sensitivity because, as Samuel Taylor Coleridge noted, the productive power is "suspended and, as it were, quenched in the product."[21] Nature as generativity is also emphasized in Alfred North Whitehead's process philosophy, according to which nature is "a continuous stream of occurrence."[22]

Gilles Deleuze and Guattari, drawing on Spinoza, Romanticism, Whitehead, and others (including Friedrich Nietzsche, Franz Kafka, and Henri Bergson), put this spin on *natura naturans*: Nature is a "pure plane of immanence . . . upon which unformed elements and materials dance."[23] According to Spinoza's theory of bodies, sketched in chapter 2, all bodies are modes of a common substance, which can be called either

God or Nature. Perhaps wary of the connotation of a static homogeneity that tends to cling (despite Spinoza's own efforts) to the word *substance*, and also wary of Spinoza's (albeit quite heterodox) theism, Deleuze and Guattari inflect Spinozism to speak of Nature as "an immense abstract machine" of generativity, whose pieces "are the various assemblages and individuals, each of which groups together an infinity of particles entering into an infinity of more or less interconnected relations."[24] Like Spinoza's God or Nature, this abstract machine too operates not in the service of a pre-given end but for the sake of itself as process.[25]

The sense of nature as creativity also seems a part of what the ancient Greeks meant by *phusis*, of which the Latin *natura* is an equivalent. *Phusis* comes from the verb *phuo*, which probably meant to puff, blow, or swell up, conveying the sense of germination or sprouting up, bringing forth, opening out, or hatching. *Phusis* thus speaks of a process of morphing, of formation and deformation, that is to say, of the becoming otherwise of things in motion as they enter into strange conjunctions with one another.

The point is this: an active becoming, a *creative not-quite-human force capable of producing the new*, buzzes within the history of the term nature. This vital materiality congeals into bodies, bodies that seek to persevere or prolong their run. Here the onto-tale again draws from Spinoza, who claims that conatus-driven bodies, to enhance their power or vitality, form alliances with other bodies. Despite this, it would be too much to say that Spinoza was a vital materialist. And it is beyond the scope of the present study to take up the vexed issue of whether his view that each mode can be understood interchangeably as a body or as an idea disqualifies him from any kind of materialism. But Spinoza's theory of bodies and their affective encounters can and does inspire ecological thinking today.

Michel Serres, for example, suggests that the process of collaboration and contestation between bodies is not random or unstructured, but conforms to the strange logic of vortices, spirals, and eddies, and this logic encompasses politics as much as physics, economics as much as biology, psychology as much as meteorology: it recurs at all scales and locations. Serres, here following Lucretius, posits but one isomorphic process, that of "flood and fire, of plethora and exhaustion, of vertical growth and sudden fall, of accumulation and drought, in which history

. . . rises and descends, as if on the high seas under the movements of the hurricane."[26] It is one vortical process, though it can be parsed theoretically into stages: first a "fall" or conative impulse of matter-energy,[27] then an aleatory swerve that produces crash encounters between protean bits, then a stage of confused turbulence, then a congealment or crystallization of matter into bodies, then a decay, decline, and dissemination of the form. And finally: a new fall, a fresh swerve, a different configuration of turbulent forces, another set of formations, a different rate and sequence of decay and decline. The vortical logic holds across different scales of size, time, and complexity, and the sequence of stages repeats, but each time with slight differences: "This is the stroke of genius in [Lucretian] . . . physics: there is no circle, there are only vortices . . . , spirals that shift, that erode."[28] Serres offers an account of the strange structuralism of vital materiality, a structuralism that includes the aleatory.

Blocks to and for a New Self-Interest

The monism I have just described is a story that may or may not resonate with the reader's experience. Even if, I as believe, the vitality of matter is real, it will be hard to discern it, and, once discerned, hard to keep focused on. It is too close and too fugitive, as much wind as thing, impetus as entity, a movement always on the way to becoming otherwise, an effluence that is vital and engaged in trajectories but not necessarily intentions. What is more, my attention will regularly be drawn away from it by deep cultural attachments to the ideas that matter is inanimate and that real agency belongs only to humans or to God, and by the need for an action-oriented perception that must overlook much of the swirling vitality of the world. In composing and recomposing the sentences of this book—especially in trying to choose the appropriate verbs, I have come to see how radical a project it is to think vital materiality. It seems necessary and impossible to rewrite the default grammar of agency, a grammar that assigns activity to people and passivity to things.

Are there more everyday tactics for cultivating an ability to discern the vitality of matter? One might be to allow oneself, as did Charles Darwin, to anthropomorphize, to relax into resemblances discerned across ontological divides: you (mis)take the wind outside at night for your father's wheezy breathing in the next room; you get up too fast and see stars; a plastic topographical map reminds you of the veins on the back of your hand; the rhythm of the cicada's reminds you of the wailing of an infant; the falling stone seems to express a conative desire to persevere. If a green materialism requires of us a more refined sensitivity to the outside-that-is-inside-too, then maybe a bit of anthropomorphizing will prove valuable. Maybe it is worth running the risks associated with anthropomorphizing (superstition, the divinization of nature, romanticism) because it, oddly enough, works against anthropocentrism: a chord is struck between person and thing, and I am no longer above or outside a nonhuman "environment." Too often the philosophical rejection of anthropomorphism is bound up with a hubristic demand that only humans and God can bear any traces of creative agency. To qualify and attenuate this desire is to make it possible to discern a kind of life irreducible to the activities of humans or gods. This material vitality is me, it predates me, it exceeds me, it postdates me.

Another way to cultivate this new discernment might be to elide the question of the human. Postpone for a while the topics of subjectivity or the nature of human interiority, or the question of what really distinguishes the human from the animal, plant, and thing. Sooner or later, these topics will lead down the anthropocentric garden path, will insinuate a hierarchy of subjects over objects, and obstruct freethinking about what agency really entails. One might also try to elide or not get defensive about the perfectly reasonable objection that the "posthumanist" gestures of vital materialism entail a performative contradiction: "Is it not, after all, a self-conscious, language-wielding human who is articulating this philosophy of vibrant matter?" It is not so easy to resist, deflect, or redirect this criticism.[29] One can point out how dominant notions of human subjectivity and agency are belied by the tangles and aporias into which they enter when the topics are explored in philosophical detail. One can invoke bacteria colonies in human elbows to show how human subjects are themselves nonhuman, alien, outside, vital materiality. One can note that the human immune system depends on parasitic helminth worms for its proper functioning or cite other instances of our cyborgization to show how human agency is always an assemblage of microbes, animals, plants, metals, chemicals, word-sounds, and the like—indeed, that insofar as anything "acts" at all, it has already entered an agentic assemblage:[30] for example, Hurricanes-FEMA-GlobalWarming; or StemCells-NIH-Souls; or Worms-Topsoil-Garbage; or Electricity-Deregulation-Fire-Greed; or E.Coli-Abattoirs-Agribusiness.

The voice of reason or habit is, however, unlikely to be mollified by such tactics and will again grasp for that special something that makes *human* participation in assemblages radically *different*. Here one might try to question the question: Why are we so keen to distinguish the human self from the field? Is it because the assumption of a uniquely human agency is, to use Kantian language, a "necessary presupposition" of assertion as such? Or is the quest motivated by a more provincial demand that humans, above all other things on earth, possess souls that make us eligible for eternal salvation? I do not imagine that any of these replies will end the conversation, but some of them together may open up new avenues within it.

There are many other pitfalls on the road to a vital materialism. For example, while I agree with Latour and Guattari that techno-fixes (smart ones that respect the vitality or quasi autonomy of materialities) must be pursued, and that there is nothing intrinsically wrong with them, I am ambivalent about Latour's claim that life (for Americans and Europeans) has simply become too technologized for the idea of pristine nature to wield any inspirational value. As the popularity of Thoreau and his heirs (such as Wendell Berry and Barry Lopez) shows, the ideal of nature as the Wild continues to motivate some people to live more ecologically sustainable lives. But even if Latour is correct in his prediction that the power of this ideal will dwindle, attracting fewer and fewer human bodies to it, he has not thought through all the normative implications of its demise.

Neither, of course, have I. But one thing I have noticed is that as I shift from environmentalism to vital materialism, from a world of nature versus culture to a heterogeneous monism of vibrant bodies, I find the ground beneath my old ethical maxim, "tread lightly on the earth," to be less solid. According to this maxim, I should try to minimize the impact of my actions so as to minimize the damage or destruction of other things with which I share existence. The ecologist James Nash describes this as the "earth-affirming norm" of frugality, a sparing "of the resources necessary for human communities and sparing of the other species that are both values in themselves and instrumental values for human needs."[31] If I live not as a human subject who confronts natural and cultural objects but as one of many conative actants swarming and competing with each other, then frugality is too simple a maxim. Sometimes ecohealth will require individuals and collectives to back off or ramp down their activeness, and sometimes it will call for grander, more dramatic and violent expenditures of human energy. I know that this last point is pitched at a very high level of abstraction or generality (as maxims must be, I suppose). And I know that more needs to be said to specify the normative implications of a vital materialism in specific contexts. I am, for now, at the end of my rope. So I will just end with a litany, a kind of Nicene Creed for would-be vital materialists: "I believe in one matter-energy, the maker of things seen and unseen. I believe that this pluriverse is traversed by heterogeneities that are continually *doing things*.[32] I believe it is wrong to deny vitality to nonhuman bodies, forces, and forms, and that a careful course of anthropomorphization can help reveal that vitality, even though it resists full translation and exceeds my comprehensive grasp.[33] I believe that encounters with lively matter can chasten my fantasies of human mastery, highlight the common materiality of all that is, expose a wider distribution of agency, and reshape the self and its interests."

Notes

Preface

1. "The partition of the sensible is the cutting-up of the world and of world . . . a partition between what is visible and what is not, of what can be heard from the inaudible." Rancière, "Ten Theses on Politics."
2. Rancière claims that "politics in general is about the configuration of the sensible," meaning that politics consists in the contestation over just what *is* "the given." It is "about the visibilities of the places and abilities of the body in those places" (Rancière, "Comment and Responses"). I agree that politics is the arranging and rearranging of the landscape that humans can sense or perceive, but I, unlike Rancière, am also interested in the "abilities" of nonhuman bodies — of artifacts, metals, berries, electricity, stem cells, and worms. I consider Rancière's theory of democracy in chapter 7.
3. Bergson, *Creative Evolution*, 45.
4. Latour, *Politics of Nature*, 237.
5. On this point Latour says that the phrase *name of action* is more appropriate than *actant*, for "only later does one deduce from these performances a competence" (Latour, *Pandora's Hope*, 303, 308).
6. Deleuze and Guattari, *Thousand Plateaus*, 351–423.
7. Spinoza, preface to *Ethics*, 102–3.

8. Deleuze, *Expressionism in Philosophy*, 67.

9. Serres, *Birth of Physics*.

10. As Michael Saler notes, enchantment, at least since the Middle Ages, has "signified both [human] 'delight' in wonderful things and the potential to be placed under *their* spell, to be beguiled" (Saler, "Modernity, Disenchantment, and the Ironic Imagination," 138; my emphasis).

11. Deleuze and Guattari, *Thousand Plateaus*, 257.

12. Cole, "Affective Literacy," 5–9.

13. See Derrida, "The Animal That Therefore I Am (More to Follow)."

14. Adorno, *Negative Dialectics*, 14. I discuss Adorno's clownishness in chapter 1.

15. Bruno Latour describes this as treating people and things "symmetrically." For a good account of this, see Crawford, "Interview with Bruno Latour."

16. Brown, *Regulating Aversion*, 11, 203.

17. "Justification is not to be confused with motivation. The current imperial policies of the United States are wrought from power-political motivations that have little to do with the . . . discourses I have been discussing here" (Brown, *Regulating Aversion*, 175n251).

18. See Sargisson, *Utopian Bodies*.

19. See Dean, *Publicity's Secret*, for a good example of demystification at work. It is in the context of assessing the political power of Slavoj Žižek's work that she asks: "If all we can do is evaluate, critique, or demystify the present, then what is it that we are hoping to accomplish? Perhaps we can start and lay the groundwork for revealing the limits of communicative capitalism, to think the unthought of the present, in order to free ourselves for a new possibility. And if Žižek can use his celebrity to work toward this goal, than all the better, right?" (http://jdeanicite.typepad.com/i_cite/2005/05/what_is_the_unt.html; accessed 18 February 2009).

20. Foucault, "Confinement, Psychiatry, Prison," 209.

21. Diana Coole offers a history of this motif in *Negativity and Politics*.

22. For a good discussion of the place of the notion of active materiality in historical materialism, see Diana Coole's contribution to Coole and Frost, *New Materialism*.

23. Adorno, *Negative Dialectics*, 183.

24. Darwin, *Formation of Vegetable Mould*, 305.

1. The Force of Things

Sections of this chapter appeared previously as "The Force of Things: Steps toward an Ecology of Matter," *Political Theory* 32, no. 3 (2004).

1. There is too much good work in feminist theory, queer studies, and cul-

tural studies to cite here. The three volumes of Feher, Naddaff, and Tazi, *Fragments for a History of the Human Body*, offer one map of the terrain. See also Rahman and Witz, "What Really Matters?"; Butler, *Bodies That Matter*; Butler, "Merely Cultural"; Brown, *States of Injury*; Ferguson, *Man Question*; and Gatens, *Imaginary Bodies*.

2. Mitchell, *What Do Pictures Want*, 156–57.

3. Spinoza, *Ethics*, pt. 3, proposition 6.

4. Mathews, *For Love of Matter*, 48.

5. Spinoza, *Ethics*, pt. 4, proposition 37, scholium 1.

6. Ibid., 4, preface.

7. Spinoza links, in this famous letter, his theory of conatus to a critique of the notion of human free will: "Now this stone, since it is conscious only of its endeavor [conatus] and is not at all indifferent, will surely think that it is completely free, and that it continues in motion for no other reason than that it so wishes. This, then, is that human freedom which all men boast of possessing, and which consists solely in this, that men are conscious of their desire and unaware of the causes by which they are determined" (Spinoza, *The Letters*, epistle 58). Hasana Sharp argues that the analogy between humans and stones "is not as hyperbolic as it seems at first glance. For Spinoza, all beings, including stones, . . . include a power of thinking that corresponds exactly to the power of their bodies to be disposed in different ways, to act and be acted upon. . . . Likewise every being, to the extent that it preserves its integrity amidst infinitely many other beings, as a stone surely does, is endowed with . . . a desire to . . . preserve and enhance its life to the extent that its nature allows" (Sharp, "The Force of Ideas in Spinoza," 740).

8. Levene, *Spinoza's Revelation*, 3. Yitshak Melamed goes further to say that "since the doctrine of the conatus . . . provide[s] the foundations for Spinoza's moral theory, it seems likely that we could even construct a moral theory for hippopotamuses and rocks" (Melamed, "Spinoza's Anti-Humanism," 23n59).

9. De Vries, introduction to *Political Theologies*, 42.

10. Ibid., 6.

11. De Vries seems to affirm this association when he wonders whether Baruch Spinoza's picture of interacting, conatus-driven *bodies* could possibly account for the creative emergence of the new: "It would seem that excess, gift, the event . . . have no place here" (de Vries, introduction to *Political Theologies*, 22). Why? Because the only plausible locus of creativity is, for de Vries, one that is "quasi-spiritual," hence Spinoza's second attribute of God/Nature, that is, *thought* or ideas. But what if materiality itself harbors creative vitality?

12. Gould, *Structure of Evolutionary Theory*, 1338.

13. On the effectivity of trash, see the fascinating Edensor, "Waste Matter"; and Hawkins, *The Ethics of Waste*.

14. See Dumm, *Politics of the Ordinary*, 7, for a subtle reckoning with the "obscure power of the ordinary." My attempt to speak on behalf of "things" is a companion project to Dumm's attempt to mine the ordinary as a potential site of resistance to conventional and normalizing practices.

15. Thoreau, *Writings*, 111 (Thoreau trained his gaze on things with the faith that "the perception of surfaces will always have the effect of miracle to a sane sense" [Thoreau, *Journal*, 2: 313]); Spinoza, *Ethics*, pt. 2, proposition 13, scholium 72; Merleau-Ponty, *Phenomenology of Perception*, 197.

16. For a good analysis of the implications of the trash-and-waste culture for democracy, see Buell and DeLuca, *Sustainable Democracy*.

17. Sullivan, *Meadowlands*, 96–97.

18. De Landa, *Thousand Years of Nonlinear History*, 16.

19. Kafka, "Cares of a Family Man," 428.

20. Ibid.

21. Ibid.

22. Deleuze, *Bergsonism*, 95.

23. Margulis and Sagan, *What Is Life*, 50.

24. Latour, "On Actor-Network Theory."

25. Latour, *Politics of Nature*, 75.

26. De Landa, *Intensive Science and Virtual Philosophy*, 123.

27. Tiffany, "Lyric Substance," 74. Tiffany draws an analogy between riddles and materiality per se: both are suspended between subject and object and engage in "transubstantiations" from the organic to the inorganic and from the earthly to the divine. In developing his materialism out of an analysis of literary forms, Tiffany challenges the long-standing norm that regards science as "the sole arbiter in the determination of matter" (75). He wants to pick "the lock that currently bars the literary critic from addressing the problem of material substance" (77).

28. Pietz, "Death of the Deodand."

29. Frow, "A Pebble, a Camera, a Man," 283.

30. De Landa, *A Thousand Years of Nonlinear History*, 26; my emphasis.

31. Ibid., 26–27.

32. Although, as I will argue in chapter 2, it is more accurate to say that this efficacy belongs less to minerals alone than to the combined activities of a variety of bodies and forces acting as an agentic assemblage.

33. Margulis and Sagan, *What Is Life*, 49; my emphasis.

34. Lyotard, *Postmodern Fables*, 98.

35. Rorty, *Rorty and Pragmatism*, 199.

36. I will also argue, at the end of chapter 2, that the efficacy of moralism in addressing social problems is overrated. The antimoralism that is one of

the implications of a vital materialism is a dangerous game to play, and not one I wish to play out to its logical extreme. I aim not to eliminate the practice of moral judgment but to increase the friction against the moralistic reflex.

37. Adorno, *Negative Dialectics*, 189. Further references to this title will be made in the running text as ND.

38. Romand Coles offers a sustained interpretation of Adorno as an ethical theorist: negative dialectics is a "morality of thinking" that can foster generosity toward others and toward the nonidentical in oneself. Coles argues that Adorno seeks a way to acknowledge and thereby mitigate the violence done by conceptualization and the suffering imposed by the quest to know and control all things. Coles, *Rethinking Generosity*, chap. 2.

39. Adorno also describes this pain as the "guilt of a life which purely as a fact will strangle other life" (ND, 364). Coles calls it the "ongoing discomfort that solicits our critical efforts" (Coles, *Rethinking Generosity*, 89). Adorno does not elaborate or defend his claim that the pain of conceptual failure can provoke or motivate an ethical will to redress the pain of social injustice. But surely some defense is needed, for history has shown that even if the pangs of nonidentity engender in the self the idea that "things should be different," this moral awakening does not always result in "social change in practice." In other words, there seems to be a second gap, alongside the one between concept and thing, that needs to be addressed: the gap between recognizing the suffering of others and engaging in ameliorative action. Elsewhere I have argued that one source of the energy required is a love of the world or an enchantment with a world of vital materiality; Adorno sees more ethical potential in suffering and a sense of loss. He "disdained the passage to affirmation," contending that the experience of the "fullness of life" is "inseparable from . . . a desire in which violence and subjugation are inherent. . . . There is no fullness without biceps-flexing" (ND 385, 378). Nonidentity is dark and brooding, and it makes itself known with the least distortion in the form of an unarticulated feeling of resistance, suffering, or pain. From the perspective of the vital materialist, Adorno teeters on the edge of what Thomas Dumm has described as "the overwhelming sense of loss that could swamp us when we approach [the thing's] unknowable vastness" (Dumm, *Politics of the Ordinary*, 169).

40. "Preponderance of the object is a thought of which any pretentious philosophy will be suspicious. . . . [Such] protestations . . . seek to drown out the festering suspicion that heteronomy might be mightier than the autonomy of which Kant . . . taught. . . . Such philosophical subjectivism is the ideological accompaniment of the . . . bourgeois I" (ND, 189).

41. The gap between concept and thing can never be closed, and, according

to Albrecht Wellmer, Adorno believes that this lack of conciliation can be withstood only "in the *name* of an absolute, which, although it is veiled in black, is not nothing. Between the being and the non-being of the absolute there remains an infinitely narrow crack through which a glimmer of light falls upon the world, the light of an absolute which is yet to come into being" (Wellmer, *Endgames*, 171; my emphasis).

42. Thanks to Lars Tønder for alerting me to the messianic dimension of Adorno's thinking. One can here note Adorno's admiration for Kant, who Adorno read as having found a way to assign transcendence an important role while making it inaccessible in principle: "What finite beings say about transcendence is the semblance of transcendence; but as Kant well knew, it is a necessary semblance. Hence the incomparable metaphysical relevance of the rescue of semblance, the object of esthetics" (*ND*, 393). For Adorno, "the idea of truth is supreme among the metaphysical ideas, and this is why . . . one who believes in God cannot believe in God, why the possibility represented by the divine name is maintained, rather, by him who does not believe" (*ND*, 401–2). According to Coles, it does not matter to Adorno whether the transcendent realm actually exists; what matters is the "demand . . . placed on thought" by its promise (Coles, *Rethinking Generosity*, 114).

43. There is, of course, no definitive way to prove either ontological imaginary. Morton Schoolman argues that Adorno's approach, which explicitly leaves open the possibility of a divine power of transcendence, is thus preferable to a materialism that seems to close the question. See Schoolman, *Reason and Horror*.

44. Lucretius, "On the Nature of the Universe," 128.

45. In response to Foucault's claim that "perhaps one day, this century will be known as Deleuzean," Deleuze described his own work as "naive": "[Foucault] may perhaps have meant that I was the most naive philosopher of our generation. In all of us you find themes like multiplicity, difference, repetition. But I put forward almost raw concepts of these, while others work with more mediations. I've never worried about going beyond metaphysics . . . I've never renounced a kind of empiricism. . . . Maybe that's what Foucault meant: I wasn't better than the others, but more naive, producing a kind of *art brut*, so to speak, not the most profound but the most innocent" (Deleuze, *Negotiations*, 88–89). My thanks to Paul Patton for this reference.

46. Mitchell, *What Do Pictures Want*, 149.

47. Lucretius, "On the Nature of the Universe," 126. There are no supernatural bodies or forces for Lucretius, and if we sometimes seem to have spiritual experiences, that is only because some kinds and collections of bodies exist below the threshold of human sense perception.

48. Althusser, "Underground Current of the Materialism of the Encounter,"
    169. "Without swerve and encounter, [primordia] would be nothing but
    abstract elements. . . . So much so that we can say that [prior to] . . . *the
    swerve and the encounter* . . . they led only a phantom existence" (ibid.).
49. Lucretian physics is the basis for his rejection of religion, his presentation
    of death as a reconfiguration of primordia made necessary by the essential
    motility of matter, and his ethical advice on how to live well while existing
    in one's current material configuration.
50. For Adorno, Heidegger, "weary of the subjective jail of cognition," became
    "convinced that what is transcendent to subjectivity is immediate for sub-
    jectivity, without being conceptually stained by subjectivity" (ND, 78). But
    it does not seem to me that Heidegger makes a claim to immediacy. See
    Heidegger, *What Is a Thing*.
51. For Marx, too, naive realism was the philosophy to overcome. He wrote
    his doctoral dissertation on the "metaphysical materialism" of Democri-
    tus, and it was against that naive objectivism that Marx would eventually
    define his own "historical materialism." Historical materialism would not
    focus on matter but on human power–laden socioeconomic structures.
52. This is Bill Brown's account of Arjun Appadurai's *The Social Life of Things*
    in "Thing Theory" (6–7).

2. The Agency of Assemblages

A version of this chapter appeared previously as "The Agency of Assemblages and the North American Blackout," *Public Culture* 17, no. 3 (2005),
which was reprinted in *Political Theologies: Public Religions in a Post-Secular
World*, eds. Hent deVries and Lawrence E. Sullivan (New York: Fordham
University Press, 2006).

1. This list could be expanded to include Maurice Merleau-Ponty's radi-
   ant matter, for example, his scissors and leather pieces that "offer themselves to the subject as action" or the "motor intentionality" of a human
   arm whose directional impetus is irreducible to any subjective decision
   (Merleau-Ponty, *Phenomenology of Perception*, 106, 110). We could also add
   the athletic entities (basketballs that move like gymnasts, and vice versa;
   a group of cyclists that flow like a flock of birds, and vice versa) featured in
   a Nike television advertisement. Thanks to Matthew Scherer for drawing
   my attention to this ad.
2. Deleuze, *Expressionism in Philosophy*, 93.
3. Substance, writes Spinoza, "cannot be produced by anything external to
   itself. For in the universe nothing is granted, save substances and their
   modifications" (*Ethics*, pt. 1, proposition 6, corollary). Also, "By substance,

I mean that which is in itself, and is conceived through itself" (*Ethics*, pt. 1, definition 3).

4. Lin, "Substance, Attribute, and Mode in Spinoza," 147.

5. "Individual things are nothing but modifications of the attributes of God, or modes by which the attributes of God are expressed in a fixed and definite manner" (*Ethics*, pt. 1, proposition 25, corollary).

6. Deleuze, *Expressionism in Philosophy*, 201.

7. Lucretius, "On the Nature of the Universe," 135.

8. See Deleuze, *Expressionism in Philosophy*, 230.

9. Rosi Braidotti underscores the place of conflict in Spinozism: "Another word for Spinoza's conatus is . . . self-preservation, not in the liberal individualistic sense . . . , but rather as the actualization of one's essence, that is to say, of one's ontological drive to become. This is neither an automatic nor an intrinsically harmonious process, insofar as it involves interconnection with other forces and consequently also conflicts and clashes. Negotiations have to occur as stepping-stones to sustainable flows of becoming. The bodily self's interaction with his/her environment can either increase or decrease that body's conatus" (Braidotti, "Affirmation versus Vulnerability," 235).

10. Spinoza, *Ethics*, pt. 4, appendix, no. 27.

11. See Latour, *Reassembling the Social*; Varela, "Organism"; Hardt and Negri, *Empire*; and Hardt and Negri, *Multitude*.

12. The term is Patrick Hayden's in "Gilles Deleuze and Naturalism." For Bergson, too, the universe is a nontotalizable sum, a "whole that is not given" because its evolution produces *new* members and thus an ever-changing array of effects. The world is "an indivisible process" of movement and creation, where there is "radical contingency in progress, incommensurability between what goes before and what follows — in short, duration." See Bergson, *Creative Evolution*, 29n1; and chapter 4 of the present volume.

13. Mark Bonta and John Protevi define an assemblage (*agencement*) as "an intensive network or rhizome displaying 'consistency' or emergent effect by tapping into the ability of the self-ordering forces of heterogeneous materials to mesh together" (Bonta and Protevi, *Deleuze and Geophilosophy*, 54).

14. Glanz, "When the Grid Bites Back."

15. Nosovel, "System Blackout Causes and Cures."

16. U.S.-Canada Power Outage Task Force, "Initial Blackout Timeline."

17. Ibid., 6. According to Nosovel, the "evaluation of disturbances shows that protection systems have been involved in 70% of the blackout events" (Novosel, "System Blackout Causes and Cures," 2).

18. Di Menna, "Grid Grief!"

19. The task force was appointed by the Canadian prime minister Jean Chré-
tien and the U.S. president George W. Bush. The first report of the task
force (issued 12 September 2003) was a description of about twenty grid
"events" occurring from 2:02 p.m. until 4:11 p.m. (EST) on 14 August
2003.
20. The grid is an AC (alternating current) system. For a fascinating historical
account of the development of electrical systems, see Jonnes, *Empires of
Light.*
21. U.S.-Canada Power Outage Task Force, "Initial Blackout Timeline," 2.
22. Novosel, "System Blackout Causes and Cures," 2.
23. Lerner, "What's Wrong with the Electric Grid?"
24. Hardin, "Tragedy of the Commons."
25. Latour, *Pandora's Hope*, 281. See also my discussion in chapter 7 of the
current volume.
26. Ibid.
27. Casazza and Loehr, *Evolution of Electric Power Transmission.*
28. U.S.-Canada Power Outage Task Force, "Initial Blackout Timeline," 7; my
emphasis.
29. Wald, "Report on Blackout." FirstEnergy was formed from the merger of
seven utilities (Toledo Edison, Cleveland Electric, Ohio Edison, Pennsylvania Power, Pennsylvania Electric, Metropolitan Edison, and Jersey Central Power and Light) and has very close ties to George W. Bush. As indi-
cated by Tyson Slocum, the "FirstEnergy President Anthony Alexander
was a Bush Pioneer in 2000 — meaning he raised at least $100,000 — and
then served on the Energy Department transition team. H. Peter Burg, the
company's CEO and chairman of the board, hosted a June event that raised
more than half a million dollars for Bush-Cheney '04" (Slocum, "Bush
Turns Blind Eye to Blackout Culprit").
30. See chapter 4, "Habit and the Will," in Augustine's *Confessions.* See also
chapter 1, note 7 in the present work.
31. Connolly, *Why I Am Not a Secularist*, 166. Connolly cites this passage from
Kant: "Now if a propensity to this does lie in human nature, there is in
man a natural propensity to evil; and since this very propensity must in
the end be sought in a will which is free, and can therefore be imputed,
it is morally evil. This evil is *radical*, because it corrupts the ground of
all maxims; it is, moreover, as natural propensity, *inextirpable* by human
powers, since extirpation could occur only through good maxims, and
cannot take place when the ultimate subjective ground of all maxims is
postulated as corrupt; yet at the same time it must be possible to *overcome*
it, since it is found in man, a being whose actions are free" (Kant, *Religion
within the Limits of Reason Alone*, 18).
32. On this point, see Kauffman, *Reinventing the Sacred*, chap. 6.

33. Brumfield, "On the Archaeology of Choice," 249. Or, as the sociologist Margaret Archer puts it, human agents are "both free and enchained, capable of shaping our own future and yet confronted by towering . . . constraints" (Archer, *Realist Social Theory*, 65).

34. "The subject, when put in front of his scissors, needle and familiar tasks, does not need to look for his hands or his fingers, because they are not objects . . . but potentialities already mobilized by the perception of scissors or needles, the central end of those 'intentional threads' which link him to the objects given" (Merleau-Ponty, *Phenomenology of Perception*, 106).

35. As Diana Coole puts it, "the operation of agentic capacities in politics will always exceed the agency exercised by rational subjects" because the latter "acquire differential agentic capacities depending upon their intersubjective context" (Coole, "Rethinking Agency," 125–26).

36. Ibid., 128.

37. See Latour, *Aramis*. See also the elegant account of *Aramis* in Laurier and Philo, "X-Morphising."

38. Latour, qtd. in Barron, "Strong Distinction," 81.

39. See Stiegler, *Technics and Time*. I am grateful to Ben Corson for this point. See his "Speed and Technicity."

40. It would be interesting to compare the idea of a swarm to Adorno's "constellation." See Adorno, *Negative Dialectics*, 166.

41. Mathews, *For Love of Matter*, 35.

42. Derrida, "Marx and Sons," 248. Disappointment is absolutely essential to messianicity: the "promise is given only under the premises of the possible retraction of its offering" (Hamacher, "Lingua Amissa," 202). Derrida argues that it is not only phenomena that obey this logic: language, and thus thought, also operate only in the promissory mode (Derrida, "Marx and Sons," 253–56).

43. Connolly, "Method, Problem, Faith," 342–43.

44. Arendt, "On the Nature of Totalitarianism." My thanks to John Docker for this reference. See also his "*Après la Guerre*."

45. Arendt, "On the Nature of Totalitarianism."

46. Jullien, *Propensity of Things*, 13.

47. Archer, *Realist Social Theory*, 66.

48. Recall that reactive power is when the waves of current and voltage in an electron stream are ninety degrees out of sync.

49. Hayden, "Gilles Deleuze and Naturalism," 187.

50. Latour, *Politics of Nature*, 67.

51. Marres, "Issues Spark a Public into Being," 216.

3. Edible Matter

A version of this chapter appeared previously in *New Left Review*, no. 45 (2007).

1. Mario Bunge, *Causality and Modern Science* (1979), qtd. in De Landa, *Intensive Science and Virtual Philosophy*, 137. Bunge notes that the belief in brute matter is "still held in esteem by those quantum theorists who hold that it is the experimenter who produces all atomic-scale phenomena," and De Landa adds that it is also assumed "by those critics of science who think that all phenomena are socially constructed" (ibid.).

2. Bayliss, *Physiology of Food*, 1.

3. This represents a 39 percent increase from 1950 and includes 440 twelve-ounce cans of soda per person per year, according to Warner, "Sweetener with a Bad Rap."

4. This amounts to seven pounds more red meat and forty-six pounds more poultry per year than in 1950.

5. This represents a 67 percent increase from 1950.

6. All food statistics, unless otherwise noted, are taken from U.S. Department of Agriculture, Office of Communications, "Profiling Food Consumption in America." In the *Agriculture Fact Book*, from which the chapter is taken, the term *consumption* refers to what is used up of the aggregate food supply; because of "spoilage, plate waste, and . . . other losses," "consumption" amounts are likely to be greater than the actual amount of food ingested or taken into human bodies. For example, if, as is estimated, Americans waste twenty of those fifty-three teaspoons of sugar, the ingestion of sugar could be as low as thirty-two teaspoons per day per person. The term *added fats* refers to fats "used directly by consumers, such as butter on bread, as well as shortenings and oils used in commercially prepared cookies, pastries, and fried foods. All fats naturally present in foods, such as in milk and meat, are excluded."

7. Gesch et al., "Influence." The modern Western diet has entailed a "staggering rise in the consumption of seed oils . . . , whose polyunsaturated fatty acid content is predominantly omega-6, at the expense of omega-3" (Hallahan and Garland, "Essential Fatty Acids and Mental Health," 277).

8. Richarson and Montgomery, "Oxford-Durham Study."

9. Su, Shen, and Huang, "Omega-3 Fatty Acids."

10. Perhaps the links among omega-3, mental health, and cognitive functions should not surprise, given that "the dry weight of the mammalian brain is approximately 80% lipid (the highest of any organ)" (Hallahan and Garland, "Essential Fatty Acids and Mental Health," 186).

11. Carroll, "Diets Heavy in Saturated Fats."

12. I take these points from John Buell, who directed me to the nonlinearity of the vying going on in the body-flesh-psyche-food assemblage (email correspondence, 2008).

13. Grégoire Nicolis and Ilya Prigogine, *Exploring Complexity: An Introduction* (1989), qtd. in De Landa, *Intensive Science and Virtual Philosophy*, 131.

14. De Landa, *Intensive Science and Virtual Philosophy*, 144.

15. Deleuze and Guattari, *Thousand Plateaus*, 324–25.

16. Serres, *Parasite*, 191. Serres suggests that it is the *human* that is the passive one in the eater-eaten relationship. For him, the eater is utterly dependent on (exists in a "parasitic" relation to) foodstuff. We eat only at the expense (on the tab) of another who is our host: "The host comes before and the parasite follows"(14). Thus the eater *owes* the eaten. (Perhaps this is why many say grace before meals.) I think Serres is right to note the moral obligations entailed by eating, but I also think that the figure of the parasite goes too far: it does not acknowledge the active power of the human body or any agentic capacity.

17. Goodman, "Ontology Matters," 183.

18. Nietzsche, *On the Genealogy of Morals and Ecce Homo*, third essay, sec. 17, 130.

19. Nietzsche, *Daybreak*, 39.

20. Friedrich Nietzsche, "Why I Am So Clever," *On the Genealogy of Morals and Ecce Homo*, sec. 1, 239.

21. The complete quotation is: "My virile food taketh effect, my strong and savoury sayings: and verily, I did not nourish them with flatulent vegetables! But with warrior-food, with conquerer-food: new desires did I awaken" (Nietzsche, *Thus Spoke Zarathustra*, pt. 4, "The Awakening").

22. Cornaro, *Art of Living Long*, 55. In Cornaro's "Second Discourse, Written at the Age of Eight-Six," he gives a fuller inventory of his diet: "First, bread; then, bread soup or light broth with an egg, or some other nice little dish of this kind; of meats, I eat veal, kid, and mutton; I eat fowls of all kinds, as well as partridges and birds like the thrush. I also partake of such salt-water fish as the goldney and the like; and, among the various fresh-water kinds, the pike and others" (87).

23. Ibid., 94.

24. Nietzsche, *Twilight of the Idols*, sec. 1, 47. Nietzsche seems not to have read Cornaro carefully enough, for Cornaro explicitly says that his particular diet is not for everyone: "No one need feel obliged to confine himself to the small quantity to which I limit myself. . . . For I eat but little; and my reason in doing so is that I find a little sufficient for my small and weak stomach" (Cornaro, *Art of Living Long*, 62); "I was compelled to be extremely careful with regard to the quality and quantity of my food and drink. However those persons who are blessed with strong constitutions

may make use of many other kinds and qualities of food and drink, and partake of them in greater quantities, than I do" (ibid., 97).

25. The full quotation reads: "I . . . do not like these latest speculators in ideal-ism, the anti-Semites, who . . . rouse up all the horned-beast elements in the people by a brazen abuse of the cheapest of all agitator's tricks, moral attitudinizing (that *no* kind of swindle fails to succeed in Germany today is connected with the undeniable and palpable stagnation of the German spirit; and the cause of that I seek in a too exclusive diet of newspapers, politics, beer, and Wagnerian music)" (Nietzsche, *On the Genealogy of Morals and Ecce Homo*, third essay, sec. 26, 158–59; my emphasis).

26. Nietzsche, *On the Genealogy of Morals and Ecce Homo*, first essay, sec. 6, 32.

27. See Haraway, *Modest_Witness@Second_Millennium*, 2.

28. Nietzsche, "Why I am So Clever," *On the Genealogy of Morals and Ecce Homo*, sec. 10, 256.

29. Thoreau, *Walden and Resistance to Civil Government*, 140.

30. Whitman, "Song of Myself," lines 389–90, *Leaves of Grass*. My thanks to Hadley Leach for this reference.

31. Thoreau, *Walden and Resistance to Civil Government*, 143. Thoreau notes in his journal that though his "coarse and hurried outdoor work compels me to . . . be inattentive to my diet," "left to my own pursuits, I should never . . . eat meat" (qtd. in Robinson, *Thoreau and the Wild Appetite*, 9).

32. Thoreau, *Walden and Resistance to Civil Government*, 143. "Most men would feel shame if caught preparing with their own hands" the bloody meat dinner that is "everyday prepared for them by others," that is, by women (144).

33. Ibid., 144.

34. To those who wonder why he gives so much heed to little things like ber-ries, Thoreau confidently replies that what are to the conformist self "great things are not great but *gross*. . . . little things are not little but fine—they are some huckleberries" (qtd. in Keiser, "New Thoreau Material," 253–54).

35. Thoreau, *Walden and Resistance to Civil Government*, 146. He calls the blue-berry the "Berry of berries," but he also offers high praise to wild blackber-ries, blueberries, raspberries, huckleberries, cranberries, and strawberries. Robinson notes that "it is hard to tell which berry Thoreau cherished most." Thoreau's promiscuity with regard to berry loving and berry eating leads Robinson to note a "kind of ritualistic ceremony of pagan exaltation" in Thoreau's description of himself as "going from water spring to water spring, his hands reddened afresh between successive water springs by wild strawberries" (Robinson, *Thoreau's Wild Appetite*, 22).

36. Thoreau, *Walden and Resistance to Civil Government*, 116–17.

37. Thanks to Patchen Markell for this point.
38. Kass, *Hungry Soul*, 25–26. Kass was appointed by George W. Bush to the President's Council on Bioethics in 2001 and was at one time its chair.
39. Ibid., 55.
40. Ibid., 15.
41. Roe, "Material Connectivity." Rachel Colls makes a related point in her study of bodily "flab" as *"mobile* flesh," which is neither fully "material" nor fully "discursive" (Colls, "Materialising Bodily Matter").
42. Maud Ellman, *The Hunger Artists* (1993), qtd. in Eagleton, "Edible Écriture," 207.
43. Deleuze, "Metal, Metallurgy, Music, Husserl, Simondon."
44. See Slow Food USA, "Manifesto."
45. Kingsolver, "Good Farmer," 13.
46. Jackson et al., "Manufacturing Meaning along the Food Commodity Chain." Michael Pollan's *The Omnivore's Dilemma* serves as a good example here. It gives a genealogy of four American meals — one from McDonald's, one made from items bought at a Whole Foods supermarket, one whose ingredients come from a small, self-sustaining farm, and one created from items that Pollan has hunted or gathered.
47. Good examples here include Cheri Lucas Jennings's and Bruce H. Jennings's exposé of the poverty wages and poisonous working conditions embedded in the shiny red, wormless supermarket apple and Greg Critser's account of the link between agribusiness interests, subsidized corn production, high-fructose corn syrup, and obesity. See Jennings and Jennings, "Green Fields/Brown Skin"; and Critser, *Fat Land*. For a critique of its claim that high-fructose corn syrup is a significant factor in America's obesity problem, see Warner, "Does This Goo Make You Groan?"

4. A Life of Metal

1. Kafka, "Report to an Academy," 257.
2. For a good summary of the relevant research, see Kate Douglas, "Six 'Uniquely' Human Traits Now Found in Animals."
3. The geographer Nick Bingham develops a notion of "nonhuman friendship" as a "certain quality of being open," or a "capacity to learn to be affected" by an out-side. Though his examples of nonhumans are organisms (bees and butterflies), his essay raises the question of whether it is possible to "befriend" inorganic material. See his "Bees, Butterflies, and Bacteria."
4. Deleuze, "Immanence," 3–4.
5. Ibid., 4. In "The Novelty of Life" (unpublished manuscript), Paola Marrati

argues that the concept of life in Deleuze has no empirical or biological content but is closer to the Bergsonian idea of duration. Life "becomes coextensive with the virtual reality of time and its open-ended power of differentiation, which is to say of the creation of novelty" (7). A copy of this source is on file in my private collection.

6. Deleuze, "Immanence," 5.

7. Das, *Life and Words*, 97.

8. Deleuze and Guattari, *Thousand Plateaus*, 407; my emphasis.

9. Deleuze, "Immanence," 5.

10. Deleuze and Parnet, "On the Superiority of Anglo-American Literature," 50.

11. Deleuze and Guattari also affirm Nietzsche's criticism of a metaphysics of "atoms" or stable "objects." There are only, says Nietzsche in *The Will to Power*, entry 522, "complexes of events apparently durable in comparison with other complexes." But Deleuze and Guattari eschew the tendency toward a linguistic constructionism occasionally evident in Nietzsche's formulations, wherein the event is reduced to the *human* forces operative in it. This occurs, for example, when Nietzsche says that "things . . . atoms, too . . . do not exist at all. . . . A 'thing' is the sum of its effects, synthetically united by a concept, an image" (Nietzsche, *Will to Power*, entry 551). It also occurs when he makes this note to himself: "What things . . . may be like, apart from our sense receptivity and the activity of our understanding, must be rebutted with the question: how could we know that things exist? 'Thingness' was first created by us. The question is . . . whether that which 'posits things' is not the sole reality; and whether the 'effect of the external world upon us' is not also only the result of such active subjects" (entry 569).

12. Aeschylus, *Prometheus Bound*, 65.

13. Deleuze and Guattari, *Thousand Plateaus*, 411.

14. "So how are we to define this matter-movement, this matter-energy, this matter-flow, this matter in variation that enters assemblages and leaves them? It is a destratified, deterritorialized matter. . . . [It is] a region of *vague and material essences* (. . . vagabond, anexact and yet rigorous), distinguishing them from fixed, metric and formal, essences. . . . They relate to a *corporeality* (materiality) that is not to be confused either with an intelligible, formal essentiality or a sensible, formed and perceived, thinghood" (ibid., 407).

15. Hobbes, "De Corpore," pt. 2, 8.10.

16. Deleuze and Guattari, *Thousand Plateaus*, 262.

17. Ibid., 407–11.

18. Ibid., 411.

19. Kass, *Hungry Soul*, 36.

20. Ibid., 41.
21. Marks, "Introduction," 5.
22. Latham and McCormack, "Moving Cities," 701. Massumi's phrase is quoted on page 705.
23. Foucault, "Theatrum Philosophicum," 169–70. Jonathan Goldberg notes that "Foucault in fact recalls a controversy that haunts Epicureanism from the start: if atoms are themselves imperceptible, colorless, tasteless—if they lack almost every feature by which bodies can be known, virtually every characteristic that characterizes matter—in what sense are atoms material?" (Goldberg, *The Seeds of Things*, 34). Goldberg continues to explore the strange fact that the condition of the possibility of visibility or of the phenomenological experience of things is *unseen* matter in "Lucy Hutchinson Writing Matter."
24. Where Foucault speaks of an "incorporeal materiality," Latham and McCormack speak of "the immaterial" within the material. "The immaterial" is that which gives materiality "an expressive life and liveliness independent of the human subject" (Latham and McCormack, "Moving Cities," 703). I hesitate about this definition because of its implication that materiality requires something *else*, something other to itself, to animate it. In so doing, it recalls the nineteenth-century vitalist claim that while matter is (in its essence) inert, because material bodies move, there must be at work a vital principle that while profoundly implicated in matter, is not "of" matter. Latham and McCormack repeat this gesture when they assign to "thinking" and its "conceptual vehicles" the task of "charg[ing] . . . and activat[ing] . . . the detail of the world with an enlivening potential" (709).
25. Ibid., 702.
26. Anderson, "Time-Stilled Space-Slowed." Anderson makes a persuasive case for how the affect of boredom—which is "stilling and slowing" rather than vital and generative—complicates an image of materiality that assumes "an almost unlimited [internal] plenitude [and] . . . 'richness'" (745). In a lucid introduction to a special issue on materiality in *Geoforum*, Ben Anderson and Divya Tolia-Kelly note "two specific figurations of matter." The first is the realist equation of matter with "unmediated, static, physicality" and "the second is the use of 'the material,' or 'material conditions,' to refer to an ostensive social structure that over-determines 'the cultural'" (Anderson and Tolia-Kelly, "Matter(s) in Social and Cultural Geography," 669–70).
27. Smith, "Texture of Matter," 8–9n.
28. Smith, *A History of Metallography*, 134.
29. Smith, "Texture of Matter," 8–9n.
30. Ibid., 27; my emphasis.

31. Smith, *A History of Metallography*, 73.
32. Ibid., 101.
33. Ibid., 134.
34. Ibid., 244.
35. The durability of a particular metal is a function of how much internal resistance is offered to the flow of the crack: if "populations of these line defects are free to move in a material, they will endow it with the capacity to yield locally without breaking, that is, they will make the material tough. On the other hand, restricted movement of dislocations will result in a . . . more brittle material. . . . Toughness or strength are emergent properties of a metallic material that result from the complex dynamic behaviour of some of its components" (De Landa, "Uniformity and Variability").
36. Deleuze, "Metal, Metallurgy, Music, Husserl, Simondon."
37. This may also be what they mean by the perverse notion of "a materiality possessing a *nomos*" of its own (Deleuze and Guattari, *Thousand Plateaus*, 408).
38. Qtd. in Margulis and Sagan. *What Is Life?* 49.
39. Smith also celebrates the metallurgical focus on "middle-sized aggregates," whereas more theoretical inquiry into nature has tended to focus on the infinite universe (as in cosmology) or the infinitesmal bit (as in particle and subparticle physics). See Smith, "Texture of Matter," 3. Heidegger makes a similar point about the methodological bias of modern science in favor of scales of organization that reside at the extremes: "Everywhere . . . the gigantic is making its appearance. In so doing, it evidences itself simultaneously in the tendency toward the increasingly small" (Heidegger, "Age of the World Picture," 134). *A Thousand Plateaus* is sometimes pitched at the level of the minuscule, as when Deleuze and Guattari focus on the motility of intensities, and also sometimes pitched at the level of the gigantic, as when they invoke a vagabond or deterritorializing matter constituting a veritable cosmos of becoming. This is not, however, a big, undifferentiated flow of becoming, but a self-parsing, self-splaying "life" that has always already distributed itself into various subgroupings or swarms, eddies, circuits, cascades, and assemblages. *A Thousand Plateaus* proceeds both by grand metaphysics and by analyses of material processes operating more "locally," as capitalism, militarism, music, metallurgy.
40. Perniola defines the human as a "feeling thing" (*cosa che sente*). See Contardi and Perniola, "Sex Appeal of the Inorganic"; and Perniola, *Sex Appeal of the Inorganic*, 2–4. In the first piece, Perniola says: "The notion of 'feeling thing' derives from an encounter between two different traditions of thought: that which meditated around the thing [das Ding] and that which meditated around feeling [das Fühlen]. The first goes back to Kant (the thing-in-itself), Heidegger (the question of the thing), and Lacan (the

Freudian thing); the second also goes back to Kant (sentiment), to Hegel (pathos) and the aesthetics of empathy. I took away the dimension of feeling that this second tradition attributes to the subjective feature. I replace 'I feel' [io sento] with an anonymous and impersonal 'it is felt' [si sente], something which I had laid out in my previous book *Del sentire*. . . . In *The Sex Appeal of the Inorganic*, the 'it is felt' assumes a more specific sexual connotation" (brackets in original).

5. Neither Vitalism nor Mechanism

1. Frederick Burwick and Paul Douglass argue that "critical vitalism" emerged "in the 19th century transition from a matter-based physics to an energy-based physics" (Burwick and Douglass, introduction, 1). For a good conceptual history of "energy," see Caygill, "Life and Energy."

2. Quirk, *Bergson and American Culture*, 1–2. Quirk also places the works of Willa Cather and Wallace Stevens in this context: "Both Cather and Stevens believed in the 'creative power,' and both . . . linked this power to a vital force, biological in nature and primordial in origin" (8). See also the debates between Arthur O. Lovejoy and H. S. Jennings about vitalism during the period 1911–15: Lovejoy, "Meaning of Vitalism"; Lovejoy, "Import of Vitalism"; Jennings, "Driesch's Vitalism and Experimental Indeterminism"; Lovejoy, "Meaning of Driesch and the Meaning of Vitalism"; and Jennings, "Doctrines Held as Vitalism."

3. Driesch, *The Science and Philosophy of the Organism* . . . *1908*, 321.

4. Quirk, *Bergson and American Culture*, 1. Linked to the public discussion of vitalism was the political movement of Progressivism; see Eisenach, *Social and Political Thought of American Progressivism*.

5. In his *The History and Theory of Vitalism*, Driesch makes "an exception" to the book's usual practice of providing only brief summaries of each theory of vitalism: "In the case of Kant, [we will] . . . analyse his *Critique of Judgment* with particular thoroughness, our reason [being] . . . the extraordinary and far-reaching influence which this book has exerted up to the present day" (66).

6. Kant, *Critique of Judgment*, sec. 78, #411. Further references to this title will be made in the running text.

7. Because of the nature of our understanding, which Kant says requires us to explain the relation between things through the idea of mechanistic causality, we run up against an impasse when we encounter organisms. Organisms exceed mechanistic causality, but we do not have an adequate concept to capture the excess.

8. Before he invokes the *Bildungstrieb*, Kant speaks in the text of a "formative

force" (*bildende Kräfte*) operative in organisms but not in dead matter: "An organized being is not a mere machine. For a machine has only *motive* force. But an organized being has within it *formative* force [*bildende Kräfte*], and a formative force that this being imparts to the kinds of matter that lack it (thereby organizing them). This force is therefore a formative force that propagates itself" (*Judgment* sec. 65, #374).

9. The translation is Robert J. Richards's in "Kant and Blumenbach on the *Bildungstrieb*."

10. *Bildungstrieb* can be placed alongside other notable figures of vital force in the eighteenth century, including Georges Buffon's *moule intérieur*, Albrecht von Haller's *irritability* (a force in muscles that made them twitch in response to stimuli), and Caspar Wolff's *vis essentialis*. For a broader history of figures of vital force, see Battye, *What Is Vital Force*; Driesch, *The History and Theory of Vitalism*; and Wheeler, *Vitalism*.

11. Qtd. in Richards, "Kant and Blumenbach on the *Bildungstrieb*," 11.

12. Ibid., 11–12.

13. Johann Friedrich Blumenbach, *Über den Bildungstrieb und das Zeugungsgeschäfte* (1781), qtd. ibid., 18.

14. By allowing that *Bildungstrieb* is "a principle that is inscrutable to us," Blumenbach "leaves an indeterminable and yet unmistakable share to natural mechanism" (*Judgment* sec. 81).

15. Lenoir, "Kant, Blumenbach, and Vital Materialism," 84. According to Blumenbach, "The cause of the *Bildungstrieb* is no more capable of explanation than attraction or gravity or any other generally recognized natural forces. It suffices that it is an independent force whose undeniable existence and extensive effects manifest themselves through experience of the entire organized creation and whose constant phenomena give an easier and brighter insight into development and several other important facets of life than any other theory" (Johann Friedrich Blumenbach, *Handbuch der Naturgeschichte* [1791], qtd. in Lenoir, "Kant, Blumenbach, and Vital Materialism," 89n39).

16. Lenoir puts the point this way: "Having lost a substantial portion of its primary generative substance, the force of the *Bildungstrieb* had been weakened" (Lenoir, "Kant, Blumenbach, and Vital Materialism," 84).

17. In the debates of Kant's time over how to explain the growth of organisms and their reproduction across generations, one camp favored the theory of "preformation," as in Charles Bonnet's notion of *emboîtement*, according to which "God had created a multitude of germs, each encapsulating an embryonic organism, which in turn carried yet smaller organisms within its own germs, down through ever smaller encased individuals"; and another camp affirmed "epigenesis," or the theory that transformations within the organism entailed the gradual movement from less to

more specialization, from formless matter to an increasingly articulated structure of parts. See Richards, "Kant and Blumenbach on the *Bildungstrieb*," 14–18. Kant was more or less on the side of epigenesis, as long as that could "also be entitled the system of generic preformation, because the productive faulty of the generator, and consequently the specific form would be *virtually* preformed according to the inner pruposive capacities [*Anlagen*] which are part of its stock [*Stamm*]" (*Judgment* sec. 81, qtd. in Lenoir, "Kant, Blumenbach, and Vital Materialism," 88).

18. In the system of natural causality of which humans form a part, humans make for a *special* part: "There is only one kind of being with a causality that is teleological, i.e., *directed* to purposes, but also so constituted that the law of which these beings must determine their purposes is presented . . . as *unconditioned* and *independent of conditions in nature*" (*Judgment* sec. 84, #323; my emphasis).

19. See Serres, *Birth of Physics*.

20. Driesch, *The Science and Philosophy of the Organism . . . 1908*, 115.

21. Driesch, *The History and Theory of Vitalism*, 208.

22. Driesch, *The Science and Philosophy of the Organism . . . 1908*, 144.

23. Ibid., 250.

24. Ibid., 316.

25. Ibid., 115. "In Nature conceived scientifically—as here-now-such, there is no room for 'psychical' entities at all" (Driesch, *The Problem of Individuality*, 33). Driesch makes the same point in Driesch, *The Science and Philosophy of the Organism . . . 1908*, where he says that "there 'are' no souls . . . in the phenomenon called nature in space" (82).

26. Driesch, *The Science and Philosophy of the Organism . . . 1907*, 50; my emphasis. On this point Driesch echoes Kant's claim that in judging *organized* beings, "we must always presuppose some original organization that itself *uses* mechanism" (*Judgment* sec. 80, #418; my emphasis).

27. Driesch, *The Problem of Individuality*, 34.

28. Driesch does not elaborate on his differences with Aristotle and says only that he will retain Aristotle's idea that "there is at work a something in life phenomena 'which bears the end in itself'" (Driesch, *The Science and Philosophy of the Organism . . . 1907*, 144).

29. Blumenbach had said that *Bildungstrieb* "initially bestows on creatures their form, then preserves it, and, if they become injured, where possible restores their form"; Driesch here describes the tasks of entelechy in similar terms. (Blumenbach, *Über den Bildungstrieb*, qtd. in Richards, "Kant and Blumenbach on the *Bildungstrieb*," 18). A blastocyst is the name for the developmental stage of a fertilized egg at which it has changed from a solid mass of cells into a hollow ball of cells around a fluid-filled cavity.

30. "The organism is different . . . from all combinations of crystals, such as

those called dendrites . . . which consists of a typical arrangement of iden-
tical units. . . . For this reason, dendrites . . . must be called aggregates;
but the organism is not an aggregate" (Driesch, *The Science and Philosophy
of the Organism . . . 1907*, 25).

31. Driesch, *The Science and Philosophy of the Organism . . . 1908*, 61; my emphasis.

32. Ibid., 79. Here Driesch echoes Kant's claim that organisms actively "produce" themselves rather than blindly follow a path of "development." Kant
writes: "For in considering those things whose origin can be conceived
only in terms of a causality of purposes," we must regard "nature as itself
producing them rather than as merely developing them" (*Judgment* sec. 81,
#424).

33. Driesch, *The History and Theory of Vitalism*, 213. Or, as he puts the point in
The Science and Philosophy of the Organism . . . 1908, there is an "'individuality of correspondence' between stimulus and effect" (67).

34. Driesch, *The Problem of Individuality*, 38. In the vocabulary of today, it
might be said that the stem cells have not yet been channeled into their
respective "fate paths."

35. Ibid., 39.

36. Driesch, *The History and Theory of Vitalism*, 213.

37. Driesch, *The Science and Philosophy of the Organism . . . 1908*, 72; my emphasis.

38. "Indeed, as far as morphogenesis and physiological adaptation and instinctive reactions are concerned, there *must* be a something comparable meta-
phorically with specified knowing and willing" (Driesch, *The Science and
Philosophy of the Organism . . . 1908*, 143).

39. Ibid.

40. Joseph Chiari defends Bergson's vitalism precisely because *élan vital* is
"the informing spirit which, through man, evolves into consciousness and
therefore gives man his favored position as the goal and the apex of creation" (Chiari, "Vitalism and Contemporary Thought," 254).

41. Driesch, *The History and Theory of Vitalism*, 210. On this point Driesch follows Kant quite closely. Kant writes: "If parts are removed from the watch,
it does not replace them on its own; nor, if parts were missing . . . , does
it compensate for this [lack] by having the other parts help out, let along
repair itself on its own when out of order: yet all of this we can expect
organized nature to do. Hence an organized being is not a mere machine"
(*Judgment* sec. 65, #374).

42. Driesch, *The Science and Philosophy of the Organism . . . 1907*, 110.

43. Driesch distinguishes, in his empirical proofs for vitalism (which are
better described as disproofs of the sufficiency of a mechanistic account
of morphogenesis), between the process of "the *differentiation* of the har-

monious systems" and the development of the original cell within which differentiation will occur. The latter is "not what comes out of the complex systems, but what they themselves come from. And we shall take the ovary as one instance standing for them all. The ovary develops from one special single cell which is its *Anlage*, to use a German word not easy to translate" (Driesch, *The Problem of Individuality*, 21–22).

44. Driesch, *The History and Theory of Vitalism*, 212.
45. Bakhtin, "Contemporary Vitalism," 89.
46. Driesch, *The Science and Philosophy of the Organism . . . 1908*, 169. What could it mean to be exclusively an "order of relation"? Driesch sheds some light on this notion by describing entelechy as an "agent that arranges" elements into a harmonious whole. Driesch sees evidence of this arranging power in instinctive movements: although "physiological factors" play a role in instincts, "there would be something else also at work, a 'something' that may be said to *make use* of the factors"(Driesch, *The Science and Philosophy of the Organism . . . 1908*, 51). This "new and autonomic natural factor . . . unknown to the inorganic world" (ibid., 114) is also "at the root of the transformism of the species" (Driesch, *The Science and Philosophy of the Organism . . . 1907*, 287). In addition, such an arrangement must have been operative in the process of inheritance. A mechanical explanation would speak only of the transfer of material units "localized in the nucleus," but, again, these material conditions cannot be "*the main thing*. Some agent that *arranges* is required, and this arranging agent of inheritance *cannot* be of a machine-like, physico-chemical character" (Driesch, *The Problem of Individuality*, 23). Why not? Because, the physico-chemical is by definition incapable of the arranging agency required. Arranging agency requires both precision and flexibility, an ad hoc judging exquisitely attuned to the singularity of the parts it is to arrange and the singularity of the context in which the organism swims. Physico-chemical elements, qua inert matter, are too obedient to generic laws to perform the required juggling, too routinized to arrange artfully.
47. Driesch, *The Science and Philosophy of the Organism . . . 1907*, 16.
48. Driesch, *The Science and Philosophy of the Organism . . . 1908*, 295.
49. Ibid., 180.
50. *Psuche* marks the difference between a living human and an inactive corpse. It is "composed of a very tenuous stuff, which resides in the body while the individual is alive, flies away through some orifice at death and goes down to Hades"; it is "simply that whose presence ensures that the individual is alive" (Adkins, *From the Many to the One*, 15).
51. Driesch, *The Science and Philosophy of the Organism . . . 1908*, 326.
52. Bakhtin, "Contemporary Vitalism," 95–96. Bakhtin names this alternative machine-image "modern dialectical materialism," in contrast to Driesch's

"naive-mechanist point of view with its fixed and immovable machines" (96). K. S. Lashley made a similar point in 1923: "The vitalist cites particular phenomena—morphogenesis, regeneration, habit-formation, complexities of speech, and the like—and denies the possibility of a mechanistic account of them. But he thereby commits what we might term the egoistic fallacy. On analysis his argument reduces every time to the form, '*I* am not able to devise a machine which will do these things; therefore no one will ever conceive of such a machine.' This is the argument from inconceivability of Driesch and McDougall, put badly. To it we may answer, 'You overvalue your own ingenuity.'" (Lashley, "Behavioristic Interpretation of Consciousness," 242).

53. Bakhtin, "Contemporary Vitalism," 95–96.
54. So do Deleuze and Guattari. In *A Thousand Plateaus* they describe Nature as a plane of morphogenesis, which they call a "war-machine." Paul Patton suggests that a better term would have been "metamorphosis machine": "The 'war-machine' . . . is a concept which is betrayed by its name since it has little to do with actual war and only a paradoxical and indirect relation to armed conflict. [Its] . . . real object . . . is not war but the condition of creative mutation and change" (Patton, *Deleuze and the Political*, 110).
55. "All reality is . . . tendency, if we agree to call tendency a nascent change of direction." Bergson, *The Creative Mind*, 188.
56. Bergson, *Creative Evolution*, 202–3. Further references to this title will be made in the running text as CE.
57. Driesch, *The Science and Philosophy of the Organism* . . . 1907, 50.
58. Deleuze describes *élan vital* as "a virtuality in the process of being actualized, a simplicity in the process of differentiating, a totality in the process of dividing up" (Deleuze, *Bergsonism*, 94).
59. The first quote is taken from Bergson, *The Creative Mind*, 95.
60. Deleuze, *Bergsonism*, 106.
61. Bergson, *The Creative Mind*, 93.
62. Bergson continues, "Now, it finds only one way of succeeding in this, namely, to secure such an accumulation of potential energy from matter, that it can get, at any moment, . . . by pulling a trigger. The effort itself possesses only that power of releasing" (CE, 115).
63. Bergson, *The Creative Mind*, 31.
64. Driesch, *The Science and Philosophy of the Organism* . . . 1907, 108.

6. Stem Cells and the Culture of Life

1. Driesch, *Problem of Individuality*, 80, 74–75.
2. Canguilhem, *Aspects du vitalisme*, 124.

3. Harrington, *Reenchanted Science*, 190. After Hitler came to power in 1933, "Driesch was one of the first non-Jewish German professors to be forcibly retired," she writes (191).

4. Stolberg, "House Approves a Stem Cell Bill."

5. Cole, "Bush Stands Against 'Temptation to Manipulate Life.'"

6. The lower estimate is from iraqbodycount.org, the larger one from Les Roberts and Gilbert M. Burnham of the Center for International Emergency, Disaster, and Refugee Studies at the Johns Hopkins Bloomberg School of Public Health; Richard Garfield of Columbia University; and Riyadh Lafta and Jamal Kudhairi of Baghdad's Al-Mustansiriya University College of Medicine.

7. George W. Bush said, "We should not legislate defeat in this vital war" (United States, Office of the White House Press Secretary, "President Bush Discusses Iraq War Supplemental").

8. It is not, as Driesch put the point before the concept of the stem cell was invented, a "potency" able to "play every *single* part in the totality of what will occur in the whole system" (Driesch, *Science and Philosophy of the Organism* . . . 1907, 120–21). See also U.S. Department of Health and Human Services, National Institutes of Health, "Stem Cells."

9. Maienschein, "What's in a Name."

10. Tom DeLay, qtd. in Baer, "In Vitro Fertilization." There is some dispute over whether a pregastrulated mass is an "embryo." If an embryo is defined as a fertilized egg, then the answer is yes. But others define an embryo as a dividing egg that has passed *through* gastrulation: "Many biologists . . . don't call these early stages of development an embryo, but a preimplantation embryo or pre-embryo. The preimplantation embryo passes through three stages during its week of development: a zygote (one cell), morula (multiple cells in a cluster, all the same), and blastocyst [blastula] (when it develops sections, including a yolk sac, and has an inside and outside but still none of the defined structures of an embryo)" (Spike, "Bush and Stem Cell Research," 45).

11. In November of 2007 two research laboratories reported "a new way to turn ordinary human skin cells into what appear to be embryonic stem cells without ever using a human embryo" (Kolata, "Researcher"). The new technique has many obstacles to overcome if it is to translate into human medical treatments: "Scientists have yet to fully understand how DNA is programmed and reprogrammed for therapeutic use. In addition, initial experiments were done with retroviruses that can cause tumors and cancer. . . . Still, the production of the stem cells avoids the moral and ethical objections raised by President Bush and others to the harvesting of cells from discarded human embryos" ("Stem Cell Breakthrough").

12. Paulus PP, "Evangelium Vitae."

13. Best, "Prepared Statement."
14. Ibid.
15. Driesch, *The History and Theory of Vitalism*, 1. Bergson affirms something close to this when he says that "while analysis will undoubtedly resolve the process of organic creation into an ever-growing number of physico-chemical phenomena, . . . it does not follow that chemistry and physics will ever give us the key to life" (Bergson, *Creative Evolution*, 31). Driesch says that he "know[s] very well that . . . 'autonomy' usually means the faculty of *giving* laws to oneself, and . . . is applied with regard to a community of men; but in our phrase autonomy is to signify the *being subjected* to laws peculiar to the phenomena in question" (Driesch, *Science and Philosophy of the Organism* . . . *1907*, 143). Although Driesch means to focus on the ability of organisms to self-arrange and self-restore, his use of the term *autonomy* still retains something of the Kantian sense of freedom, freedom from determinism.
16. Driesch, *The History and Theory of Vitalism*, 57–58.
17. It is worth noting here that one need not be an atheist to reject the particular constellation of ideas inside the culture of life: pantheisms of various sorts discern divinity in *all* things, human and nonhuman, organic and inorganic; many "Jewish and Muslim scholars . . . regard life as starting . . . 40 days" after fertilization; some believers affirm that God would approve of embryonic stem cell research as a fuller realization of the potential within the process of morphogenesis. See Maienschien, "What's in a Name," 14.
18. Cole, "Bush Stands Against 'Temptation to Manipulate Life.'"
19. Driesch, *The History and Theory of Vitalism*, 223–24.
20. Bakhtin, "Contemporary Vitalism," 92. The fuller quotation reveals Bakhtin's own deterministic materialism: "It obviously goes without saying that at every place and every time, some specific conditions prevail. Therefore it is completely absurd to say [as Driesch does] that any particular possibility of development is really contained in a given blastomere. The potential is contained within it . . . to the same degree that it is part of the complex of its surrounding conditions. What is Driesch doing? He strays from any real conditions, locating abstract blastomere outside of the frames of time and space. . . . Talk of several potentials and possibilities serves only one purpose: it allows for the presupposition that they are all equally possible . . . and that therefore it is possible to choose one of them freely. Freedom of choice, not determinism in organic life, is the ground of all of Driesch's constructions" (ibid.).
21. Driesch, *Science and Philosophy of the Organism* . . . *1908*, 72; my emphasis.
22. Bergson, *Creative Evolution*, 47.
23. Two quotes: Terrorists kill because "they hate freedom" (United States,

Office of the White House Press Secretary, "Remarks by President and Mrs. Bush"); "The more free the Iraqis become, the more electricity is available, the more jobs are available, the more kids that are going to school, the more desperate these killers become, because they can't stand the thought of a free society. They hate freedom. They love terror" (United States, Office of the White House Press Secretary, "President Bush, Ambassador Bremer Discuss Progress in Iraq").

24. Canguilhem, *Aspects du vitalisme*, 121.

25. Sumner, Review of *The History and Theory of Vitalism*.

26. Deleuze and Guattari, *Thousand Plateaus*, 255.

27. Althusser, "Underground Current of the Materialism of the Encounter," 190.

28. Serres, *Birth of Physics*.

29. "Executive Summary" in U.S. Department of Health and Human Services, "Stem Cells," 9; my emphasis.

30. For a discussion of Bergson and the open whole, see Marrati, "Time, Life, Concepts."

31. Emerson, *Journals and Miscellaneous Notebooks*, 10:335.

32. Johann Gottfried von Herder, "God: Some Conversations" (1787), qtd. in Zammito, *Genesis of Kant's Critique of Judgment*, 244.

7. Political Ecologies

1. Darwin, *Formation of Vegetable Mould*, 313. Further references to this title will be made in the running text.

2. These "small agencies" ought not to be "undervalued" simply because they are undesigned (ibid., 2).

3. In the sixteenth century, a miller was put on trial for heresy for a similarly materialist view, as Carlo Ginzburg recounts in his *The Cheese and the Worms*. God did not create the world out of nothing at all, Mennochio opined, for in the beginning, "all was chaos, that is, earth, air, water, and fire were mixed together; and out of that bulk a mass formed—just as cheese is made out of milk—and worms appeared in it, and these were the angels. . . . among that number of angels, there was also God, he too having been created out of that mass at the same time" (6).

4. The story is told in Latour, *Pandora's Hope*, chap. 2; the quotation is from page 53.

5. Ibid., 76.

6. Deleuze and Guattari, *Thousand Plateaus*, 324–25.

7. Levine, *Darwin Loves You*, 150.

8. Lorimer, "Nonhuman Charisma." Lorimer notes that "jizz" has affinities

with what Deleuze and Guattari term "a 'singularity'—the congealing of a particular mode of individuation" (915). The article offers a rich account of the degrees of "detectability" (for us) of different bodies.

9. Jullien, *Propensity of Things*, 113, 115. Unlike the European system of assigning to each sound a note or symbol on a written score, "Chinese musical notation does not indicate the sounds themselves . . . but simply the precise gesture required to produce them" (116).

10. Johnson, *Emergence*, 18. In contrast both to simple systems with linear causality and to giant systems best described in terms of statistical probability, systems of "organized complexity" are marked by self-organizing patterns created from the bottom up, where no single element plays the role of a central or higher authority. There is no "pacemaker," only a creative "swarm." Organized complexity produces outcomes that are "emergent," that is, do not issue from *either* a consummate central agent *or* an automatic process.

11. Noortje Marres notes that for Dewey (and also Walter Lippmann), the "public is precisely not a social community. . . . those who are jointly implicated in the issue must organize a community. What the members of the public share is that they are all affected . . . , but they do not already belong to the same community" (Marres, "Issues Spark a Public into Being," 214).

12. "The ramification of the issues . . . is so wide and intricate, the technical matters involved are so specialized, the details are so many and so shifting, that the public cannot for any length of time identify and hold itself. It is not that there is no public, . . . there are too many publics" (Dewey, *Public and Its Problems*, 137).

13. A public "consists of all those who are affected by the indirect consequences of transactions to such an extent that it is deemed necessary to have those consequences systematically cared for" (ibid., 16).

14. Ibid., 137.

15. Dewey, *Art as Experience*, 59.

16. "Humans, for millions of years, have extended their social relations to other actants with which, with whom, they have swapped many properties, and with which, with whom, they form collectives" (Latour, *Pandora's Hope*, 198). Latour says in that book that he rejects the category of "Nature" (as a pure realm devoid of human culture), because such an idea "renders invisible the political process by which the cosmos is collected in one livable whole" (304). I would emphasize that it is equally important to reject the idea of passive matter, because that renders invisible the material agencies at work in a polity.

17. "Action is not what people do, but is instead the *'fait-faire,'* the making-do, accomplished along with others in an event, with the specific opportuni-

ties provided by the circumstances. These others are not ideas, or things, but nonhuman entities, or . . . *propositions*" (ibid., 288; my emphasis).

18. Ibid., 288.

19. Ibid., 247. But this fermentation seems to require some managing to ensure, for example, that all the ingredients are in the pot. It seems to require humans to exercise this "executive" function.

20. "Whenever we make something *we* are not in command, we are slightly overtaken by the action: every builder knows that." And, likewise, the momentum of nonhumans is also slightly overtaken by "the *clinamen* of our action" (ibid., 281).

21. Dewey, *Public and Its Problems*, 16.

22. A democratic collective is one "which brings together starts, prions, cows, heavens, and people . . . into a 'cosmos' instead of an 'unruly shambles'" (Latour, *Pandora's Hope*, 261).

23. "The most urgent concern for us today," says Latour, "is to see how to fuse together humans and non-humans in the same hybrid forums and open, as fast as possible, this Parliament of things" (Latour, "What Rules of Method"). Kevin Murray notes that the suggestion to include nonhuman voices at first provokes "the medieval comedy of endangered Amazonian forests tapping microphones to be heard above the bellowing megafauna. Yet, such a mind change is necessary if the planet is not to be speedily consumed by the interests of short-term capital" (Murray, "Cabinet of Helmut Lueckenhausen," 19).

24. "I call the distribution of the sensible the system of self-evident facts of sense perception that simultaneously discloses the existence of something in common and the delimitations that define the respective parts and positions within it. A distribution of the sensible therefore establishes at one and the same time something common . . . and exclusive parts. . . . The distribution of the sensible reveals who can have a share in what is common to the community based on what they do and on the time and space in which this activity is performed. . . . There is . . . an 'aesthetics' at the core of politics that has nothing to do with Benjamin's discussion of the 'aestheticization of politics.' . . . This aesthetics . . . can be understood . . . as the system of a priori forms determining what presents itself to sense experience. It is a delimitation of spaces and times, of the visible and invisible, of speech and noise. . . . Politics revolves around what is seen and what can be said about it, around who has the ability to see and the talent to speak, around the properties of spaces and the possibilities of time" (Rancière, *Politics of Aesthetics*, 12–13).

25. Rancière, *Disagreement*, 99.

26. Rancière and Panagia, "Dissenting Words," 125.

27. Rancière, *Disagreement*, 33. Democracy is the "staging of the very contra-

diction between police logic and political logic," as when the feminist Jeanne Deroin presented herself, in 1849, "as a candidate for a legislative election in which she cannot run" (41).

28. "One does not practice democracy except under the form of these mise-en-scènes that reconfigure the relations of the visible and the sayable" (Rancière and Panagia, "Dissenting Words," 125).

29. Rancière, *Disagreement*, 79. Democracy happens when the incommensurability between "the order of the inegalitarian distribution of social bodies" and "the order of the equal capacity of speaking beings in general" becomes visible (42).

30. Ibid., 99.

31. Ibid., 24–25. The plebes forced the patricians to relate to them as if they had intelligence, as if they were worthy of discoursing with. The plebs erected "a sphere for the name of the people to appear," carving out "in the heart of the city [a] . . . place where liberty is to be exercised, . . . where the power of the demos that brings off the part of those who have no part is to be exercised" (66).

32. I posed the question to Rancière at a conference engaging his work. It was called "Fidelity to the Disagreement" and was sponsored by the Post-structuralism and Radical Politics group of the British Political Studies Association, held at Goldsmiths College, London, 16–17 September 2003.

33. Rancière and Panagia, "Dissenting Words," 124.

34. For Mark Warren, for example, participation in the (voluntary) associations he says are central to a democratic culture depends on a fluency in "talk, normative agreement, cultural similarity, and shared ambitions— that is, forms of communication that are rooted in speech, gesture, self-presentation" (Warren, *Democracy and Association*, 39).

35. Connolly, *Pluralism*, 76. Connolly also describes the politics of "enactment" through which "new identities are forged out of old differences, injuries, and energies" in *The Ethos of Pluralization* (xiv). Unlike Rancière, Connolly emphasizes the interdependence between new drives to pluralization (new entrants into the demos) and existing pluralist settlements.

36. According to the *Encyclopaedia Britannica*, the Diet of Worms was "a meeting of the Diet (assembly) of the Holy Roman Empire held at Worms, Germany, in 1521 that was made famous by Martin Luther's appearance before it to respond to charges of heresy" (online edition, http://www.britannica.com).

37. Are they "agencies" or "agents"? As I struggle to choose the right term, I confront a profound ambiguity in both terms regarding wherein lies the cause and wherein the effect.

38. It might even be said that humans need nonhumans to function more than nonhumans need humans, for many nonhumans—from a can rusting at

the bottom of a landfill to a colony of spores in the Arctic — fester or live beyond the proximity of humans.

39. A public is what Karen Barad describes as an "intra-action" of humans and nonhumans: she coins the term "to signify *the inseparability of 'objects' and 'agencies of observation'* (in contrast to 'interaction,' which reinscribes the contested [subject-object] dichotomy)" (Barad, "Scientific Literacy," 232).

40. Latour, *Pandora's Hope*, 297.

8. Vitality and Self-interest

1. I take the phrase "fatalistic passivity" from Félix Guattari: "The increasing deterioration of human relations with the socius, the psyche and 'nature,' is due not only to environmental and objective pollution but is also the result of a certain incomprehension and fatalistic passivity towards these issues as a whole, among both individuals and governments. Catastrophic or not, negative developments [*evolutions*] are simply accepted without questions. . . . We need to 'kick the habit' of sedative discourse" (Guattari, *Three Ecologies*, 41; brackets in original).

2. "'Blowback' is a CIA term first used in March 1954 in a recently declassified report on the 1953 operation to overthrow the government of Mohammed Mossadegh in Iran. It is a metaphor for the unintended consequences of the U.S. government's international activities that have been kept secret from the American people. The CIA's fears that there might ultimately be some blowback from its egregious interference in the affairs of Iran were well founded. Installing the Shah in power brought twenty-five years of tyranny and repression to the Iranian people and elicited the Ayatollah Khomeini's revolution. The staff of the American embassy in Teheran was held hostage for more than a year. This misguided 'covert operation' of the U.S. government helped convince many capable people throughout the Islamic world that the United States was an implacable enemy" (Johnson, "Blowback").

3. Nature writers such as Barry Lopez and Wendell Berry have also found the category of "environment" wanting: it is for them unable to express the beautiful complexity of nonhuman nature or the degree of our intimacy with it. Though they also seek to cultivate an enhanced attentiveness to the out-side, they do not go as far as I do in playing up the essential role of the nonhuman in the human.

4. See Mathews, *For Love of Matter*; Latour, *Politics of Nature*; Haraway, *How Like a Leaf*; Hawkins, *Ethics of Waste*; Ingold, *The Perception of the Environment*; Hayles, *How We Became Posthuman*; Barad, *Meeting the Universe*

Halfway; Whatmore, "Materialist Returns"; Bingham and Hinchliffe, "Reconstituting Natures"; Ihde, *Postphenomenology and Technoscience*; and Mitchell, *What Do Pictures Want*.

5. Wade, "Bacteria Thrive in Crook of Elbow."

6. Guattari, *Three Ecologies*, 28. He speaks of "social ecology, mental ecology and environmental ecology" (41).

7. Ibid., 27.

8. Ibid., 38.

9. See, for example, Luke, *Capitalism, Democracy, and Ecology*; and Luke, *Ecocritique*.

10. Guattari, *Three Ecologies*, 51.

11. The environmentalist Scott Russell Sanders, for example, makes the same point in "Stillness": "We need to resist attacks on air, soil, water, and wild lands. But we also need to change our culture, not just our leaders and technology. We need to speak out and act for more conserving, more sustainable, more peaceful, and more just practices in our homes, our workplaces, our schools, and our public assemblies. We must refuse to shut up, refuse to give up, in the face of corporate consumerism and a mass culture peddling the narcotics of entertainment. We need to articulate and demonstrate a more decent and joyous way of life" (5).

12. "*The Trinity is One*. We do not confess three Gods, but one God in three persons, the 'consubstantial Trinity.' The divine persons do not share the one divinity among themselves but each of them is God whole and entire." And yet, "*The divine persons are really distinct from one another*. 'God is one but not solitary.' 'Father,' 'Son,' 'Holy Spirit' are not simply names designating modalities of the divine being, for they are really distinct from one another: 'He is not the Father who is the Son, nor is the Son he who is the Father, nor is the Holy Spirit he who is the Father or the Son.' . . . The divine Unity is Triune'" ("The Dogma of the Holy Trinity"; emphasis added).

13. Guattari, *Three Ecologies*, 41–42.

14. Latour, "It's the Development, Stupid," 6–7.

15. "Second Nature" was the title of the 2007 Graduate Student Conference in Political Theory at Northwestern University. For papers from this conference, see Archer, Maxwell, and Ephraim, eds., *Second Nature*.

16. Latour, *Politics of Nature*, 12.

17. Guattari, *Three Ecologies*, 68.

18. Ibid., 66–67. Latour echoes Guattari's advocacy of an active, energetic, and pro-technological greening. This call to arms is also at the heart of Shellenberger and Nordhaus, *Break Through*, the book to which Latour is responding in "It's the Development, Stupid." *Break Through* argues that environmentalism is inadequate to the new ecological crises. Overcoming

global warming, for example, will require a new kind of economic development, that is, big and bold technological investments in the future.

19. The historian of ideas A. O. Lovejoy lists sixty-six senses of the term. See
the appendix of Lovejoy and Boas, *Primitivism and Related Ideas in Antiquity*; see also Lovejoy, "Nature as Aesthetic Norm."

20. The first sense is the "nature" of a Hobbesian or Lockean or Rousseauian
"state of nature," but it also resonates with what Sigmund Freud calls
drives and instincts and what Martin Heidegger points to in calling our
thrownness primordial. Maurice Merleau-Ponty describes the relationship between nature as stable substrate and nature as creativity as "chias-
matic," as flowing into and back from one another endlessly.

21. Coleridge, *The Literary Remains of Samuel Taylor Coleridge*, 2:341. Spinoza,
Ethics, pt. 1, proposition 29: "By nature viewed as active (natura naturans)
. . . we should understand . . . those *attributes* of substance . . . , in other
words . . . God, in so far as he is considered as a free cause. By nature
viewed as passive (natura naturata) I understand all that which follows
from the *necessity* of [God or nature] . . . that is, all the modes of the attributes of God, in so far as they are considered as *things*" (my emphasis).

22. Whitehead, *Concept of Nature*, 172.

23. Deleuze and Guattari, *A Thousand Plateaus*, 255.

24. Ibid., 254.

25. Here is how Spinoza puts the point: "There is no need to spend time in
going on to show that Nature has no fixed goal and that all final causes are
but figments of the human imagination" (*Ethics*, pt. 4, appendix).

26. Serres, *The Birth of Physics*, 64. Serres argues that Lucretius's text, *De Rerum Natura*, exemplifies this isomorphism: "The Book V, on the world and
nascent humanity, is traversed by the same laws as the Book IV, on perception; and these are the laws of matter found in Book II. Always the
same whole, a multiplicity of elements, and always the same operations at
work on these wholes. The method by structural invariants, generalised to
the global stability of flowing movements, establishes materialism" (ibid.,
54).

27. "The world, objects, bodies, my very soul are, at the moment of their birth,
in decline. This means, in the everyday sense, that they are mortal and
bound for destruction. It also means that they form and arise. Nature de-
clines and this is its act of birth. And its stability. Atoms join together, conjunction is the strength of things, through declination. This signifies the
whole of time. The past, the present, the future, the dawn of appearance
and death, tenacious illusions, are only the declinations of matter. They
decline and are declined like the tenses of a verb, a word made up of atom-
letters. . . . Existence, time, meaning and language go down the inclined
plane together" (ibid., 34).

28. Ibid., 58.
29. For a thoughtful account of the performative contradiction, see Gulshan Ara Khan, "Habermas's Charge of a Performative Contradiction: Paradox of Contradiction?" (unpublished manuscript, 2008). A copy of this source is on file in my private collection.
30. Velasquez-Manoff, "Worm Turns," 17.
31. Nash, "On the Subversive Virtue," 427.
32. See also Pickering, *Mangle of Practice*, 6.
33. The phrase "resists full translation and exceeds our comprehensive grasp" is Romand Coles's in "The Wild Patience of Radical Democracy," 78.

Bibliography

Adkins, A. W. D. *From the Many to the One: A Study of Personality and Views of Human Nature in the Context of Ancient Greek Society, Values, and Beliefs*. Ithaca: Cornell University Press, 1970.

Adorno, Theodor. *Negative Dialectics*. Trans. E. B. Ashton. New York: Continuum, 1973.

Aeschylus. "Prometheus Bound." *Greek Tragedies*, vol. 1, ed. David Grene and Richmond Lattimore, 61–106. Chicago: University of Chicago Press, 1960.

Althusser, Louis. "The Underground Current of the Materialism of the Encounter." *Philosophy of the Encounter: Later Writings, 1978–87*, trans. G. M. Goshgarian, ed. François Matheron, 163–207. New York: Verso, 2006.

Anderson, Ben. "Time-Stilled Space-Slowed: How Boredom Matters." *Geoforum* 35, no. 6 (2004): 739–54.

Anderson, Ben, and Divya Tolia-Kelly. "Matter(s) in Social and Cultural Geography." *Geoforum* 35, no. 6 (2004): 669–74.

Appadurai, Arjun, ed. *The Social Life of Things: Commodities in Cultural Perspective*. Cambridge: Cambridge University Press, 1986.

Archer, Crina, Lida Maxwell, and Laura Ephraim, eds. *Second Nature: Rethinking the Natural through Politics*. Minneapolis: University of Minnesota Press, forthcoming.

Archer, Margaret S. *Realist Social Theory: The Morphogenetic Approach*. Cambridge: Cambridge University Press, 1995.

Arendt, Hannah. "On the Nature of Totalitarianism: An Essay in Understanding." 1953. Hannah Arendt Papers at the Library of Congress, http://www.loc.gov.

Augustine. *Confessions*. Trans. Garry Wills. New York: Penguin, 2006.

Baer, Susan. "In Vitro Fertilization, Stem Cell Research Share Moral Issues." *Baltimore Sun*, 4 June 2005.

Bakhtin, Mikhail. "Contemporary Vitalism." *The Crisis in Modernism: Bergson and the Vitalist Controversy*, ed. Frederick Burwick and Paul Douglass, 76–97. Cambridge: Cambridge University Press, 1992.

Barad, Karen. *Meeting the Universe Halfway: Quantum Physics and the Entanglement of Matter and Meaning*. Durham, N.C.: Duke University Press, 2007.

———. "Scientific Literacy → Agential Literacy = (Learning + Doing) Science Responsibly." *Feminist Science Studies: A New Generation*, ed. Maralee Mayberry, Banu Subramaniam, and Lisa Weasel, 226–46. New York: Routledge, 2001.

Barron, Colin. "A Strong Distinction between Humans and Non-humans Is No Longer Required for Research Purposes: A Debate between Bruno Latour and Steve Fuller." *History of the Human Sciences* 16, no. 2 (2003): 77–99.

Battye, Richard Fawcett. *What Is Vital Force? Or, A Short and Comprehensive Sketch, Including Vital Physics, Animal Morphology, and Epidemics; To Which Is Added an Appendix upon Geology: Is the Detrital Theory of Geology Tenable?* London: Truber, 1877.

Bayliss, William Maddock. *The Physiology of Food and Economy in Diet*. London: Longmans, Green, 1917.

Bergson, Henri. *Creative Evolution*. Trans. Arthur Mitchell. New York: Dover, 1998.

———. *The Creative Mind: An Introduction to Metaphysics*. Trans. Mabelle Andison. New York: Citadel, 1974.

Best, Robert. "Prepared Statement to the Subcommittee on Science, Technology, and Space of the Committee on Commerce, Science, and Transportation." *U.S. Senate Hearing on Human Cloning*, 107th Cong., 1st sess., 2 May 2001.

Bingham, Nick. "Bees, Butterflies, and Bacteria: Biotechnology and the Politics of Nonhuman Friendship." *Environment and Planning A* 38, no. 3 (2006): 483–98.

Bingham, Nick, and Steve Hinchliffe. "Reconstituting Natures: Articulating Other Modes of Living Together," *Geoforum* 39, no. 1 (2008): 83–87.

Bonta, Mark, and John Protevi, eds. *Deleuze and Geophilosophy: A Guide and Glossary*. Edinburgh: Edinburgh University Press, 2004.

Braidotti, Rosi. "Affirmation versus Vulnerability: On Contemporary Ethical

Debates." *Symposium: Canadian Journal of Continental Philosophy* 10, no. 1 (2006): 235–54.

Brown, Bill. "Thing Theory." *Critical Inquiry* 28, no. 1 (2001): 1–22.

Brown, Wendy. *Regulating Aversion: Tolerance in the Age of Identity and Empire.* Princeton: Princeton University Press, 2006.

———. *States of Injury: Power and Freedom in Late Modernity.* Princeton: Princeton University Press, 1995.

Brumfield, Elizabeth. "On the Archaeology of Choice." *Agency in Archaeology,* ed. Marcia-Anne Dobres and John E. Robb, 249–56. New York: Routledge, 2000.

Buell, John, and Tom DeLuca. *Sustainable Democracy: Individuality and the Politics of the Environment.* Thousand Oaks, Calif.: Sage, 1996.

Burwick, Frederick, and Paul Douglass. Introduction to *The Crisis in Modernism: Bergson and the Vitalist Controversy,* ed. Burwick and Douglass, 1–12. Cambridge: Cambridge University Press, 1992.

Butler, Judith. *Bodies That Matter: On the Discursive Limits of "Sex."* New York: Routledge, 1993.

———. "Merely Cultural." *New Left Review,* no. 227 (1998): 33–44.

Canguilhem, Georges. *Aspects du vitalisme: La connaissance de la vie.* Paris: Hachette, 1952.

Carroll, Linda. "Diets Heavy in Saturated Fats May Lead to Fading Memories." *Neurology Today* 4, no. 12 (2004): 31–32.

Casazza, John A., and George C. Loehr, eds. *The Evolution of Electric Power Transmission under Deregulation: Selected Readings.* Hoboken, N.J.: Wiley, 2000.

Caygill, Howard. "Life and Energy." *Theory, Culture, and Society* 24, no. 6 (2007): 19–27.

Chiari, Joseph. "Vitalism and Contemporary Thought." *The Crisis in Modernism: Bergson and the Vitalist Controversy,* ed. Frederick Burwick and Paul Douglass, 245–73. Cambridge: Cambridge University Press, 1992.

Cole, David. "Affective Literacy." Paper presented at the ALEA/AATE National Conference, Gold Coast, Queensland, Australia, 2005.

Cole, Ethan. "Bush Stands against 'Temptation to Manipulate Life.'" *Christian Post Reporter,* 13 April 2007.

Coleridge, Samuel Taylor. *The Literary Remains of Samuel Taylor Coleridge.* Vol. 2. Ed. Henry Nelson Coleridge. London: William Pickering, 1836.

Coles, Romand. *Rethinking Generosity: Critical Theory and the Politics of Caritas.* Ithaca: Cornell University Press, 1997.

———. "The Wild Patience of Radical Democracy: Beyond Žižek's Lack." *Radical Democracy: Politics Between Abundance and Lack,* ed. Lars Tønder and Lasse Thomassen, 68–85. Manchester: Manchester University Press, 2005.

Colls, Rachel. "Materialising Bodily Matter: Intra-action and the Embodiment of 'Fat.'" *Geoforum* 38, no. 2 (2007): 353–65.

Connolly, William E. *The Ethos of Pluralization*. Minneapolis: University of Minnesota Press, 1995.

———. "Method, Problem, Faith." *Problems and Methods in the Study of Politics*, ed. Ian Shapiro, Rogers Smith, and Tarek E. Masoud, 332–49. Cambridge: Cambridge University Press, 2004.

———. *Pluralism*. Durham, N.C.: Duke University Press, 2005.

———. *Why I Am Not a Secularist*. Minneapolis: University of Minnesota Press, 1999.

Contardi, Sergio, and Mario Perniola. "The Sex Appeal of the Inorganic: A Conversation." *Journal of European Psychoanalysis*, nos. 3–4 (1996–1997): http://www.psychomedia.it/jep.

Coole, Diana. *Negativity and Politics: Dionysus and Dialectics from Kant to Post-structuralism*. New York: Routledge, 2000.

———. "Rethinking Agency: A Phenomenological Approach to Embodiment and Agentic Capacities." *Political Studies* 53, no. 1 (2005): 124–42.

Coole, Diana, and Samantha Frost, eds. *New Materialisms*. Durham, N.C.: Duke University Press, forthcoming.

Cornaro, Luigi. *Art of Living Long*. Milwaukee: William F. Butler, 1915.

Corson, Ben. "Speed and Technicity: A Derridean Exploration." PhD diss., Johns Hopkins University, 2000.

Crawford, T. Hugh. "An Interview with Bruno Latour." *Configurations* 1, no. 2 (1993): 247–68.

Critser, Greg. *Fat Land: How Americans Became the Fattest People in the World*. New York: Mariner Books, 2004.

Darwin, Charles. *The Formation of Vegetable Mould, through the Action of Worms, with Observations on Their Habits*. London: John Murray, 1881.

Das, Veena. *Life and Words: Violence and the Descent into the Ordinary*. Berkeley: University of California Press, 2007.

Dean, Jodi. *Publicity's Secret: How Technoculture Capitalizes on Democracy*. Ithaca: Cornell University Press, 2002.

De Landa, Manuel. *Intensive Science and Virtual Philosophy*. London: Continuum, 2002.

———. *A Thousand Years of Nonlinear History*. New York: Zone, 1997.

———. "Uniformity and Variability: An Essay in the Philosophy of Matter." Paper presented at the "Doors of Perception 3" conference, Netherlands Design Institute, Amsterdam, 7–11 November 1995.

Deleuze, Gilles. *Bergsonism*. Trans. Hugh Tomlinson and Barbara Habberjam. New York: Zone, 1991.

———. *Expressionism in Philosophy: Spinoza*. Trans. Martin Joughin. New York: Zone Books, 1992.

————. "Immanence: A Life . . ." *Theory, Culture, and Society* 14, no. 2 (1997): 3–7.

————. "Metal, Metallurgy, Music, Husserl, Simondon." Web Deleuze, "Sur *Anti-Oedipe* et *Mille Plateaux*: Cours Vincennes — 27/02/1979," http://www .webdeleuze.com.

————. *Negotiations*. Trans. Martin Joughin. New York: Columbia University Press, 1995.

————. *Spinoza: Practical Philosophy*. Trans. Robert Hurley. San Francisco: City Lights Books, 1988.

Deleuze, Gilles, and Félix Guattari. *A Thousand Plateaus: Capitalism and Schizophrenia*. Trans. Brian Massumi. Minneapolis: University of Minnesota Press, 1987.

Deleuze, Gilles, and Claire Parnet. "On the Superiority of Anglo-American Literature." *Dialogues*, trans. Hugh Tomlinson and Barbara Habberjam, 36–76. New York: Columbia University Press, 1987.

Derrida, Jacques. "The Animal That Therefore I Am (More to Follow)." Trans. David Wills. *Critical Inquiry* 28, no. 2 (2002): 369–418.

————. "Marx and Sons." *Ghostly Demarcations: A Symposium on Jacques Derrida's Specters of Marx*, ed. Michael Sprinker, 213–69. London: Verso, 1999.

de Vries, Hent. Introduction to *Political Theologies: Public Religions in a Postsecular World*, ed. Vries and Lawrence Sullivan, 1–88. New York: Fordham University Press, 2006.

Dewey, John. *Art as Experience*. New York: Minton, Balch, 1934.

————. *The Public and Its Problems*. New York: Henry Holt, 1927.

Di Menna, Jodi. "Grid Grief!" *Canadian Geographic*, http://www.canadian geographic.ca/blackout_2003/grid.html (accessed 14 April 2009).

Docker, John. "*Après la Guerre*: Dark Thought, Some Whimsy." *Arena Journal*, n.s., no. 20 (2002–3), http://www.arena.org.au.

Douglas, Kate. "Six 'Uniquely' Human Traits Now Found in Animals." *NewScientist*, 22 May 2008, http://www.newscientist.com.

Driesch, Hans. *The History and Theory of Vitalism*. Trans. C. K. Ogden. London: Macmillan, 1914.

————. *The Problem of Individuality: A Course of Four Lectures Delivered before the University of London in October 1913*. London: Macmillan, 1914.

————. *The Science and Philosophy of the Organism: The Gifford Lectures Delivered before the University of Aberdeen in the Year 1907*. London: Adam and Charles Black, 1908.

————. *The Science and Philosophy of the Organism: The Gifford Lectures Delivered before the University of Aberdeen in the Year 1908*. London: Adam and Charles Black, 1908.

Dumm, Thomas L. *A Politics of the Ordinary*. New York: New York University Press, 1999.

Eagleton, Terry. "Edible Écriture." *Consuming Passions: Food in the Age of Anxiety*, ed. Sian Griffiths and Jennifer Wallace, 203–8. Manchester: Manchester University Press, 1998.

Edensor, Tim. "Waste Matter: The Debris of Industrial Ruins and the Disordering of the Material World." *Journal of Material Culture* 10, no. 3 (2005): 311–32.

Eisenach, Eldon J., ed. *The Social and Political Thought of American Progressivism*. Indianapolis: Hackett, 2006.

Emerson, Ralph Waldo. *Journals and Miscellaneous Notebooks: 1847–1848*. Vol. 10. Cambridge, Mass.: Belknap, 1960.

Feher, Michel, Ramona Naddaff, and Nadia Tazi, eds. *Fragments for a History of the Human Body*. 3 vols. New York: Zone, 1989.

Ferguson, Kathy E. *The Man Question: Visions of Subjectivity in Feminist Theory*. Berkeley: University of California, 1993.

Fletcher, Angus. *A New Theory for American Poetry: Democracy, the Environment, and the Future of Imagination*. Cambridge: Harvard University Press, 2004.

Foucault, Michel. "Confinement, Psychiatry, Prison." *Politics, Philosophy, Culture: Interviews and Other Writings, 1977–84*, trans. Alan Sheridan, ed. Lawrence D. Kritzman, 178–210. New York: Routledge, 1988.

————. "Theatrum Philosophicum." *Language, Counter-memory, Practice: Selected Essays and Interviews*, ed. Donald F. Bouchard, 165–98. Ithaca: Cornell University Press, 1977.

Fraser, Nancy. *Justice Interruptus: Critical Reflections on the Postsocialist Condition*. New York: Routledge, 1997.

Frow, John. "A Pebble, a Camera, a Man." *Critical Inquiry* 28, no. 1 (2001): 270–85.

Gatens, Moira. *Imaginary Bodies: Ethics, Power, and Corporeality*. New York: Routledge, 1996.

Gesch, C. Bernard, et al. "Influence of Supplementary Vitamins, Minerals, and Essential Fatty Acids on the Antisocial Behaviour of Young Adult Prisoners: Randomised, Placebo-Controlled Trial." *British Journal of Psychiatry*, no. 181 (2002): 22–28.

Ginzburg, Carlo. *The Cheese and the Worms: The Cosmos of a Sixteenth-Century Miller*. Trans. John and Anne Tedeschi. Baltimore: Johns Hopkins University Press, 1980.

Glanz, James. "When the Grid Bites Back: More Are Relying on an Unreliable System." *International Herald Tribune*, 18 August 2003.

Goldberg, Jonathan. "Lucy Hutchinson Writing Matter." ELH 73, no. 1 (2006): 275–301.

————. *The Seeds of Things: Theorizing Sexuality and Materiality in Renaissance Representations*. New York: Fordham University Press, 2009.

Goodman, David. "Ontology Matters: The Relational Materiality of Nature and Agro-Food Studies." *Sociologia Ruralis* 41, no. 2 (2001): 182–200.

Gould, Stephen Jay. *The Structure of Evolutionary Theory*. Cambridge: Belknap, 2002.

Guattari, Félix. *The Three Ecologies*. Trans. Ian Pindar and Paul Sutton. London: Athlone, 2000.

Habermas, Jürgen. *The Future of Human Nature*. Cambridge: Polity, 2003.

Hallahan, Brian, and Malcolm R. Garland. "Essential Fatty Acids and Mental Health." *British Journal of Psychiatry*, no. 186 (2005): 275–77.

Hamacher, Werner. "Lingua Amissa: The Messianism of Commodity-Language and Derrida's *Specters of Marx.*" *Ghostly Demarcations: A Symposium on Jacques Derrida's Specters of Marx*, ed. Michael Sprinker, 168–212. London: Verso, 1999.

Haraway, Donna J. *How Like a Leaf*. New York: Routledge, 2000.

———. *Modest_Witness@Second_Millennium. FemaleMan©Meets_Onco-Mouse: Feminism and Technoscience*. New York: Routledge, 1997.

Hardin, Garrett. "The Tragedy of the Commons." *Science*, 13 December 1968, 1244–48.

Hardt, Michael, and Antonio Negri. *Empire*. Cambridge: Harvard University Press, 2000.

———. *Multitude: War and Democracy in the Age of Empire*. New York: Penguin, 2004.

Harrington, Anne. *Reenchanted Science: Holism in German Culture from Wilhelm II to Hitler*. Princeton: Princeton University Press, 1996.

Hawkins, Gay. *The Ethics of Waste: How We Relate to Rubbish*. Sydney: University of New South Wales Press, 2006.

Hayden, Patrick. "Gilles Deleuze and Naturalism: A Convergence with Ecological Theory and Politics." *Environmental Ethics* 19, no. 2 (1997): 185–204.

Hayles, N. Katherine. *How We Became Posthuman*. Chicago: University of Chicago Press, 1999.

Heidegger, Martin. "The Age of the World Picture." *The Question Concerning Technology, and Other Essays*, trans. William Lovitt, 115–54. New York: Harper and Row, 1982.

———. *What Is a Thing?* Trans. W. B. Barton Jr. and Vera Deutsch. South Bend, Ill.: Gateway, 1967.

Hobbes, Thomas. "De Corpore." *The English Works of Thomas Hobbes*, vol. 1, ed. William Molesworth, n.p. London: John Bohn, 1839.

Ihde, Don. *Postphenomenology and Technoscience: The Peking University Lectures*. Albany, N.Y.: SUNY Press, 2009.

Ingold, Tim. *The Perception of the Environment: Essays on Livelihood, Dwelling, and Skill*. New York: Routledge, 2000.

"Iraq Body Count," August 2007. Iraq Body Count, http://www.iraqbodycount .org.

Jackson, Peter, et al. "Manufacturing Meaning along the Food Commodity Chain." *Cultures of Consumption Research Programme* (London: Birkbeck College), http://www.consume.bbk.ac.uk/researchfindings/meaningfood .pdf.

Jennings, Cheri Lucas, and Bruce H. Jennings. "Green Fields / Brown Skin: Posting as a Sign of Recognition." *In the Nature of Things: Language, Politics, and the Environment*, ed. Jane Bennett and William Chaloupka, 173–94. Minneapolis: University of Minnesota Press, 1993.

Jennings, H. S. "Doctrines Held as Vitalism." *American Naturalist*, July 1913, 385–417.

———. "Driesch's Vitalism and Experimental Indeterminism." *Science*, 4 October 1912, 434–35.

Johnson, Chalmers. "Blowback." *Nation*, 15 October 2001, 4–9.

Johnson, Steven. *Emergence: The Connected Lives of Ants, Brains, Cities, and Software*. New York: Touchstone, 2001.

Jonnes, Jill. *Empires of Light: Edison, Tesla, Westinghouse, and the Race to Electrify the World*. New York: Random House, 2003.

Jullien, François. *The Propensity of Things: Toward a History of Efficacy in China*. Trans. Janet Lloyd. New York: Zone, 1995.

Kafka, Franz. "Cares of a Family Man." *Complete Stories*, ed. Nahum N. Glatzer, 427–29. New York: Schocken, 1971.

———. "A Report to an Academy." *Complete Stories*, ed. Nahum N. Glatzer, 250–59. New York: Schocken, 1971.

Kant, Immanuel. *Critique of Judgment*. Trans. Werner Pluhar. Indianapolis: Hackett, 1987.

———. *Religion within the Limits of Reason Alone*. Trans. Theodore M. Greene and Hoyt H. Hudson. New York: Harper Torchbooks, 1960.

Kass, Leon. *The Hungry Soul: Eating and the Perfecting of Our Nature*. Chicago: University of Chicago Press, 1994.

Kauffman, Stuart. *Reinventing the Sacred: A New View of Science, Reason, and Religion*. New York: Basic Books, 2008.

Keiser, Albert. "New Thoreau Material." *Modern Language Notes* 44, no. 4 (1929): 253–54.

Kingsolver, Barbara. "A Good Farmer." *Nation*, 3 November 2003, 7–11.

Kolata, Gina. "Researcher Who Helped Start Stem Cell War May Now End It." *New York Times*, 22 November 2007.

Lashley, K. S. "The Behavioristic Interpretation of Consciousness." *Psychological Bulletin*, no. 30 (1923): 237–72; 329–53.

Latham, Alan, and Derek P. McCormack. "Moving Cities: Rethinking the Materialities of Urban Geographies." *Progress in Human Geography* 28, no. 6 (2004): 701–24.

Latour, Bruno. *Aramis; or, The Love of Technology*. Trans. Catherine Porter. Cambridge: Harvard University Press, 1996.

———. "'It's the Development, Stupid!' or, How to Modernize Modernization?" EspacesTemps website, http://www.espacestemps.net (accessed 15 April 2009).

———. "On Actor-Network Theory: A Few Clarifications." *Soziale Welt* 47, no. 4 (1996): 369–81.

———. *Pandora's Hope: Essays on the Reality of Science Studies*. Cambridge: Harvard University Press, 1999.

———. *Politics of Nature: How to Bring the Sciences into Democracy*. Trans. Catherine Porter. Cambridge: Harvard University Press, 2004.

———. *Reassembling the Social: An Introduction to Actor-Network Theory*. Oxford: Oxford University Press, 2005.

———. "What Rules of Method for the New Socio-scientific Experiments?" Plenary lecture for the Darmstadt Colloquium, 30 March 2001.

Laurier, Eric, and Chris Philo. "X-Morphising: Review Essay of Bruno Latour's *Aramis, or the Love of Technology*." *Environment and Planning A* 31, no. 6 (1999): 1047–71.

Lenoir, Timothy. "Kant, Blumenbach, and Vital Materialism in German Biology." *Isis* 71, no. 1 (1980): 77–108.

Lerner, Eric J. "What's Wrong with the Electric Grid?" *Industrial Physicist* 9, no. 5 (2003), http://www.aip.org/tip.

Levene, Nancy K. *Spinoza's Revelation: Religion, Democracy, and Reason*. Cambridge: Cambridge University Press, 2004.

Levine, George. *Darwin Loves You: Natural Selection and the Re-enchantment of the World*. Princeton: Princeton University Press, 2006.

Lin, Martin. "Substance, Attribute, and Mode in Spinoza." *Philosophy Compass* 1, no. 2 (2006): 144–53.

Lorimer, Jamie. "Nonhuman Charisma." *Environment and Planning D: Society and Space* 25, no. 5 (2007): 911–32.

Lovejoy, Arthur O. "The Import of Vitalism." *Science*, 21 July 1911, 75–80.

———. "The Meaning of Driesch and the Meaning of Vitalism." *Science*, 15 November 1912, 672–75.

———. "The Meaning of Vitalism." *Science*, 21 April 1911, 610–14.

———. "Nature as Aesthetic Norm." *Essays in the History of Ideas*, 69–77. Baltimore: Johns Hopkins University Press, 1948.

Lovejoy, Arthur O., and George Boas. *Primitivism and Related Ideas in Antiquity*. Baltimore: Johns Hopkins University Press, 1935.

Lucretius. "On the Nature of the Universe: De Rerum Natura." *The Epicurean*

Philosophers, trans. C. Bailey, R. D. Dicks, and J. C. A. Gaskin, ed. John Gaskin, 78–304. London: J. M. Dent, 1995.

Luke, Timothy W. *Capitalism, Democracy, and Ecology: Departing from Marx.* Urbana: University of Illinois Press, 1999.

———. *Ecocritique: Contesting the Politics of Nature, Economy, and Culture.* Minneapolis: University of Minnesota Press, 1997.

Lyotard, Jean-François. *Postmodern Fables.* Trans. Georges van den Abbeele. Minneapolis: University of Minnesota Press, 1997.

Maienschein, Jane. "What's in a Name: Embryos, Clones, and Stem Cells." *American Journal of Bioethics* 2, no. 1 (2002): 12–19.

Margulis, Lynn, and Dorion Sagan. *What Is Life?* Berkeley: University of California Press, 2000.

Marks, John. "Introduction." "Deleuze and Science," ed. Marks, special issue, *Paragraph* 29, no. 2 (2006): 1–18.

Marrati, Paola. "Time, Life, Concepts: The Newness of Bergson." "Comparative Literature Issue," ed. Suzanne Guerlac, special issue, MLN 120, no. 5 (2005): 1099–111.

Marres, Noortje. "Issues Spark a Public into Being: A Key But Often Forgotten Point of the Lippmann-Dewey Debate." *Making Things Public*, ed. Bruno Latour and Peter Weibel, 208–17. Cambridge: MIT Press, 2005.

Mathews, Freya. *For Love of Matter: A Contemporary Panpsychism.* Albany: State University of New York Press, 2003.

Melamed, Yitzhak. "Spinoza's Anti-Humanism." *The Rationalists*, ed. C. Fraenkel, D. Perinetti, and J. Smith. New York: Kluwer, forthcoming.

Merleau-Ponty, Maurice. *The Phenomenology of Perception.* Trans. Colin Smith. New York: Routledge and Kegan Paul, 1981.

Mitchell, W. J. T. *What Do Pictures Want? The Lives and Loves of Images.* Chicago: University of Chicago Press, 2005.

Murray, Kevin. "The Cabinet of Helmut Lueckenhausen." *Craft Victoria*, no. 29 (1999): 17–19.

Nash, James A. "On the Subversive Virtue: Frugality," *Ethics of Consumption: The Good Life, Justice, and Global Stewardship*, ed. David A. Cricker and Toby Linden, 416–36. Lanham, Md.: Rowman and Littlefield, 1998.

Nietzsche, Friedrich. *Daybreak: Thoughts on the Prejudices of Morality.* Trans. R. J. Hollingdale. Cambridge: Cambridge University Press, 1997.

———. *On the Genealogy of Morals and Ecce Homo.* Trans. Walter Kaufmann and R. J. Hollingdale. New York: Vintage, 1969.

———. *Thus Spake Zarathustra.* Trans. Thomas Common. New York: Dover, 1999.

———. *Twilight of the Idols and The Anti-Christ.* Trans. R. J. Hollingdale. London: Penguin, 1983.

————. *The Will to Power*. Trans. Walter Kaufmann and R. J. Hollingdale. New York: Random House, 1967.

Nosovel, Damir. "System Blackout Causes and Cures." Energy Central Network, 6 October 2003, http://www.energypulse.net.

Patton, Paul. *Deleuze and the Political*. New York: Routledge, 2000.

Paulus PP. II, Ioannes. "Evangelium Vitae: To the Bishops, Priests, and Deacons, Men and Women, Religious, Lay, Faithful, and All People of Good Will, on the Value and Inviolability of Human Life." Libreria Editrice Vaticana, 25 March 1995, http://www.vatican.va.

Perniola, Mario. *Sex Appeal of the Inorganic: Philosophies of Desire in the Modern World*. Trans. Massimo Verdicchio. New York: Continuum, 2004.

Petulla, Joseph M. *American Environmentalism: Values, Tactics, Priorities*. College Station: Texas A&M University Press, 1980.

Pickering, Andrew. *The Mangle of Practice: Time, Agency, and Science*. Chicago: University of Chicago Press, 1995.

Pietz, William. "Death of the Deodand: Accursed Objects and the Money Value of Human Life." "The Abject," ed. Francesco Pellizzi, special issue, *Res*, no. 31 (1997): 97–108.

Pollan, Michael. *The Omnivore's Dilemma: A Natural History of Four Meals*. New York: Penguin, 2006.

Quirk, Tom. *Bergson and American Culture: The Worlds of Willa Cather and Wallace Stevens*. Chapel Hill: University of North Carolina Press, 1990.

Rahman, Momin, and Anne Witz. "What Really Matters? The Elusive Quality of the Material in Feminist Thought." Paper presented at the Annual Congress of the Canadian Sociology and Anthropology Association, University of Toronto, 28–31 May 2002.

Rancière, Jacques. "Comment and Responses." *Theory and Event* 6, no. 4 (2003): n.p.

————. *Disagreement: Politics and Philosophy*. Trans. Julie Rose. Minneapolis: University of Minnesota Press, 1999.

————. *The Politics of Aesthetics: The Distribution of the Sensible*. Trans. Gabriel Rockhill. London: Continuum, 2004.

————. "Ten Theses on Politics." *Theory and Event* 5, no. 3 (2001): n.p.

Rancière, Jacques, and Davide Panagia. "Dissenting Words: A Conversation with Jacques Ranciere." *Diacritics* 30, no. 2 (2000): 113–26.

Richards, Robert J. "Kant and Blumenbach on the *Bildungstrieb*: A Historical Misunderstanding." *Studies in the History and Philosophy of Biology and Biomedical Sciences* 31, no. 1 (2000): 11–32.

Richardson, Alexandra J., and Paul Montgomery. "The Oxford-Durham Study: A Randomized, Controlled Trial of Dietary Supplementation with Fatty Acids in Children with Developmental Coordination Disorder." *Pediatrics* 115, no. 5 (2005): 1360–66.

Roberts, Les, et al. "Mortality before and after the 2003 Invasion of Iraq: Cluster Sample Survey." *Lancet* 364, no. 9448 (2004): 1857–64.

Robinson, Kenneth Allen. *Thoreau and the Wild Appetite.* New York: AMS Press, 1957.

Roe, Emma J. "Material Connectivity, the Immaterial, and the Aesthetic of Eating Practices: An Argument for How Genetically Modified Foodstuff Becomes Inedible." *Environment and Planning A* 38, no. 3 (2006): 465–81.

Rorty, Richard. *Rorty and Pragmatism: The Philosopher Responds to His Critics.* Ed. Herman J. Saatkamp Jr. Nashville, Tenn.: Vanderbilt University Press, 1995.

Saler, Michael. "Modernity, Disenchantment, and the Ironic Imagination." *Philosophy and Literature* 28, no. 1 (2004): 137–49.

Sanders, Scott Russell. "Stillness." *Orion* 20, no. 2 (2001): 64–71.

Sargisson, Lucy. *Utopian Bodies and the Politics of Transgression.* New York: Routledge, 2000.

Schoolman, Morton. *Reason and Horror: Critical Theory, Democracy, and Aesthetic Individuality.* New York: Routledge, 2001.

Serres, Michel. *The Birth of Physics.* Trans. Jack Hawkes. Ed. David Webb. Manchester: Clinamen, 2000.

———. *The Parasite.* Trans. Lawrence R. Schehr. Baltimore: Johns Hopkins University Press, 1982.

Sharp, Hasana. "The Force of Ideas in Spinoza." *Political Theory* 35, no. 6 (2007): 732–55.

Shellenberger, Michael, and Ted Nordhaus. *Break Through: From the Death of Environmentalism to the Politics of Possibility.* Boston: Houghton Mifflin, 2007.

Sikorski, Wade. *Modernity and Technology.* Tuscaloosa: University of Alabama Press, 1993.

Slocum, Tyson. "Bush Turns Blind Eye to Blackout Culprit." CorpWatch, 21 August 2003, http://www.corpwatch.org.

Slow Food USA. "Manifesto." Slow Food USA, http://www.slowfoodusa.org (accessed 25 February 2009).

Smith, Cyril S. *A History of Metallography.* Chicago: University of Chicago Press, 1960.

———. "The Texture of Matter as Viewed by Artisan, Philosopher, and Scientist in the Seventeenth and Eighteenth Centuries." *Atoms, Blacksmiths, and Crystals: Practical and Theoretical Views of the Structure of Matter in the Seventeenth and Eighteenth Centuries.* Los Angeles: William Andrews Clark Memorial Library, University of California, Los Angeles, 1967.

Spike, Jeffrey. "Bush and Stem Cell Research: An Ethically Confused Policy." *American Journal of Bioethics* 2, no. 1 (2002): 45–46.

Spinoza, Baruch. *Ethics: Treatise on the Emendation of the Intellect, and Selected Letters*. Trans. Samuel Shirley. Ed. Seymour Feldman. Indianapolis: Hackett, 1992.

———. *The Letters*. Trans. Samuel Shirley. Indianapolis: Hackett, 1995.

"Stem Cell Breakthrough." *Washington Post*, 24 November 2007.

Stiegler, Bernard. *The Technics and Time*. Vol. 1, *The Fault of Epimetheus*. Trans. Richard Beardsworth and George Collins. Stanford: Stanford University Press, 1998.

Stolberg, Sheryl Gay. "House Approves a Stem Cell Bill Opposed by Bush." *New York Times*, 25 May 2005.

Su, Kuan-Pin, Winston W. Shen, and Shih-Yi Huang. "Omega-3 Fatty Acids as a Psychotherapeutic Agent for a Pregnant Schizophrenic Patient." *European Neuropsychopharmacology* 11, no. 4 (2001): 295–99.

Sullivan, Robert. *The Meadowlands: Wilderness Adventures on the Edge of a City*. New York: Doubleday, 1998.

Sumner, Francis B. Review of *The History and Theory of Vitalism*, by Hans Driesch. *The Journal of Philosophy, Psychology, and Scientific Methods* 13, no. 4 (1916): 103–9.

"The Dogma of the Holy Trinity." Catechism of the Catholic Church, Libreria Editrice Vaticana, http://www.vatican.va (accessed 25 February 2009).

Thoreau, Henry David. *The Journal of Henry David Thoreau*. Vol. 2. Ed. Bradford Torrey and Francis H. Allen. New York: Houghton Mifflin, 1949.

———. *Walden and Resistance to Civil Government*. 2nd edn. Ed. William Rossi. New York: W. W. Norton, 1992.

———. *The Writings of Henry David Thoreau: Walden*. Ed. J. Lyndon Shanley. Princeton: Princeton University Press, 1973.

Tiffany, Daniel. "Lyric Substance: On Riddles, Materialism, and Poetic Obscurity." *Critical Inquiry* 28, no. 1 (2001): 72–98.

U.S.-Canada Power Outage Task Force. "Initial Blackout Timeline: August 14, 2003, Outage Sequence of Events." Canadian Department of Natural Resources, 12 September 2003, http://www.nrcanrncan.gc.ca.

U.S. Department of Agriculture, Office of Communications. "Profiling Food Consumption in America." *Agriculture Fact Book: 2001–2002*, chap. 2. March 2003, http://www.usda.gov.

U.S. Department of Health and Human Services. National Institutes of Health. "Stem Cells: Scientific Progress and Future Research Directions." June 2001, stemcells.nih.gov.

United States. Office of the White House Press Secretary. "President Bush, Ambassador Bremer Discuss Progress in Iraq." 27 October 2003, http://www.whitehouse.gov.

———. "President and Mrs. Bush's Remarks in an Interview by Television of Spain." 12 March 2004, http://www.whitehouse.gov.

————. "President Bush Discusses Iraq War Supplemental." 16 April 2007, http://www.whitehouse.gov.

Varela, Francesco. "Organism: A Meshwork of Selfless Selves." *Organisms and the Origin of Self*, ed. Alfred I. Tauber, 79–107. Dordrecht: Kluwer Academic, 1991.

Velasquez-Manoff, Moises. "The Worm Turns: Could We Cure Some Diseases by Reintroducing Parasites?" *New York Times Magazine*, 29 June 2008, 7.

Wade, Nicholas. "Bacteria Thrive in Crook of Elbow, Lending a Hand." *New York Times*, 23 May 2008.

Wald, Matthew L. "Report on Blackout Is Said to Describe Failure to React." *New York Times*, 12 November 2003.

Warner, Melanie. "A Sweetener with a Bad Rap." *New York Times*, 2 July 2006.

————. "Does This Goo Make You Groan?" *New York Times*, 2 July 2006.

Warren, Mark E. *Democracy and Association*. Princeton: Princeton University Press, 2001.

Wellmer, Albrecht. *Endgames: The Irreconcilable Nature of Modernity*. Trans. David Midgley. Cambridge: MIT Press, 1998.

Whatmore, Sarah. "Materialist Returns: Practicing Cultural Geography in and for a More-Than-Human World." *Cultural Geographies* 13, no. 4 (2006): 600–609.

Wheeler, Leonard Richmond. *Vitalism: Its History and Validity*. London: H. F. and G. Witherby, 1939.

Whitehead, Alfred North. *The Concept of Nature: Tarrner Lectures Delivered in Trinity College November 1919*. Cambridge: Cambridge University Press, 1920.

Whitman, Walt. *Leaves of Grass and Other Writings*. 2nd edn. Ed. Donald Moon. New York: W. W. Norton, 2002.

Zammito, John H. *The Genesis of Kant's Critique of Judgment*. Chicago: University of Chicago Press, 1992.

Index

Thermal exciter, 42

Thing-power, xiii, xvii, 2–6, 8, 10–11, 13–14, 16–18, 29; definition of, xvi; individualism and atomism, 20

Things: Adorno's nonidentity and, 13–15; becoming of, 8, 118–19; "feeling," 139n40; force of, vii–ix, xii–xiv, xvi–xvii, 1–6, 18, 20–22, 29–31, 35, 47, 63, 65, 89, 92, 107, 111; as *natura naturata*, 154n21; Nietzsche on, 137n11; objects vs., vii, xvi–xvii, 2, 5, 12–13, 18, 22, 61; "parliament of," 104; people vs., x, 4, 9–10, 12, 37, 86, 119–21; recalcitrance of, 1, 50. *See also* Thing-power

Thoreau, Henry David, viii, xii, xiv, 5, 62, 121, 126n15; on diet, xvii, 40, 45–48; "the Wild" concept of, xv, 2, 20, 121

Thumos, 38

Tool, 7, 25, 38–39, 51, 108; stone, 31

"Tragedy of the commons" concept (Hardin), 27, 37

Trajectory, viii, 61, 119; of actants, 62; of action, 103; of assemblages, 24, 31–32, 35–38; of fats, 43; of organic growth, 72–73

Transformation, 98, 108; entelechy and, 72; epigenetic, 141n17; between human and nonhuman, 40, 48–49; of life, 54; of matter into life, 56; of metal, 59; techno-

scientific, 113; "thermal exciter" and, 42

Trash, vii–viii, x, 5–6, 10, 39, 107, 115; in the Meadowlands, 5–6, 20. *See also* Litter

Value, xiii, 121–22; distribution of, 13

Vernadsky, Vladimir Ivanovich, 8, 11, 19, 60

Vital force, xviii, 24, 38, 47, 64–67, 69, 78–79, 81–84, 87, 140n2

Vitalism, xiii, 56, 143n43; of Bergson, viii, xviii, 48, 61, 63–65, 76–83, 87, 90, 92–93, 143n40; critical, 63–65, 84, 140n1; of Driesch, viii, xviii, 48, 61, 63–67, 69–84, 87, 89–90, 92–93; of Kant, xviii, 48, 64–71, 73, 82–83; latter-day, 81–91; of Nietzsche, 54

Vitality: definition of, viii; as energy, 74, 76, 79–80; metallic, 59; violence and, 53–54, 61, 69, 85, 88–90

Whitehead, Alfred North, 117

Whitman, Walt, xii, xiv, 46

Will, 43, 73, 97; free, viii–x, 21, 28–33, 45, 68, 90, 98, 102, 125n7; to mastery, xvii, 15; political, 10; to power, xiv

Will to Power (Nietzsche), 54

Worms, xiii, xviii, 99–100, 103, 120–21, 123n2, 136n47; "small agency" of, 94–98, 108–9

JANE BENNETT

is a professor of political science at Johns Hopkins University. She is the author of *The Enchantment of Modern Life: Attachments, Crossings, Ethics* (2001), *Thoreau's Nature: Ethics, Politics, and the Wild* (1994), and *Unthinking Faith and Enlightenment* (1986).